The Education of Black Philadelphia

The Education of Black Philadelphia

The Social and
Educational History of a
Minority Community,
1900–1950

Vincent P. Franklin

University
of
Pennsylvania
Press
1979

Library of Congress Cataloging in Publication Data

Franklin, Vincent P
    The Education of Black Philadelphia.
    Bibliography: p. 277
    Includes index.
    1. Afro-Americans—Education—Pennsylvania—
Philadelphia.   2. Philadelphia—Race relations.
I. Title.
LC2802.P4F72   370'.9748'11   79-5045
ISBN 0-8122-7769-4

To my parents,
Vincent F. and Cecilia S. Franklin,
my family,
and my friends

Contents

Illustrations

Maps

Tables

Preface

Afro-Americans historically have had a great attachment to learning and education. The enslaved physical condition of Africans in America well into the second half of the nineteenth century made that aspect of education that liberates the mind especially valuable. The African slaves who through great effort and risk had learned to read and write would be literate for the remainder of their lives. They may have been slaves one year, and freed people the next; responsible landowners one day, and impoverished sharecroppers a few days later; these changes in their social and economic conditions would not have any effect on their status as "educated" men and women. The significance of education to black Americans meant that they would go out of their way to become educated, and to provide education for their children. This, of course, was far from easy in many parts of the United States, but in Philadelphia the educational activities of black citizens began in the late eighteenth century.

This study examines the public and community education of black Philadelphia, primarily between 1900 and 1950, within the changing social, political, and economic context for the black minority. From the perspective of the black community, the major social purpose of public and community educational activities was the advancement of Afro-Americans in the city. Given the discrimination leveled against blacks in employment, housing, and public accommodations, education was perceived as an important vehicle for improving the depressed social and economic conditions for black citizens. Community educational programs were also geared toward the specific social, political, and economic problems facing the black population; and black leaders, parents, and educators struggled persistently to insure that the schooling that was made available to black children and adults at public expense also functioned to bring about improvements in the overall social status of black Philadelphians.

Over the last six years this study has gone through a number of

xi

phases, and at each phase I accumulated many debts, only some of which I will be able to acknowledge formally in this preface. Initially, I was interested in documenting and analyzing the persistence of segregation in the Philadelphia public schools. I prepared a seminar paper on the topic for Professor Edgar G. Epps at the University of Chicago, and he and my advisor, Professor Robert L. McCaul, encouraged me to pursue the topic for my doctoral dissertation. Once I began the research, however, it became clear that I was going to have to expand my area of focus beyond blacks in the public schools to the educational activities within the black community because the public schools were generally only one of the more significant agencies providing education for black Philadelphians. Professors William J. Wilson and John Hope Franklin also supported me as I gradually moved beyond public schooling into the murky area of "community education."

Several other scholars, including Diane Ravitch of Teachers College and James D. Anderson, Clarence Karier, and Paul C. Violas of the University of Illinois, read sections or the entire dissertation and made many helpful suggestions and asked many pointed questions that forced me to re-examine the relationships between the schools and the community. I set to work again, expanding my analysis of the political nature of the relationship between the public schools and black Philadelphia, and gathered more information on community educational activities.

The first draft of the manuscript was sent to Professor Lawrence D. Reddick at Harvard University, who immediately recognized that my heart was in the right place, but suggested that there was still a need to make clear why all these educational activities were taking place, and to define the relationship between education and the larger social and political context for blacks in the city. After several long discussions and meetings, I returned to the drawing board. This book is the latest "re-examination." Although it is traditional to mention that despite the assistance and criticism offered by other scholars and friends, the faults of the work are my own, I would have to maintain that, indeed, I am the main perpetrator of any crimes herein committed against the canons of historical scholarship and interpretation, but my friends are open to the charge of guilt by association.

In my research the staffs of various libraries and archives were particularly helpful in providing me with resources and much information about educational activities and organizations in the Philadelphia area. Peter Parker of the Historical Society of Pennsylvania, Dr. Fred Miller and Dr. Peter Silverman at the Temple University Urban Archives, and most importantly, Mrs. Evelyn Boyer, director of the Newspaper Department of the Free Library of Philadelphia, and her colleagues, Frank

Green and Annette Murdock, made my long hours of research both fruitful and personally rewarding. Former Deputy Superintendent Robert L. Poindexter was instrumental in my gaining access to the records of the Philadelphia Board of Public Education stored at the Kennedy Center in Southwest Philadelphia, and Anne Howe at the Pedagogical Library of the Board of Education assisted me in locating more recent materials.

Many informal interviews were conducted with former teachers, administrators, and students in the Philadelphia public school system. I also spent many hours with various community leaders of black Philadelphia in an attempt to gain their personal insights into social conditions and public and community education. The late Floyd L. Logan of the Educational Equality League was more than generous with his time and allowed me access to the voluminous files of his organization. Dr. Ruth Wright Hayre also provided me with a great deal of information about the public school system in the 1940s and 1950s. Doris Bullock, Eustace Gay, Nellie Bright, Ruby Boyd, Eloise Owens Strothers, John Thomas, and the late Raymond Pace Alexander, in brief conversations or long hours of discussion, were extremely helpful in providing me with guidance and information about the educational activities in the city over the last thirty or forty years.

A Spencer Postdoctoral Fellowship from the National Academy of Education was an important source of funds for the typing and copying of the manuscript in its various phases. An earlier version of chapter 4 appeared as an essay in *New Perspectives on Black Educational History*, which I co-edited with James Anderson. Among the other individuals who were more than generous with their time and information about black Philadelphia were Ernest Batchelor, Ronald Batchelor, Jack T. Franklin, Helen Oakes, Glenn Taylor, Dr. Alfred Morris, and the late Alvin Lester ben-Moring. I have been sustained in this effort over the last few years by more than a little help from my family and friends, and I have dedicated this book to them. It is my hope that this examination of the education of black Philadelphia will stimulate other, comparative analyses of the social and educational history of racial and cultural minorities in urban America.

VINCENT P. FRANKLIN
NEW HAVEN, CONNECTICUT

Introduction

Historians of American education have recently begun to redefine and expand their primary field of investigation. Moving beyond the narrow institutional histories of the first half of the twentieth century that recounted the genesis, rise, and triumph of the public schools, the present generation of educational historians has begun to examine the nature and uses of education in specific periods of American history and to describe the various agencies and institutions, formal and informal, which, according to Lawrence A. Cremin, "have shaped American thought, character, and sensibility over the years . . . and the relationships between the agencies and the society that has sustained them."

> Whereas an earlier generation was understandably preoccupied with school organization and structure, more recent studies have emphasized the modes and processes of education. Whereas an earlier generation stressed formal legal arrangements and statements of educational aim, more recent works have inquired into actual educational practice. Whereas an earlier generation underscored the separation of education from politics, more recent interpretations have reasserted the complex network of relationships between education and politics.[1]

In the first volume of his projected three-volume history of American education, Cremin provides a comprehensive definition of "education" that will be used throughout the work:

> I shall view education as the deliberate, systematic, and sustained effort to transmit or evoke knowledge, attitudes, values, skills, and sensibilities, a process that is more limited than what the anthropologist would term enculturation or the sociologist socialization, though obviously inclusive of some of the same elements. Education, defined thus, clearly produces outcomes in the lives of individuals, many of them discernible, though other phenomena, varying from politics to commerce to technology to earthquakes, may prove more influential at particular times and in particular circumstances.[2]

Cremin recognized the all-inclusive nature of this view of education, however, and in a more recent work, *Traditions of American Education*, he stressed the need to describe "the changing configurations of education at different times in American history and the various ways in which individuals have interacted with those configurations." In towns in colonial New England, for example, Cremin believes the educational configuration consisted of the household, church, school, college, and printing press, which "were essentially complementary and mutually reinforcing in the knowledge, values, attitudes, and sensibilities they taught." He contrasts the educational configuration of the Puritans in colonial Massachusetts with those of the Quakers and German Lutherans in Pennsylvania and the Anglicans in Virginia, and suggests that each configuration was organized into "an explicit and well-articulated *paideia* —a vision of life itself as deliberate cultural and ethical aspiration." Cremin describes the education of several early Americans, including Thomas Jefferson and John Adams, emphasizing the interaction between the colonial educational configurations and the personal aims and objectives of the individuals.[3]

During the first century of the American nation (1776–1876), Cremin notes the proliferation of educational agencies and institutions, especially following the decline of the family and household as the major socializing agencies in local communities. Through an examination of the educations of various individuals, black and white, Cremin details the shifting educational practices of the period in light of the changing social, political, and economic conditions. Here again he identifies an "American *paideia*," forged out of popular "democratic hopes, evangelical pieties, and millennial expectations" and supporting the changing educational structures. For Cremin the key to understanding the educational configurations of a group or community is its underlying *paideia*, or "vision of life."[4]

Although Cremin's explanation is useful, when one attempts to analyze the educational process for minority groups, especially Afro-Americans, it becomes necessary to contrast the *paideia* of the dominant (white) majority, which is supporting financially educational institutions and agencies, and that of the minority group. For example, the social purposes to be served by the opening of the free, universal, common schools in the 1830s and 1840s were not the same for all citizens. Whereas a major objective of the public schools was to provide an equal opportunity to basic education in order to allow individuals to compete for the limited resources of the society on a relatively equal footing, this was not a major objective of public schooling for racial minorities in general and Afro-Americans in particular. The general belief of the dominant white majority in the innate inferiority of blacks determined not only the social status of Africans in American society, but also the amount and type of schooling made available to blacks at public expense. Thus, an examination of the evolving American *paideia* between 1776 and 1876 may help to explain the lack of equal educational opportunities for blacks in the public schools, but it would not necessarily account for the actual educational configurations in black communities during the period.[5]

In Philadelphia, which contained one of the largest urban black communities in the United States throughout the nineteenth and twentieth centuries, the public education available to blacks was generally inferior to that of whites because the white majority in the city held certain beliefs and attitudes about the character and capacities of Africans, and public schooling reflected these beliefs. Black Philadelphians, however, did not agree with the perceptions of the whites, and conflicts often arose over public educational policies and practices with regard to black students and teachers. The fact that blacks were never more than 10 percent of the city's population before 1900 meant that they exercised only limited control over educational decisions affecting black children. As the number of blacks in the city and the school system increased throughout the first half of the twentieth century, blacks began to demand greater input into and control over educational decisions affecting them.

Changes in the public education of black Philadelphia in the twentieth century were inextricably tied to larger social, political, and economic changes for blacks in the city—improvements in race relations, increases in black political power, economic depressions, and the like. Thus, in order to understand fully the evolution of black public education in Philadelphia between 1900 and 1950, we must examine it within the larger social context for the black minority.

Within the overall educational configuration of black Philadelphia in the nineteenth and twentieth centuries, the community educational activities of black (and a few white) social and religious organizations were extremely significant. Throughout the nineteenth century, the social, political, economic, and educational situation of blacks in the City of Brotherly Love was the subject of discussion and debate at community-wide educational forums sponsored by black social organizations. In the first half of the century, these organizations sponsored programs to educate blacks about the various campaigns to end slavery in the United States. Following the Civil War, they were active in raising funds and other support for their newly emancipated brothers and sisters in the South, while keeping black Philadelphians informed of the changing social conditions there and throughout the country.

In the twentieth century there was a proliferation of organizations and institutions in black Philadelphia and an increase in community-wide educational programs. Many of these community forums dealt with some aspect of public education, but most did not. Black history and culture, employment conditions, the influx of southern migrants, race relations, juvenile delinquency, and a number of related issues and problems were also important topics of discussion. In 1921, for example, a community education program was sponsored by the local branch of the National Association for the Advancement of Colored People (NAACP) to insure that black citizens knew which white Republican politicians were responsible for the demise of the Asbury equal rights bill in the state assembly. The *Philadelphia Tribune*, the leading black newspaper throughout this period, sponsored a series of community meetings in 1926 to educate black citizens about the campaign to end the practice of official segregation in the city's public schools and to raise funds to reopen litigation against school officials.

Newspapers are important sources of information on public and community educational programs within the Philadelphia black community. Newspaper accounts of programs and events provide an important record of the education of the community, which then can be compared with other sources, such as oral testimony and organizational records. Moreover, in Philadelphia, the *Tribune* not only reported the news, but it often *made* the news. Thus, an account of a public meeting or conference in the *Tribune* may not be merely a record of the event but also an important statement from the black community on an issue. The newspaper's editorials, articles, and special features provide information on the social dynamics within the black community and important leads for determining the consensus within the community on various social and political questions.

The *Philadelphia Tribune* was usually in the vanguard of activities to improve the overall social conditions within the black community. Chris J. Perry, G. Grant Williams, E. Washington Rhodes, and Eustace Gay, who published and edited the paper between 1884 and 1950, generally supported the positions that would help the largest number of black Philadelphians to get from where they were, socially, politically, or economically, to where they wanted to be. For example, during the 1920s, when some black Philadelphians favored separate public schools for blacks because they would very likely mean more jobs for black teachers, E. Washington Rhodes and the *Tribune* reported the position of these individuals and groups, but continued to support and lead the movement to desegregate the public school system. In this instance the interests of the hundreds of black children who were being officially segregated were placed ahead of those of the few black teachers who would be guaranteed positions in the separate black public schools. However, during the 1930s the *Tribune* supported the campaign for the creation of two separate black battalions of the National Guard in Pennsylvania. Some might claim that Rhodes, the editor, was inconsistent in supporting desegregation of the public schools and segregation in the National Guard. But here again, the newspaper was supporting the interests of the largest number of black citizens: it was either separate units or no blacks in the Pennsylvania National Guard during the 1930s. The *Tribune* also supported efforts to improve interracial understanding and cooperation, and publicized the meetings, conferences, and rallies held to educate Philadelphians about the social problems of racial, cultural, and religious minorities in the United States.

This study attempts to describe and analyze the educational process within black Philadelphia, especially between 1900 and 1950, within this larger social, political, and economic context. Just as public and community educational activities were affected by changes in social, political, and economic conditions, changes in the policies and practices of the public school system or in the thrust of community education programs often affected the overall socioeconomic conditions of black citizens. The first part of the book concentrates on the period from the turn of the century and the publication of W. E. B. Du Bois's *The Philadelphia Negro* (1899) to the onset of the Great Depression. Chapter 1 presents a discussion of the origins and development of the Philadelphia black community in the eighteenth and nineteenth centuries and a detailed examination of social conditions before 1920, especially the impact of the Great Migration. Chapter 2 examines the public and private schooling of black Philadelphians in the nineteenth and early twentieth centuries. The Progressive education movement had a significant impact upon public education in Philadelphia as school officials attempted to come to grips with the problem of increasing black and immigrant enrollments. The increase in public school segregation in the wake of the Great Migration led in the 1920s to a campaign by members of the black community to change official school board policies and practices. Chapter 3 examines the social, political, economic, and educational conditions in black Philadelphia during the 1920s, and describes the unsuccessful campaign to end the practice of segregating black students and teachers in the public school system. The lack of black political power in the city meant that demands for the desegregation of the public schools would not be met in that decade.

Various historical and literary societies, church and fraternal groups, and social improvement associations organized community-wide educational activities to inform black Philadelphians about their heritage and contemporary social issues and problems. Chapter 4 presents an analysis of the educational programs that flourished between 1900 and 1930.

In part II the major concern is the impact of the Great Depression, New Deal, World War II, and changing race relations upon black Philadelphia. The economic depression of the 1930s caused even greater poverty and discrimination against blacks in the local (and national) job market. Chapter 5 examines the social, economic, and most importantly, the political changes for black Philadelphia during the decade. Self-help activities and the problems for blacks in the various New Deal programs in the city are given particular attention. The re-emergence of the Democratic Party in Philadelphia during the early 1930s led to increased competition between the two major parties for the large black vote. Chapter 6 details the successful campaigns for the appointment of a black to the school board and the official desegregation of the public school system. The increase in black political power in the city at large was extremely important in bringing about a change in the policies of the politically appointed Board of Public Education.

The national defense mobilization in the late 1930s signaled the beginning of a major shift in black-white, majority-minority relations in the United States. In Philadelphia the increased demand for skilled workers led to the training and hiring of blacks in areas from which they had previously been barred. Chapter 7 describes race relations in Philadelphia in the 1930s and 1940s and the campaigns to educate black and white citizens about the need for greater interracial cooperation and understanding. Chapter 8 examines conditions in the public secondary schools of the city and the vocational training available to black youth, whose high dropout and unemployment rates became an important topic of discussion at many educational programs in the black community. This chapter also describes attempts to improve the social and educational environment for black teenagers in Philadelphia. In the final chapter the question of change and continuity in the social and educational conditions of black Philadelphia is examined. Although the first half of the century brought many significant changes in the socioeconomic status and educational conditions of black Philadelphians, there were also important continuities in the problems blacks faced and the way they dealt with them.

The educational configurations for the black minority in Philadelphia during this period were determined not only by the developing Afro-American *paideia* and social conditions in the city, but also by the minority status imposed upon blacks by the dominant white majority. Physical and cultural differences, as well as political power, served as the basis for discrimination against the black population, and the social deprivation that resulted led to educational activities by blacks to try to improve their status. Other racial, religious, and cultural minority groups have been the victims of discrimination in American society and in the cities in particular, and have used public schooling and community educational programs to improve their socioeconomic conditions.[6] Thus, this examination of the education of the Philadelphia black community should provide important insights into the general patterns of minority education in twentieth-century urban America.

I pray that the Lord may undeceive my ignorant brethren, and permit them to throw away pretensions and seek after the substance of learning. I would crawl on my hands and knees through the mud and mire, to the feet of a learned man, where I would sit and humbly supplicate him to instil in me, that which neither devils nor tyrants could remove, only with my life—for coloured people to acquire learning in this country makes tyrants quake and tremble on their sandy foundation.

David Walker, *Appeal* (1829)

Part One / 1900 to 1930

1
The
Black Community
and
Race Relations
before 1920

Historical records reveal that in the 1630s blacks accompanied the Swedes and Dutch into the area that later came to encompass the city of Philadelphia. When William Penn laid out his "planned city" in 1682, many of the Quakers who joined him in launching his Holy Experiment owned black slaves. By the end of the colonial era, however, not all blacks in Philadelphia were slaves or indentured servants, who were forced to labor in the city for a specified period of time; some were members of the small but growing community of "Free People of Colour."[1]

The historic center of the free black community in colonial Philadelphia was the area extending from Fifth Street in the east to the Schuylkill River on the west, and from Spruce Street in the north to South Street. Evidence of free blacks inhabiting this area is found in court records and statutes dating from the early 1700s.[2] These same records provide a good deal of information on the peculiar status of free blacks in Philadelphia and throughout colonial Pennsylvania. The presence of black slaves in small but significant numbers in the Quaker colony meant that laws were passed detailing the particular status of "this species of property." Problems arose, however, when free blacks (or "ex-slaves") tried to exercise the rights and privileges of free citizens. As early as 1705 free blacks were being denied the right to be tried in the regular courts, and had to go through a special court system. In 1707 free blacks lost the right to trial by jury, and when they were sentenced, their punishment tended to be noticeably more capital. Before 1718 the penalty for free blacks who committed arson, burglary, or rape was usually death.[3]

In the ensuing years, the laws became more paternalistic in their focus and enforcement. The slave code of 1725–26, for example, recognized only two statuses for blacks: "slaves" and "Negro servants." The latter category encompassed all free blacks, and included servants bound out by the courts; all children of free blacks bound out until ages twenty-four (males) or twenty-one (females); blacks sold into servitude for crime; and all nonslave mulattoes under thirty-one. Edward Turner, in his famous study of the blacks in Pennsylvania from 1630 to 1861, fully documented the "legal status of the free Negro" and concluded that "before 1780 a Negro even if free was far from being as free as a white man."

> He had no political rights and could have none. He could not marry a white person and hence could never aspire to social equality. In his family relations he was not permitted to have charge of the raising of his own children. He had no access to the ordinary courts of the colony, but was subjected to special jurisdiction and trial without jury.[4]

By the end of the colonial period (1780), free blacks in Philadelphia made up the majority of the black population, but before 1751 most blacks in the city were slaves. Slavery was never an important economic institution in Pennsylvania, and initially there was little distinction drawn between the indentured servant and the slave, except that the slave was to serve indefinitely. Gradually statutes and laws began to define slave status, and the differences between slave and servant were made clear. In 1700, 1706, and 1725–26, enactments were passed that together formed what was considered Pennsylvania's "slave code." The legislation provided for the trials and punishment of slaves and black servants, the regulation of the slave trade, and duties on slaves imported into the colony.[5] Protests of free white laborers against the general employment of slaves and free blacks also date from the early eighteenth century. As a result of these protests, the act of 1726 prohibited the hiring out of slaves and placed restrictions upon manumission on the grounds that "free Negroes are an idle and slothful people."[6]

Though the slave code of 1726 imposed a fine on masters who freed their slaves, voluntary manumission continued throughout the period from 1725 to 1780. One of the earliest groups officially to oppose the slave trade and the existence of slavery in the colony of Pennsylvania was the Society of Friends. Individual Quakers, such as Francis Pastorius and George Keith, began campaigning against slavery at the end of the seventeenth and beginning of the eighteenth centuries. With the Great Awakening of the 1730s, a period of religious revival among Christian denominations in colonial America, the Society of Friends in Philadelphia became more and more vexed by "slaveholding within its ranks." The records of Quaker Monthly Meetings reveal that the issue was being hotly debated by the members of the society from the early 1740s. The Yearly Meeting of 1751 officially condemned slavery and those Quakers who owned slaves. Finally, in 1754, notice was served on Friends in Philadelphia that slaveowners would no longer be welcomed at Quaker religious services.[7]

The Friends were also among the chief organizers of the first abolition society in the United States. On 14 April 1775, at the Sun Tavern in South Philadelphia, the Society for the Relief of Free Negroes Unlawfully Held in Bondage held its first meeting. The society was initially concerned with blacks who had been enslaved illegally. Little was accomplished before wartime hostilities interrupted its activities. In March 1787 the society was reorganized and came to be known as the Pennsylvania Abolition Society.[8] The new organization would become involved in a number of activities to improve the social conditions of black Philadelphia, especially through the support of private elementary schools for the education of black children.[9]

In 1778 the Pennsylvania Assembly began to discuss seriously the possibility of ending slavery in the state. The unprofitability of slavery in Pennsylvania is generally considered by historians to have been the prime motive for early support for abolition. Other researchers have stressed ideological considerations, such as the strong opposition of the influential Society of Friends to the institution, and the antagonism between the revolutionary goal of liberty and the practice of enslaving one's fellow man. But one should also note that the British offer of freedom to black slaves who assisted in putting down the Revolution served as an added incentive to push the first Act of Gradual Manumission through the Pennsylvania legislature in 1780.[10]

Under the terms of the act, as of 1 March 1780 all children born to slaves in the state were to become free at twenty-eight years of age, and all slaves not registered with the state government by 1 November 1780 were to be free.[11] There were a number of flaws in the original law, and it had to be supported by other acts, including a supplement in 1788 that levied a fine of one thousand pounds on any Pennsylvanian convicted of engaging in the slave trade. The act did not "emancipate" the slaves in the state, but kept their numbers from increasing. The first federal census in 1790 reported 387 slaves in Philadelphia, and 2,102 free blacks. By 1800 there were only 85 slaves and almost 7,000 free blacks in the city.[12]

Though their number was small, as early as 1785 blacks were establishing a community in Philadelphia. When Richard Allen arrived there in February 1786, he found a large number of blacks in need of religious guidance and social organizations. Having been asked to minister to the needs of the free black communicants by several local elders of the newly established Methodist Episcopal denomination, Allen proceeded to hold religious services and regular prayer meetings.

Allen was born in February 1760, a slave of Benjamin Chew of Philadelphia. His mother and father and their four children were sold sometime in 1768 to a "Master Stokeley," a farmer in Dover, Delaware. Allen remained on the Stokeley farm for about thirteen years, though several members of his family were sold during periods of economic strain for their owner. While still an adolescent, Allen began attending religious revivals of Methodist circuit riders and underwent a significant "conversion experience." "One night I thought hell would be my portion," Allen later wrote:

> I cried unto Him who delighteth to hear the prayers of a poor sinner, and all of a sudden my dungeon shook, my chains flew off, and, glory to God, I cried. My soul was filled. I cried, enough for me—the Saviour died. Now my confidence was strengthened that the Lord, for Christ's sake, had heard my prayers and pardoned all my sins.[13]

The positive change in Allen and his brother following conversion was noticed by Stokeley, who eventually came to believe that "religion made slaves better not worse" and even allowed the Methodist evangelist Freeborn Garretson to preach to his farmhands. Stokeley himself was soon converted to Methodism and accepted its antislavery doctrines. He then offered Allen and his brother the opportunity to purchase their freedom, which they did in 1780. Following manumission, Allen worked at various unskilled jobs, and then began to accompany white Methodist preachers on their circuit and to spread the Methodist tenets among his people. After turning down an offer to accompany Bishop Francis Asbury, one of the founders of American Methodism, into the South, Allen accepted the Methodist elders' invitation to preach in Philadelphia. His initial success led to his suggestion that a separate black church be established for the large number of black Methodists; however, the elders voiced their opposition to the proposal in language that Allen considered "very degrading and insulting."[14]

Absalom Jones, one of the most respected blacks in the city, also saw the need for some type of social organization for black Philadelphians. Jones was born in Sussex, Delaware, in 1746 and was brought to the city in 1762 by his master, who had purchased a store. Jones worked in the store by day and attended a Quaker school in the evening. Eventually he saved enough money to purchase his freedom and that of his wife, and by 1787 he owned several houses in the city and was considered a leader of the black members of St. George's Methodist

Episcopal Church. Failing to gain sufficient support for a separate black church, Allen, Jones, and several other free blacks organized the Free African Society on 12 April 1787 for the purpose of mutual aid and self-improvement. The noted historian Charles Wesley has pointed out that this early "Negro institution had the characteristics of a benevolent and reform organization. Through it a kind of parental discipline was to be exercised over the membership, and mutual aid was to be given in time of need. This was a first step of the Negro people in the United States toward organized social life."[15]

The preamble to the charter of the Free African Society revealed that initially the group had attempted to form a religious society, "but there being too few to be found under like concern, and those who were, differed in their religious sentiments; with these circumstances they labored for sometime till it was proposed . . . that a society should be formed without regard to religious tenets." The society held monthly meetings, and those who joined were required to attend regularly. Dues were collected and became the fund out of which benefits were paid to members in need. Membership was denied to drunkards and disorderly persons, and failure to pay dues could lead to suspension. Widows of deceased members were to receive the benefits of the organization, and children of the deceased were to be "under the care of the society so far as to pay for the education of their children, if they cannot attend the free school." A committee of three was set up to monitor, on a monthly basis, the finances of the society and to oversee the distribution of food, clothing, and good counsel to the membership.

The Free African Society was active until the early 1790s and represented the beginnings of the organized Afro-American community of Philadelphia. The society ceased meaningful activity following a split that occurred when a majority of the members, excluding Allen and Jones, voted to affiliate the group with the Episcopal Church. On 17 July 1794 the African Episcopal Church of St. Thomas was dedicated, and the members of the Free African Society became the church's "Elders and Deacons." Absalom Jones eventually became the pastor. The first black Episcopal church in the United States served many of the social and emotional needs of black Philadelphians. By the end of the nineteenth century, a full range of social and religious institutions had developed in black Philadelphia.

Race relations in the nineteenth century

Although Philadelphia is famous for its antislavery activities, antiblack violence and discrimination have also been a significant part of the city's history. The period from 1800 to 1860 witnessed a rather uneven rate of increase in the size of Philadelphia's black community. In fact, in the decade between 1840 and 1850, there was a net decrease in the number of blacks (see table 1). Local social and economic factors account for these demographic fluctuations. Late eighteenth-century Philadelphia has been characterized as a "Town of Entrepreneurs."[16] The economy was dominated by "one-man shop" artisans and small businesses, and there was little demand for unskilled laborers. However, with the growing industrialization, especially in the period from 1830 to 1860, semiskilled and unskilled labor was needed to build and run the new factories, railroads, and canals. The large influx of European immigrants that accompanied this industrial growth provided the greater part of the needed labor. Blacks attracted to the city for reasons of economic improvement or freedom from slavery competed with the European immigrants for the limited employment opportunities.

Censuses of the black population in Philadelphia carried out by the Society of Friends and the Pennsylvania Abolition Society in 1837, 1847, and 1856 presented a somewhat misleading assessment of the socio-

Table 1
Black population of Philadelphia, 1790–1950

Year	Total Population	Black Population	Percentage Black	Increase (Percent)
1790	54,391	2,489	4.57	
1800	81,009	6,880	8.4	176.42
1810	111,240	10,552	9.5	52.93
1820	135,637	11,891	8.8	13.00
1830	188,797	15,624	8.3	31.39
1840	258,037	19,833	7.4	27.07
1850	408,762	19,761	4.8	(.36)[a]
1860	565,529	22,185	3.9	12.26
1870	674,022	22,147	3.2	(.17)[a]
1880	847,170	31,699	3.7	43.13
1890	1,046,964	39,371	3.8	24.20
1900	1,293,697	62,613	4.8	60.4
1910	1,549,008	84,459	5.5	33.2
1920	1,823,779	134,224	7.4	58.9
1930	1,950,961	219,599	11.3	63.5
1940	1,931,334	252,757[b]	13.1	13.6
1950	2,071,605	378,968[b]	18.3	49.9

Source: U.S. Census Reports, 1790–1950.
Notes: a. Decrease.
b. Includes all nonwhites.

economic conditions in the black community.[17] A recent examination of the occupational distribution of Philadelphia's antebellum black population by Theodore Hershberg found that although blacks were engaged in over four hundred occupations, "a stark fact emerges from the analysis: there was almost no occupational differentiation. Five occupations accounted for 70 percent of the entire male work force: laborers (38 percent), porters (11.5 percent), waiters (11.5 percent), seamen (5 percent), and carters (4 percent); another 10 percent were employed in miscellaneous laboring capacities."[18] The Hershberg study revealed that the black community in antebellum Philadelphia was plagued by high unemployment and poverty.[19]

Moreover, beginning in 1829 black Philadelphians were the victims of mob actions and violence. From the late 1820s through the 1850s, Catholics, Mormons, and abolitionists, as well as blacks, were likely to suffer as a result of the frustrations and prejudices of the white working classes. "Whoever shall write a history of Philadelphia from the Thirties to the era of the Fifties," wrote one foreign visitor, "will record a popular period of turbulence and outrages so extensive as to now appear almost incredible."[20] In August 1834, for example, a full-scale race riot took place in which at least one black was killed, many others were severely injured, and two churches and innumerable private dwellings were attacked and their contents destroyed or looted. A citizens' investigating committee conservatively estimated the damage at $4,000, which in the context of the extreme poverty of the Philadelphia black community was a considerable sum. The committee also reported that the majority of the white attackers were Irish immigrants who found "hunting the nigs" a favorite pastime. Antiblack prejudices, however, were only one aspect of the general causes of the attacks. As one writer put it, "Irish antagonism toward the Negro and his abolitionist allies arose for many complex reasons, but at the heart of the struggle lay the fact that both groups were competitors for the most menial, unskilled, and low-paid types of employment available."[21]

In the riot of August 1842, a black area of several blocks was laid completely to waste by a white mob, which was again "chiefly Irish." Hundreds of blacks were forced to flee the area and the city for several weeks in order to escape assaults at work, on the streets, and in their homes.[22] In October 1849 the general disorders surrounding an election led to an antiblack riot when a mob of white (mostly Irish) gang members decided to attack a hotel "frequented by Negroes and operated by a mulatto married to a white wife." The rioting lasted one and a half days and was finally brought under control by the local militia. George Lippard, in one of the earliest muckraking novels published in the

United States, *The Quaker City* (1844), penned the following exchange between two low-life Philadelphians.

> Why you see, a party of us one Sunday afternoon had nothin' to do so we got up a nigger riot. We have them things in Phil'delphy once or twice a year, you know? I helped to burn a nigger church, two orphan asylums and a schoolhouse. And happenin' to have a pump-handle in my hand, I aksedentally hit an old nigger on the head. Konsekance was, he died. That's why they call me Pump-Handle.
> And you was tried for this accident?
> Yes I was. Convicted, too. Sentenced in the bargain. But the Judge and the jury and the lawyers on both sides, signed a paper to the Governor. He pardoned me.[23]

Violence perpetrated against blacks in antebellum Philadelphia by native whites and immigrants is generally considered one of the major reasons for the net decline in the black population in the city between 1840 and 1850, a decade when the city's white population increased by 63 percent.[24]

The Civil War did not greatly improve race relations in the City of Brotherly Love. In his examination of Civil War issues in the local area from 1856 to 1865, William Dusinberre concluded that "most white Philadelphians regarded Negroes as members of an inferior race that might be treated contemptuously, with impunity. Anti-Negro rhetoric was a major political weapon of the Democratic Party, while non-Democratic politicians repeatedly deflected their opponents' charge that they sympathized with Negroes, sometimes using anti-Negro arguments themselves to achieve this purpose. (Anti-Negro attitudes have provided a central theme, for they appeared wherever one looked.)"[25] The participation of blacks from Philadelphia in the Civil War did little to assuage the antiblack bias. In 1862 and 1863, before blacks were allowed to serve in regiments formed in Pennsylvania, Philadelphia blacks volunteered to serve in regiments of Massachusetts and Rhode Island.[26] In the first half of 1863, blacks volunteered for duty in Pennsylvania regiments, but were rejected. It was not until the military situation had become grave that the Philadelphia Supervisory Committee for Recruiting Colored Regiments was formed in June 1863. Eventually eleven regiments of black troops were mustered from Pennsylvania.[27] These black Pennsylvanians saw action in South Carolina, Florida, and in the West, but it was in Virginia in the last months of the war that black troops witnessed the worst rigors of the war. Although their overall participation would not be described as glorious, many blacks from Philadelphia demonstrated that they were willing to fight and die for black freedom and the Union cause.[28]

The participation of blacks in the Civil War notwithstanding, the racial situation in Philadelphia did not improve. During the war and in its immediate aftermath, blacks became embroiled in violent confrontations with white Philadelphians in an attempt to end discrimination on Philadelphia streetcars and to obtain the right to vote.

In June 1858 Philadelphia's first streetcars were opened to the public, but from the outset blacks were not allowed aboard. During the Civil War years, several blacks were forcibly ejected from their seats, and the Social, Cultural, and Statistical Association of the Colored People of Pennsylvania, organized in September 1860 in Philadelphia, formally protested. The leaders of the Association were Isaiah Wears, a prominent black Philadelphian; Octavius Catto, a young schoolteacher and civil rights militant; and William Still. Considered one of the leading Philadelphians of the nineteenth century, Still had been active in the abolitionist movement and aided numerous fugitive slaves in their flight toward freedom. In 1872 he published his famous book, *The Underground Railroad*, which was based on his antislavery activities before the Civil War. Wears, Catto, and Still led the Statistical Association in its program of activities, which included petitioning the presidents of the streetcar companies, bringing litigation against segregation, and lobbying in the state legislature for redress of the grievances of black citizens. These strategies, however, met with only limited success.[29]

In the early months of 1864, a successful case was brought against a streetcar conductor by a black woman who had been ejected from a car, but the streetcar companies did not change their regulations, and blacks were still not permitted to ride. The Pennsylvania State Equal Rights League, a local offshoot of the National Convention of Colored Citizens of the United States held in Syracuse, New York, in October 1864, concentrated on winning a favorable enactment in the state legislature against discrimination on streetcars. Through the efforts of the league, a bill was drafted and ushered through the General Assembly. On 18 March 1867 a law was finally passed making it illegal to discriminate against black passengers on streetcars in any part of the state.[30] The victory was the result of both the support for the measure among legislators who desired future black votes (in various parts of the commonwealth) and the lobbying efforts of the Equal Rights League.[31]

The tense antiblack atmosphere in Philadelphia and Pennsylvania in general during the 1830s had culminated in the disenfranchisement of the black minority by the state constitutional convention of 1838 on the grounds that blacks were "inferior and degraded beings . . . naturally lawless and idle, and if allowed to vote it would prove harmful to the state."[32] In 1869 the Republicans in Congress submitted the Fifteenth Amendment to the United States Constitution to the states for approval. Republican control of the legislature allowed Pennsylvania to be one of the first states to ratify the amendment. After ratification by three-fourths of the states, the Fifteenth Amendment became law in April 1870. The first election in which black Philadelphians participated since 1838 was marked by only one minor incident.[33] During the fall elections of 1871, however, racial violence erupted and resulted in the death of three blacks, including Octavius V. Catto.[34]

The extreme antipathy of white Philadelphians toward blacks during this period has led to the suggestion that it was caused by a high percentage of southern whites living in the city. Sam Bass Warner examined the federal census of 1850 and found that the majority of native-born whites in Philadelphia were born in the state of Pennsylvania.[35] In terms of its racial practices, however, Warner correctly concludes that Philadelphia should be considered a "southern city."[36] That is, if one classified American cities in terms of the amount of violence and discrimination perpetrated against their black populations, Philadelphia would fall into the same category as the more violent urban areas south of the Mason-Dixon line.[37]

With the increasing industrialization of American cities in the post-Civil War era, labor demands were met by the large-scale immigration of southern and eastern Europeans. In 1860, for example, only nine cities had populations over 100,000. By 1900 the number of cities with this population had reached thirty-eight, and by 1920 there were sixty-eight U.S. cities with over 100,000 inhabitants.[38] European immigration in the nineteenth century reached a peak of over 5 million in the 1880s, and more than 8.2 million arrived in the first decade of the twentieth century.[39] These great demographic changes in American cities spurred a number of political and social changes as well. For some these changes meant better jobs and higher wages, but for others the new industrial city meant poverty and despair. The increase in population led to overcrowding, a rise in slums, and increased crime. Philadelphia did not receive as large an immigrant influx as did New York and Chicago, and native white migrants or native-born Philadelphians made up over 70 percent of the population from 1870 through the 1920s.[40] The foreign-born population in this period averaged less than 25 percent of the inhabitants (see table 2).[41]

Although the number of European immigrants was comparatively small, the black population in Philadelphia was quite large. In 1890 there were almost forty thousand blacks in the city, and by 1900 there were over sixty-two thousand, almost 5 percent of the city's residents.[42] The large number of blacks living in the city, however, tended only to exacerbate the social problems caused by the European immigration.

Table 2
Percentage of foreign-born in major cities

City	1870	1880	1890	1900	1910	1920
Boston	35	32	38	35	36	32
Buffalo	36.5	33	35	30	28	24
Chicago	48	41	41	35	36	30
Cleveland	42	37	37	33	35	30
Detroit	44.5	39	40	34	34	29
Milwaukee	47	40	40	31	30	24
New York	44.5[a]	40[b]	42[b]	37	41	36
Newark	34.5	29.5	30.5	29	32	28
Philadelphia	27	24	26	23	25	22
Pittsburgh	32	28.5	31	26	26	20.5

Source: U.S. Census, 1870–1920.
Notes: a. Manhattan only.
b. Does not include Brooklyn for 1880 and 1890.

The political power vacuum that was created by the changing ethnic composition of American cities in the last half of the nineteenth century was filled in part by political bosses and machines. William (Boss) Tweed in New York City, Abraham Ruef in San Francisco, and the Vare brothers in Philadelphia gained political power by offering jobs, food, and sometimes money to the immigrants and black poor in exchange for their votes.[43]

The widespread corruption and graft, plus the poverty, crime, and vice of the larger cities, helped to generate a movement for "urban reform" that exposed, challenged, and attempted to improve the negative consequences of the rise of the industrial city. Some reformers tried to beautify the urban environment and make it more livable; others worked to improve housing conditions; while still others attempted to aid the victims of the urban growth through the establishment of social centers and settlement houses.[44]

In Philadelphia in the 1880s and 1890s, the most pressing concern of urban reformers was municipal corruption. Candidates for public office were supported by the Committee of 100, a group of upper-class, reform-minded Republicans, if they pledged to work for the "modernization" of Philadelphia's municipal government. In 1881 a reform coalition of Democrats, nonmachine Republicans, and concerned Independents succeeded in electing Samuel G. King to the office of mayor on a nonpartisan ticket. But in the election of 1884, the Republican machine won back the mayor's office. In 1885 the Committee of 100 supported the passage of the Bullitt Bill, a new city charter, which "centralized power and responsibility in the hands of the mayor, consolidating the twenty-five municipal bureaus into nine departments."[45] The committee also spearheaded the movement to modernize the Philadelphia public school system that culminated in the Public School Reorganization Act of 1905.[46]

Urban reformers often approached these social and political issues utilizing the new social scientific methodologies for the investigation of "social problems." In 1896 Susan Wharton, a prominent Quaker and supporter of the College Settlement House in Philadelphia, Charles C. Harrison, the provost of the University of Pennsylvania, and several others asked W. E. B. Du Bois, then a young Doctor of Philosophy from Harvard, to carry out an investigation of the black population concentrated in the city's seventh ward.[47] Du Bois later commented on the background of the study:

> Philadelphia, then and still one of the worst governed of America's badly governed cities, was having one of its periodic spasms of reform. A thorough study of causes was called for. Not but what the underlying cause was evident to most white Philadelphians: the corrupt, semi-criminal vote of the Negro Seventh Ward. Everyone agreed that here lay the cancer; but would it not be well to elucidate the known causes by a scientific investigation, with the imprimatur of the University? It certainly would, answered Samuel McCune Lindsay of the Department of Sociology. And he put his finger on me for the task.[48]

The result was *The Philadelphia Negro—A Social Study*, which is considered by many the first, and perhaps the finest, example of engaged sociological scholarship produced in the United States.[49] In his research, Du Bois sought to "ascertain something of the geographical distribution of this race, their occupations and daily life, their homes, their organizations, and above all, their relation to their million white fellow-citizens. The final design of the work is to lay before the public such a body of information as may be a safe guide for all efforts toward the solution of many Negro problems of a great American city."[50] Du Bois provides the historical background of the black community, demographic and occupational data, statistics on schooling, health, and incomes, and a detailed description of the social conditions among blacks in the seventh ward and throughout the city. In his recommendations to the Philadelphia Negro, Du Bois urged him to attempt to "bend his energy to the solving of his own social problems—contributing to his poor, paying his share of the taxes and supporting schools and public administration." In other words, Du Bois was advocating greater "self-development."[51]

As far as white Philadelphians were concerned, Du Bois found that the "center and kernel of the Negro problem . . . is the narrow opportunities afforded Negroes for earning a decent living. Such discrimination is morally wrong, politically dangerous, industrially wasteful, and socially silly. It is the duty of the whites to stop it, and to do so primarily for their own sakes. Industrial freedom of opportunity has by long experience been proven to be generally the best for all."[52] Philadelphians thus entered the twentieth century armed with empirical data and well-researched recommendations for dealing with their so-called Negro Problem.

Black migrants to Philadelphia, 1900–1920

At the turn of the twentieth century, the black community of Philadelphia was the largest of any northern city.[53] The federal census of 1900 revealed a 60 percent increase in the black population over the previous decade, due primarily to the ongoing migration of southern blacks to the city. By 1910 the migration had helped to raise the number of blacks to over eighty-four thousand, making them 5.5 percent of the city's population.[54] As we have seen, by the late 1890s this burgeoning black population had become the concern of several leaders of the larger Philadelphia community.

The Philadelphia Negro provides a great deal of background information on the social conditions among blacks in the city for the first two decades of the twentieth century. Du Bois found that 54.3 percent of the blacks living in the seventh ward had been born in the South, and only 42.4 percent in Philadelphia, Pennsylvania, the Middle Atlantic States, or New England.[55] Literacy among blacks in the seventh ward compared favorably with that of the black population of the city as a whole. The largest percentage of illiterates (29 percent), in both the city and the seventh ward, was in the age group over forty years of age. However, illiteracy for the entire black population was low—18 percent —especially in comparison with the various immigrant minorities in the city (see table 3).[56] By 1910 the percentage of illiterates in the black population of Philadelphia (ten years of age and over), had dropped to 7.8 percent. However, this was still high when compared with the rates of illiteracy among blacks in other northern cities.[57]

With regard to occupations, Du Bois reported that in Philadelphia:

> In the half century 1840 to 1890 the proportion of Negroes who are domestic servants has not greatly changed; the mass of the remainder are still laborers; their opportunities for employment have been restricted by three causes: competition, industrial change,

Table 3
Rates of illiteracy in Philadelphia, 1894, 1896

Nationalities	Literate		Illiterate	
	Number	Percentage	Number	Percentage
Italians, 1894	1,396	36.37%	2,442	63.63%
Russians, 1894	1,128	58.08	814	41.92
Poles, 1894	828	59.73	565	40.27
Hungarians, 1894	314	69.16	140	30.84
Irish, 1894	541	74.21	188	25.79
Blacks, 7th ward, 1896	6,893	81.44	1,571	18.56
Germans, 1894	451	85.26	78	14.74

Source: W. E. B. Du Bois, *The Philadelphia Negro—A Social Study* (1899; reprint ed., New York, 1967), p. 89.

color prejudice. The competition has come in later years from the phenomenal growth of cities and the consequent hardening of conditions of life: the Negro has especially felt this change because of all the elements of the urban population he is least prepared by previous training for rough, keen competition; the industrial changes since and just before the emancipation of the slaves have had a great influence on their development, to which little notice has hitherto been given.[58]

Census data for 1910 reveal that the number of black males engaged in domestic and personal service was 8,509 out of a work force of 29,561 (almost 30 percent); another 27 percent were employed in manufacturing and mechanical industries. Over 90 percent of black females in Philadelphia were employed in domestic and personal service, while only 5.9 percent of the black female work force was employed in manufacturing and related industries.[59] The overall occupational distribution of blacks in Philadelphia in 1910 in many ways resembled the distribution of their population twenty years before, in 1890 (see table 4).

The decade from 1910 to 1920 witnessed a 58 percent increase in the black population in Philadelphia, again primarily due to the migration of southern blacks to the city. The period of greatest migration lasted from the spring of 1916 to the spring of 1918, when it was estimated that over forty thousand blacks came to Philadelphia.[60] The general causes of the Great Migration were several, and they have been the subject of a great deal of investigation. Most researchers agree that the primary reasons for the southern exodus were economic: Emmett J. Scott found that "among the immediate economic causes of the migration were the labor depression in the South in 1914 and 1915 and the

Table 4

Occupational distribution of Philadelphia workers, 1890 and 1910

Occupations	All Males	Black Males[a]	All Females	Black Females[a]
			Percentage	
1890[b]				
Agriculture, etc.	1.9	0.3	0.1	0.0
Professions	3.9	2.5	4.8	1.4
Domestic and service	17.3	61.5	37.9	88.5
Trade and transportation	29.5	28.0	11.4	1.3
Manufacturing and industries	47.4	7.7	45.8	8.8
1910[c]				
Agriculture, etc.	1.0	1.2	0.0	0.0
Professionals	4.0	1.9	6.0	1.13
Domestic and service	7.1	28.1	36.2	92.02
Trade	18.7	12.2	9.1	0.35
Transportation	9.9	20.1	1.1	0.01
Clerical and public service	12.4	5.8	11.4	0.63
Manufacturing and industries	46.7	26.7	36.0	5.91

Notes: a. Percentages for blacks in the seventh ward only.
b. From Du Bois, The Philadelphia Negro, p. 109.
c. From the U.S. Department of Commerce, Thirteenth Census of the United States, Vol. 4: Occupations, table 8, pp. 588–90.

large decrease in foreign immigration resulting from the World War."[61] The boll weevil damage to the cotton crops in 1915 and 1916, the drop in the price of cotton, floods in the summer of 1915, generally low wages, and the increasing cost of living all had the effect of driving blacks from the southland.[62]

There was also an increase in the number of jobs available to blacks in the North. In Philadelphia the Pennsylvania and Erie Railroads and "the industrial plants situated in and adjacent to Philadelphia were . . . influential in attracting Negroes to the city."[63] The increase in the black population placed an added strain on the already overcrowded housing available to blacks. Richard Robert Wright, Jr., in his 1911 study of the economic conditions for blacks in Pennsylvania, commented that in Philadelphia "the largest groups of Negroes are in the 7th and 30th wards, which contained in 1900, 10,462 and 5,242 respectively. The segregated communities were formed naturally; the first Negroes who settled for themselves settled in the places where they could secure employment. Others moved near them and so on, until there was a so-called settlement of Negroes. Race feeling, common interests, common

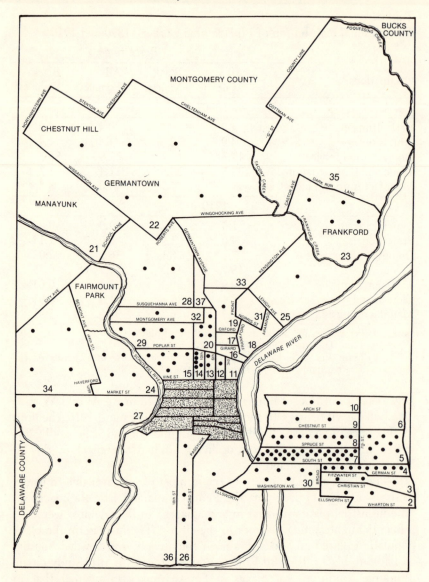

Map 1. Distribution by wards of the black population of Philadelphia in 1890. Each dot represents 250 blacks. No tabulation for wards 35, 36, and 37.

Source: John T. Emlen, "The Movement for the Betterment of the Negro in Philadelphia," The Annals 49 (September 1913): 83.

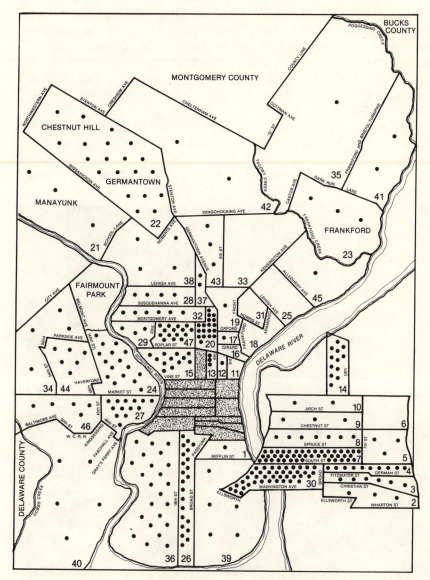

Map 2. Distribution by wards of the black population of Philadelphia, 1910.
Each dot represents 250 blacks.

Source: John T. Emlen, "The Movement for the Betterment of the
Negro in Philadelphia," The Annals 49 (September 1913): 86.

bearing of racial prejudice, were among the things which tended to keep Negroes together."[64] However, with the Great Migration, the newcomers were practically forced to seek housing in the "colored sections." Sadie T. Mossell, in a study published in 1921, reported that "the housing problem was itself a result of the determination on the part of white people that the migrant should live only in the part of the city in which Negroes had previously lived."[65]

In a later report on the black population of Pennsylvania (1927), researchers for the state Department of Public Welfare pointed out that

Typical black and immigrant residential area in South Philadelphia around 1915. (Source: Octavia Hill Association, TUUA)

as a result of the discrimination in housing, there was great overcrowding in the "Negro districts," and the rents were extremely high. "The
unskilled workingman who constitutes the mass Negro pays more for his
housing in Philadelphia and Pittsburgh than does the white man. This
is due, of course, to the fact that landlords take advantage of the great
pressure on Negro housing resulting from the large number of Negroes
in the two cities. . . . The Negro who pays the same rent as the white
man, or even the Negro who pays more rent than the white, gets much
inferior housing for his money."[66]

The response of the North to the Great Migration began very early
in the century and assumed many forms. In 1905 the Charity Organiza-
tion Society of the City of New York devoted an issue of its publication,
Charities, to the subject of "The Negro in the Cities of the North."
The living conditions of blacks in Boston, New York, Chicago, and
Philadelphia were discussed, making special note of the changes wrought
by the migration in northern industrial areas.[67] *The Annals of the
American Academy of Political and Social Science* for 1906 devoted an
entire section to the "Industrial Conditions of the Negro in the North."
Essays by Kelly Miller, Richard Robert Wright, Jr., and several others
dealt with the role of blacks in industry. The 1913 volume of *The Annals*
examined the problem of the migration in greater detail in the special
issue on "The Negro's Progress in Fifty Years."[68] Throughout the first
three decades of this century, numerous essays, articles, and reports were
published in scholarly and popular periodicals on the causes, effects, and
other aspects of the Great Migration.[69]

Various organizations sprang up in northern cities to assist first
women, and then all black migrants to these urban areas. The Association for the Protection of Colored Women (1905), the Committee
for Improving the Industrial Conditions of Negroes in New York
(1906), the National League for the Protection of Colored Women
(1906), the Committee on Urban Conditions Among Negroes (1910),
preceded the National League on Urban Conditions among Negroes
(National Urban League) (1910), which later took over many of their
projects and functions.[70] The Armstrong Association (1907), which became the Urban League affiliate in the city, and the Philadelphia Association for the Protection of Colored Women (1905) performed many
important social functions for southern migrants and other black
Philadelphians.[71]

John T. Emlen, the first president of the interracial Armstrong
Association of Philadelphia, described its activities as (1) the maintenance of the records of institutions interested in assisting the black
community. "(2) An occasional investigation in a field in which im-

provement seems possible. (3) Education of the white members of the community to make them feel sympathy with and responsibility to the other race. (4) Education of the colored members of the community to make them feel a practical interest in the progress of their race. (5) Practical work in fields needing temporarily special attention."[72] The Armstrong Association also aided southern migrants in finding employment in the city and worked with public school officials to bring about a better relationship between the schools and the black community.[73]

With the advent of World War I, there was a decided upturn in the number of southern migrants to Philadelphia, and the response of black and white citizens became more decisive. On 26 January 1917, a conference on black migration was held in New York City at the Russell Sage Foundation under the auspices of the National Urban League. Three basic subjects were discusssed: "the causes and consequences of the migration; the conditions of the migrants; and how to aid their adjustment."[74] L. Hollingsworth Wood, Kelly Miller, Oswald G. Villard, and others were joined by several representatives from Philadelphia, including John T. Emlen, John Ihlder of the Philadelphia Housing Association, and Richard Robert Wright, Jr., editor of the *Christian Recorder*.[75]

On 13 February 1917, the proceedings of the conference in New York were reported by Emlen, Wright, and Ihlder to the Round Table Conference for Work among the Colored People of Philadelphia, an organization made up of representatives of the various social and welfare agencies working in the black community.[76] At that meeting, as a direct result of the suggestions that came out of the conference held in New York, a Negro Migration Committee was formed with John Ihlder as chairman. Its purpose was to "keep in touch with the changing conditions produced by this migration so that it might prevent abuses or secure corrections."[77] Eventually, the committee was divided into eight subcommittees made up of individuals and organizations interested in various aspects of the migration.[78]

The Negro Migration Committee worked to coordinate the activities of the social agencies in the city concerned with the influx of southern blacks. In conjunction with the committee's work, the Philadelphia Housing Association, a nongovernmental organization, began conducting surveys of the housing conditions among blacks. Concentrating on the districts of heavy black in-migration, these investigations described the living conditions, especially among the migrants, and reported infractions of housing codes to the Division of Housing and Sanitation of the city government.[79] Overcrowded buildings were quickly attended to, but "sanitary improvement was not made as rapidly." The

Housing Association found that one of the main reasons these improvements were not made was "that the demand for houses was so great that a certain type of owner, knowing that his tenants had no choice and that the appropriations made by the city had been exhausted, simply disregarded orders."[80]

The Migration Committee ceased functioning in 1918, but was revived at the end of 1919. At that time it began to gather information on the migrants of the post–World War I era.[81] In August 1923 the Philadelphia Housing Association published the findings of one of the revived committee's surveys: "southern Negroes are migrating to Philadelphia in increasing numbers. The number coming to Philadelphia for the year ending June 30, 1923, approximates 10,500 persons. This is about one-third of Philadelphia's normal population yearly increment for all the races, and compared with the normal yearly increment of Negro inhabitants based on records of the previous decade, is an increase in the annual gain in such population of 200 percent over the past year." Although the later migrants were considered to be of a "higher type," housing and health conditions still presented great problems. The committee found that "many families are going into dwellings already occupied, while others are taking up residence either as tenants in one or two rooms, or as lodgers. . . . In the middle city area, where multiple occupancy is more prevalent than elsewhere in Philadelphia, many of these newcomers were taken into houses already overcrowded." The report presented graphic descriptions of the conditions in these houses and the health hazards they generated. Outbreaks of smallpox had afflicted many inhabitants of these predominantly black sections, and "within seven months medical inspectors have been obligated to quarantine forty-two different districts and to vaccinate every unvaccinated resident." The committee made two overall recommendations:

> Although many social agencies and churches are awake to the problems and are doing all that it is possible for them to do for the newcomers, the Committee feels that the real responsibility falls on the city's shoulders, and the action that can give a great deal of benefit to these migrants and to the entire city must come from the municipal government. . . .
>
> A second step is one that must be taken by the public at large. Philadelphia, for her own protection, must provide adequate housing for these families of small means who are unable to pay the high rents now being asked and those others who can pay but cannot find houses to rent.[82]

Despite the attention the migration of southern blacks received, there were no new houses built during these years in the areas they inhabited. The Octavia Hill Association, formed in 1896 to improve the housing conditions for working-class families, purchased many abandoned and deteriorating homes in black and immigrant neighborhoods, renovated them, and rented them to the black and white "working poor" who they believed could maintain them. By 1916 the organization owned over four hundred homes, and for many black migrants in the early 1920s, these provided the only decent, comfortable, and sanitary housing available.[83]

Although the Migration Committee and several other social agencies working with the southern migrants were made up of whites and blacks sympathetic to the problems of black newcomers to the city, the response of the white and black communities of Philadelphia to the migration could hardly be described as completely positive. As the black population increased, racial incidents became more frequent. The more violent ones were usually reported in detail in the city's weekly black newspapers.[84] White dailies normally confined their references to blacks to the area of "Negro Crime," but the *Philadelphia Tribune* and

Franklin Court in South Philadelphia before purchase and renovation by Octavia Hill Association. (Source: Octavia Hill Association, TUUA)

other black newspapers in the city often reported racial conflagrations on their front pages and usually commented upon them in their editorials.[85] The movement of blacks into areas that were previously all-white was a constant source of racial antagonism throughout the period of the Great Migration.[86] With the outbreak of war and the arrival of large numbers of blacks in 1917, the number of incidents increased sharply. In July 1917 a major race riot occurred in Chester, a small industrial suburb twenty-five miles south of Philadelphia. Several persons were killed, and many more were injured. The managing editor of the *Tribune*, G. Grant Williams, voiced concern about the "riot at our doors," and expressed fears that the potential for major racial violence also existed in Philadelphia.[87]

In 1918 the problem of providing housing for black workers in Philadelphia's wartime industries was settled by forcing blacks to live in the traditional "colored sections." This led to great overcrowding. Eventually the Philadelphia Housing Association succeeded in persuading realtors to rent previously white-occupied houses to blacks, especially in

Franklin Court after purchase and renovation by the Octavia Hill Association in 1912. (Source: Octavia Hill Association, TUUA)

areas where blacks were employed in wartime plants and industries.[88] The purchase of homes by blacks in predominantly white areas decreased the overcrowding in black neighborhoods, but increased the likelihood of interracial strife.

In late June 1918, a mob of white residents burned the home furnishings of two black families as they tried to move into their newly purchased homes in the 2900 block of Ellsworth Street in South Philadelphia.[89] This section of the city had attracted a large influx of blacks because of its proximity to the Hog Island Navy Yard, hiring large numbers of black workers. On Wednesday, 24 July, Mrs. Adella Bond, a black probation officer of the city, moved into her home, also in the 2900 block of Ellsworth Street. On Friday evening a crowd of whites gathered outside. Finally someone in the mob hurled a large rock through Mrs. Bond's parlor window. "I didn't know what the mob would do next," Mrs. Bond later recalled, "and I fired my revolver from my upper window to call the police. A policeman came, but wouldn't try to cope with the mob alone, so he turned in a riot call."[90] During the commotion, a white man named Joseph Kelly was shot in the leg. When the police arrived, Kelly and several other men were arrested and were later held by Magistrate Carl Baker for rioting.[91]

Saturday (27 July) was relatively quiet, but early Sunday morning white mobs began to attack blacks individually on the streets, and blacks began to arm and defend themselves. Eventually groups of blacks and whites clashed on the streets, as police and home defense reserves tried to maintain order. Rioting continued on Monday, but the onset of rain on Tuesday aided in bringing a halt to the violence. By the end of the week, four persons were dead, three whites and one black; and hundreds of others were recovering from wounds received during the four days of rioting.[92]

Attacks on blacks by groups of whites continued into the postwar period. Sailors stationed in the city were often involved in incidents of mob violence against blacks on the streets, on streetcars, and in other public places.[93] The rioting and racial violence did, however, have some positive consequences for the black community. The Colored Protective Association which was organized in the immediate aftermath of the 1918 riot by several prominent members of the black community, worked to protect the legal rights of blacks who had been arrested. Through rallies and meetings held in black churches throughout the city, the association alerted blacks to the means of gaining redress for their grievances and ending infringements upon their rights by white military personnel, residents, and police officers.[94]

It would be an exaggeration to state that all black Philadelphians greeted the newcomers with open arms. Several of the so-called Old Philadelphians voiced resentment at the disabilities they felt they were suffering as a result of the influx of the "untrained and uneducated persons" from the South.[95] An examination of the *Philadelphia Tribune* during the years of peak migration (1912–25), however, reveals that the black community generally supported the activities of individuals and groups working to assist the southern migrants in their adjustment to city life.[96] The work of the Armstrong Association on behalf of the migrants was praised and publicized almost monthly in the *Tribune's* editorial columns and in articles.[97] The Philadelphia Association for the Protection of Colored Women, a predominantly black organization that worked to provide housing and employment for girls arriving in the city from the South, also received support from the *Tribune* and the community at large for its fund-raising and educational activities.[98]

In 1916 Rev. William D. Creditt, principal of Downingtown Industrial School and later pastor of the First African Baptist Church, took the lead in investigating the needs of the black workers brought to the area by the Pennsylvania and Erie Railroads.[99] Reverend Creditt worked with the employers of the migrants to see that sanitary conditions were maintained in the housing units provided by the railroads, and made efforts to establish positive lines of communication between the southern migrants and the Old Philadelphians.[100]

In an editorial in May 1917, the managing editor of the *Tribune*, G. Grant Williams, noted that "a great hue and cry has been going up on the part of some of our citizens over the awful problem forced upon us by the incoming wave of colored men and their families from the Southland." There were complaints that some of the migrants were "loud" and that their "lack of breeding" would lead to further segregation. However, Williams pointed out that the southern migrant must be given a good example to follow, not only in order to "make him a good citizen, but [also to] help our race to achieve a higher standing in the community."[101] This sound advice was typical of the response of a large part of the Old Philadelphia black community to the Great Migration.

The wartime economy brought some improvements in social and economic conditions for blacks in Philadelphia. Unskilled and semi-skilled employment became available in many industries that had previously barred black workers. Housing in sections of the city where realtors had refused to sell to blacks now was available. Southern blacks who migrated to the city from rural areas to take advantage of the new industrial opportunities found a number of social organizations willing to assist them in their adjustment to urban life. As was noted, however, these changes in housing and employment conditions increased the likelihood of racial strife, and interracial antagonism and hostilities accompanied the social improvements.

Among the social advantages that attracted black migrants to the North was the opportunity for their children to receive a decent education.[102] The wretched public educational facilities made available to black children in most southern states often served as strong inducement to flee the Land of Cotton. Unfortunately what these southern blacks found in the City of Brotherly Love was a public school system that had developed its own almost unique form of Jim Crow schooling.

2
The Schooling of the Philadelphia Negro

In colonial Pennsylvania, because of the small size of the population, there were no statutes prohibiting the teaching of reading and writing to slaves and free blacks, as was the case in South Carolina, Virginia, and New York. Public officials in the Quaker colony appeared more interested in insuring that blacks and whites were not instructed under the same roof, and as late as 1740 a Mr. Bolton was arraigned in a Philadelphia court for teaching blacks in his private-venture school. The earliest organized attempt to provide separate schooling for blacks on an ongoing basis was made in 1758 by the Bray Associates, an Anglican philanthropic society, which opened a school in the city at the request of Benjamin Franklin, who was encouraged in the matter by a Quaker, Anthony Benezet.[1] The school was held at Christ Church and taught reading, writing, and the Anglican catechism. The Bray Associates went on to establish other schools for free blacks in New York City, in Williamsburg, Virginia, and in Newport, Rhode Island; and many were to remain in operation until the outbreak of the Revolutionary War.[2]

By the late 1760s the issue of slavery and slaveholding among the membership had been settled by the Philadelphia Quakers, and they had begun to provide for the schooling and manual training of the slaves and ex-slaves of the Friends. Again at the suggestion of Anthony Benezet, who had been instructing black children in his home from the 1750s, the Philadelphia Quaker Monthly Meeting in 1770 decided to start a class for Quaker slaves who were being prepared for freedom, and for free blacks. The school, which was attached to the Friends' School in the city, not only provided instruction in reading, writing, and arithmetic, but also offered formal religious training. Benezet, who wanted to demonstrate that blacks could be educated to the same extent as whites, became the school's instructor in 1782 and remained there until his death in 1784. The Philadelphia Friends refused to terminate Bene-

29

zet's experiment upon his death, and continued to maintain the school into the 1820s.[3]

The Pennsylvania Abolition Society, formed in 1775, re-emerged in March 1787 with one of its major goals already attained. Members of the society had lobbied successfully in the state legislature for the passage of the Act of Gradual Manumission of 1780. By 1787, however, it had become clear that the organization could accomplish much through aiding free blacks and working for the general "Improvement in the Condition of the African Race." The society initially became involved in litigation to assist free blacks who had been kidnapped or arrested as runaway slaves. On at least one occasion, members had to obtain the release from slave catchers of Richard Allen, then a minister and leader in the Philadelphia black community.[4] In 1790 James Pemberton, William Rogers, John McCree, and several other executives of the society appointed twenty-four members to the Committee for the Improvement of the Condition of the Free Negroes, which was subdivided into the Committees on Inspection, Guardians, Employment, and Education.[5] These committees would oversee all of the society's activities and programs for the local free black community.

The Committee on Inspection, later the Committee to Visit Coloured People, was charged with supervising the "morals and general conduct of the free Negroes," a duty the members discharged primarily by preparing "memorials and dissertations" to be read in churches in the free black community. This committee also periodically gathered statistics on the black population in the city. The Committee on Guardians worked to apprentice young free blacks to "suitable trades," while the Committee on Employment tried to find jobs for older blacks and new arrivals in Philadelphia.[6]

The Committee on Education, later known as the Board of Education, oversaw what was to become the most important area of activity of the Abolition Society between 1790 and 1826: the provision of schooling for black Philadelphians. The committee provided financial assistance to schools founded by blacks to allow a larger number of poor children to receive some basic schooling, and beginning in 1790, opened schools for free blacks. The records of the Pennsylvania Abolition Society contain a great deal of information on building sites, maintenance, and instruction at the various black private schools in the city in the 1790s and early 1800s. Moreover, since the Education Committee funded several schools started by blacks, these records provide important information on the efforts of free blacks to provide schooling for the children of the community. For example, in the 1790s Eleanor Harris, an educated black woman, ran a school on Cherry Street that was financed by the Abolition Society. Absalom Jones, Cyrus Buskill, and Amos White, educated free blacks, maintained schools in the city in the late 1790s and early 1800s, and received financial aid from the abolitionists.[7]

Beginning in 1802, the Committee on Education oversaw the drive to raise money to build a permanent central school for free black boys and girls in Philadelphia. The school, opened in 1813, was called Clarkson Hall in honor of the British abolitionist Thomas Clarkson. The society's membership was quite proud of Clarkson Hall, which also housed a night school and later a high school and served as the headquarters of the organization for many years. With the opening of the separate public schools for blacks in Philadelphia in the early 1820s, the enrollment at the Clarkson School began to drop. Finally, in 1826, the society decided to close the school, and thus ended its direct involvement in the provision of schooling. The benevolent venture that was Clarkson Hall was not considered a failure by the membership; in fact, many believed that "the school under our care furnish[ed] a decided refutation of the charge that the mental endowments of the descendants of Africa are inferior to those possessed by their white brethren."[8]

With the opening of the separate black churches in Philadelphia beginning in 1794, schooling in the elementary subjects was often available under the sponsorship of the various black congregations. Absalom Jones, while pastor of the African Episcopal Church of St. Thomas, established a school in the parish house in 1798. The Bethel African Methodist Episcopal Church, organized by Richard Allen, and the First African Presbyterian Church, pastored by the Reverend John Glouchester, sponsored day and Sunday schools for the free black community in the early 1800s.[9] The most ambitious educational undertaking in the black community in the early decades of the nineteenth century, however, was the opening of a grammar school. The Pennsylvania Augustine Society for the Education of People of Colour opened the school in 1822, and managed to keep it open for four years. Though the school was short-lived, black Philadelphians remained committed to education and believed that "it is our unquestionable duty which we owe to ourselves, to our posterity, and our God, who has endowed us with intellectual powers, to use the best energies of our minds and our hearts in devising and adapting the most effectual means to procure for our children a more extensive and useful education than we have heretofore had the power to effect."[10]

Individual members of the Philadelphia black community sponsored schools as private ventures throughout the nineteenth century. Instruction in reading, writing, computation, science, and foreign languages was available at nominal tuition fees. The various surveys of the black population in Philadelphia between 1827 and 1850 discussed the high quality of instruction available at many of these private black schools. With the opening of the public schools, however, almost all black children in Philadelphia received their formal schooling in these publicly financed institutions.[11]

Blacks and the Philadelphia public schools, 1822–1905

Under acts of the Pennsylvania General Assembly passed in 1802, 1804, and 1809, provisions were made for the "gratuitous education of the poor of the commonwealth."[12] In 1818 the First School District of Pennsylvania was laid out to include the city and county of Philadelphia, and in that year five schools were established for poor white children in the city.[13] After the opening of the white public schools, members of the Pennsylvania Abolition Society and the black community began to petition the local school directors to open a public school for black children in Philadelphia. The directors of the First Section school district did not respond to these initial requests, but did explain in December 1820 that they could "fully appreciate the benevolent views of this society and discovered a disposition to represent the subject to their Board in a favorable light." However, they also expressed their doubts as to the possibility of opening such a school because of a lack of "suitable rooms."[14] At this point the Abolition Society offered the directors the use of their building, Clarkson Hall, but the offer was not accepted.[15]

In 1821 the school directors ordered a survey of the number of black children in the various school districts in the city, and in April 1822 they announced that "it is expedient that a school or schools be established for the free instruction of children of indigent coloured people."[16] On 6 September 1822, the Mary Street School was opened with Henry Cooper as teacher and 199 black students.[17] It should be noted that there was no suggestion of opening racially mixed public schools during these early years. The precedent for separate schools had been established in the eighteenth century, and even the supporters of schooling for blacks did not discuss the possibility that the public schooling of black and white children could (or should) take place under the same roof.

By 1850 there were eight "colored public schools" in Philadelphia, according to the census carried out by Benjamin C. Bacon.[18] Henry Silcox, in his examination of the public schooling of blacks in antebellum Philadelphia, found that by the early 1850s educational practices with respect to blacks had crystallized. In 1828, for example, a new schoolhouse was built on Locust Street. Since the Mary Street School and the Gaskill Street School for blacks, opened in 1826, had become overcrowded, the white students of the Lombard Street School were transferred to the new school, and the black children inherited the Lombard Street School. This was the first occurrence of the practice of turning over to blacks those school buildings no longer fit for use by white children, a practice that was to be developed into a fine art by the Philadelphia Board of Public Education throughout the nineteenth and twentieth centuries.[19]

Another practice begun with the Mary Street School and continued for many years was the assignment of white teachers to all-black schools. James Bird, the principal-teacher at the Lombard Street School, was very popular with black parents. After his transfer in December 1833, however, the school experienced a high rate of turnover among instructors. Between 1833 and 1839 the school had at least six different teachers.[20] Black parents began to complain about the situation, and many decided to keep their children away from the school. Hearing of these conditions, the district board of directors threatened to close the Lombard Street School, but through the efforts of several parents and the Abolition Society, a settlement was reached, and James Bird returned to the school as principal-teacher.[21]

The overall decline in black public school enrollment in the period from 1826 to 1839 was as much due to the conditions for blacks in the city at large as to the problems in the schools. As was mentioned earlier, racial violence in Philadelphia eventually helped to bring about a net decline in the black population between 1840 and 1850.[22] More and more the black community turned inward for support, and out of this movement toward greater racial solidarity came a demand for black teachers in the separate black public schools. The Institute for Colored Youth, an industrial school for blacks founded in 1838, moved from its suburban location to Philadelphia during this period and began to offer a teacher-training program for black students. According to Henry Silcox, none of the Institute's early graduates were hired as public school teachers because of the discriminatory practices of the Philadelphia school directors.[23] However, a provision was added to the school laws of Pennsylvania of 1854 calling for the establishment of separate schools for blacks throughout the state. As a result, all of the previously established separate schools were sanctioned and legal regulations for opening others were spelled out.[24] After an initial protest by some equal rights groups, a concerted effort was made by members of the black community to get black teachers into the separate black public schools.[25]

The first black teacher in the Philadelphia public school system is believed to have been John Quincy Allen, who was hired in 1862 and taught at the Banneker School. Jacob C. White was made principal-teacher at the Roberts Vaux School in 1864 and became one of the leading spokespersons on educational issues for the black community; he participated in the movements for black civil rights and exercised a somewhat conservative influence on several of the activities for race betterment in the city until the end of the century. In 1865 even the Pennsylvania State Equal Rights League, the leading black civil rights organization, issued a statement supporting the hiring of black teachers in the state-sanctioned separate public schools.[26]

In 1870 Republicans in the Pennsylvania state legislature, to some extent following in the footsteps of the "Radical Republicans" in Congress, began introducing bills to end discrimination against blacks in the schools, hotels, and theaters, and on railroads within the state.[27] In 1874 an antidiscrimination measure passed the state senate, only to be shelved by the house of representatives. Separate schools emerged as an important political issue in 1881, when a black parent in Meadville, Pennsylvania, Elias H. Allen, appealed for a writ of mandamus to have his children admitted to the nearby white public school. The county court decided that the Pennsylvania segregation law violated the equal protection clause of the Fourteenth Amendment and ordered that black children be admitted to the school closest to their homes.[28] Meanwhile a bill was introduced into the state senate on 1 April 1881 for the repeal of the separate school provision of the school laws, supported by petitions from the Pennsylvania State Equal Rights League and several leading citizens of the state. The measure was pushed quickly through both houses and was passed with bipartisan support and signed by the governor in June 1881. The law was challenged in 1882 but was upheld by the state supreme court.[29] It should be noted, however, that this law did not end the practice of segregating black children in public schools throughout the state; it merely prohibited the legal segregation of black children by city and county governments. But the enactment was viewed as an important victory in the overall campaign for black civil rights in Pennsylvania during the nineteenth century.[30]

Between 1881 and 1905 Philadelphia's Progressive reformers who were engaged in the struggle to end corruption in municipal politics also led the campaign for a fundamental reorganization of the local public school system. The Public Education Association of Philadelphia (PEA), organized in 1881, was in the vanguard of the movement that led to the creation of a Department of Superintendence in 1882 and the appointment of the first superintendent of Philadelphia public schools in 1883. The PEA also exposed the corruption and inefficiency of various ward school districts and boards in the city. Its revelations finally forced the Board of Public Education to hold public hearings on the city's educational problems, and by 1905 the supporters of school reform were able to draw up a bill that called for the abolition of the ward school boards and an increase in the power of the central Board of Public Education. The Reorganization Act, which finally passed the Pennsylvania state legislature in April 1905, was the crowning achievement of the Progressive educational reform movement in the city. It had as one of its major objectives the "modernization" of the Philadelphia public school system.[31]

The new superintendent and the black child

Edward Brooks, the superintendent of the Philadelphia public schools, began the process of ushering the Philadelphia system into the mainstream of American educational practices, but it was Martin G. Brumbaugh, his successor, who, between 1906 and 1914, carried out the transformation and set the tone and pace of educational change in the public schools of the third largest city in the nation.[32]

That Brumbaugh was extremely well qualified for this task was admitted by most knowledgeable Philadelphians of the era. Born in Huntington County, Pennsylvania, on 14 April 1862, and educated at Juniata College and the State Normal School at Millersville, Pennsylvania, Brumbaugh served as teacher, principal, and later superintendent of the Huntington County public schools. He did graduate work at Harvard and the University of Jena, and finally received his Ph.D. from the University of Pennsylvania in 1895.[33] Provost Charles Harrison of the University of Pennsylvania decided in 1895 to create a chair of pedagogy and made Brumbaugh the first appointee to the position. In 1900 he was appointed by President William McKinley as the first commissioner of education of Puerto Rico, and after two years succeeded in establishing "a system of public schools on the American plan." Upon returning to Pennsylvania, Brumbaugh became involved in the movement to reorganize the Philadelphia public school system and in the preparation of the Reorganization Act.[34] He resumed his duties as professor of pedagogy and also served as president of Juniata College until 1906, when he was appointed superintendent of the 150,000-pupil Philadelphia public school system upon Edward Brooks's resignation. He remained in that position until 1914, when he successfully ran for governor on the Republican ticket. Between January 1915 and January 1919, Brumbaugh served as governor of the commonwealth. In 1919 he ended a successful career as a public official.[35]

As a professor of pedagogy, responsible for the training of hundreds of teachers, Brumbaugh had been exposed to many of the new trends toward "scientific management" and greater "efficiency" in the administration of public schools.[36] In his annual reports to the Board of Public Education, and in the educational policies and innovations of his administration, it is clear that Brumbaugh tried to follow through on his commitment to bring "modern public education" to Philadelphia.[37]

In his first full report to the Board of Public Education in 1907, Brumbaugh discussed several areas of educational practice that he had improved or introduced during his administration.[38] More kindergartens were opened, and a new department of physical education with ten assistants was organized. The "special" departments of music, drawing, cooking, and sewing were "moving toward better coordination . . . with the regular work of the grades." During this year one of the first public trade high schools in the United States, Edward Bok Vocational School, was opened.[39]

The bulk of this report, however, contained recommendations for the further improvement of the schools. Superintendent Brumbaugh stressed the need for the introduction of "moral education" into the classroom for the betterment of student behavior. He believed that "it is vastly more important that the growing citizen should be well mannered than he should be well informed."[40] In order to "fit the individual for participation in the interests of his kind," Brumbaugh recommended increased emphasis on the "social aspects of education."

> It is my conviction that the school plant should serve a vastly wider need than it now does. In at least five important directions, with little or no added expense to the taxpayer, it can render large good, namely: as centers for play, as centers for children, as places for School and Home Associations, as centers for illustrated lectures, and as gathering places for the alumni of the several schools.[41]

In the interest of efficiency, Brumbaugh advised the introduction of semiannual promotions. At that time, there was a "considerable group of pupils who fall below the standard of the grades, and are obliged, therefore, to repeat the work before they can secure promotion to the next grade. In Philadelphia heretofore the child that failed to secure promotion either by exemption or examination was obliged to repeat the entire year." Under a system of semiannual promotions, pupils would not have to repeat an entire year if they failed to pass only the courses of the previous semester.[42] Brumbaugh also advocated the establishment of a "Teachers' Institute," whose purpose would be "to promote the intellectual and professional efficiency of the teaching body." This institute would meet in the spring of the year around the Easter recess.[43]

Superintendent Brumbaugh then took up "the problem of the colored child" in the Philadelphia public school system. He first noted that Philadelphia had the largest black population in the North and thus "sends a larger group of colored children to the public schools than any other city in the country."[44] Most of these students attended the school nearest their homes, but in a few cases, "separate buildings have been provided in which colored children have been placed under colored teachers." This policy had two positive results, according to Brumbaugh. "First, it has given to the colored child a better opportunity to move at his own rate of progress through the materials of the curriculum, which rate of progress is in some respects different from the rate of progress of other children. Second, it has enabled the Board of Education to give employment to a group of deserving members of the colored race, who by industry and capacity have won their certificates to teach in the public schools of the city." At this point, Brumbaugh went on to discuss the importance of these results, and the policy to be pursued with respect to the black child during his administration. This official statement is extremely significant and deserves quotation in full.

> Both of these [practices] are matters of moment, and wherever the colored parents will join in petition to the Board for a school organized on this basis, I earnestly recommend that such schools be established. It is possible, however, that in some sections of the city the parents of these children will not so petition the Board, but on the contrary, will insist that their children remain in the divisions where they now attend school.
>
> Here a really difficult situation presents itself. The fact is that when the percentage of colored children reaches thirty or more the other children begin gradually to withdraw from the school. This fact, coupled with the additional fact that there are a number of qualified colored teachers in the city who are not at the present time in the employment of the Board of Education, leads me to suggest that *wherever possible separate schools should be inaugurated for the colored children, and this possibility, so far as I now can see, must be conditioned upon the petition of the parents of these children themselves.* There is a tentative solution to a part of the problem, namely, the establishment of colored divisions with colored teachers in charge in the schools now in operation in the city. This is now in successful operation in the Martha Washington School, and it may be possible in the near future to extend this method of dealing with the question to other sections of the city.
>
> I wish definitely to state that this is a serious problem; that it has given me a great amount of thought and concern; that I have a deep sympathy for these young women who have qualified themselves to teach in our schools; that I am exceedingly anxious *to pro-*

mote the most efficient educational opportunity for the colored children, and that I believe a more careful and intensive study of the entire problem will result in some solution of the matter which will be satisfactory to all fair-minded citizens.

Just what the solution will be, it is probably now unwise even to predict, but in the above analysis I have indicated what in my judgment are the lines along which immediate relief may properly be accomplished. (Italics added.)[45]

Brumbaugh concluded by announcing that the school administration was studying the "mental aptitudes of several groups of children in the public schools and the different materials which might properly be used for the best interests of the several groups, and at an early date it will

Table 5
School Census of 1908 (6 to 16 years)

Ward	Black			White			Total
	Female	Male	Number	Female	Male	Number	
1	9	11	20	4,636	4,443	9,079	9,099
2	24	33	57	3,789	3,876	7,665	7,722
3	88	106	194	2,570	2,627	5,197	5,391
4	127	119	246	1,977	2,216	4,193	4,439
5	67	39	106	1,489	1,452	2,941	3,047
6	1	3	4	584	553	1,137	1,141
7	629	583	1,212	1,019	1,005	2,024	3,236
8	68	58	126	345	312	657	783
9	68	64	132	151	128	279	411
10	44	38	82	766	705	1,471	1,553
11	1	1	2	1,022	1,040	2,062	2,064
12	14	16	30	1,066	1,089	2,155	2,185
13	33	35	68	1,113	1,168	2,281	2,349
14	127	105	232	857	799	1,656	1,888
15	152	107	259	2,791	2,694	5,485	5,744
16	2	4	6	1,465	1,501	2,966	2,972
17	12	9	21	1,421	1,453	2,874	2,895
18	1	0	1	2,409	2,493	4,902	4,903
19	8	13	21	4,566	4,461	9,027	9,048
20	296	275	571	2,975	2,853	5,828	6,399
21	48	26	74	3,084	3,044	6,128	6,202
22	245	221	466	4,536	4,349	8,885	9,351
23	70	83	153	2,645	2,594	5,239	5,392
24	240	179	419	3,882	3,893	7,775	8,194

Source: PBPE, Report of the Bureau of Compulsory Education, 1908 (Philadelphia, 1909), p. 13.

be possible for us to submit to you some plan by which great good may result to the different groups of children of all races and nationalities, that now attend our schools."[46] An analysis of the superintendent's recommendations provides an even clearer picture of the educational ideas and practices with regard to black children in a large northern public school system during the first decades of this century.

While there were nine separate black public schools in the Philadelphia school system in 1908, the majority of black children in the public schools attended mixed schools. At that time the separate schools enrolled only 2,335 of the 7,559 blacks in the elementary schools, and black children could be found in almost every ward in the city (see table 5).[47] Brumbaugh's suggestion that the black child's "rate of progress"

Table 5—Continued

Ward	Black			White			Total
	Female	Male	Number	Female	Male	Number	
25	2	12	14	3,671	3,680	7,351	7,365
26	281	226	507	4,047	4,049	8,096	8,603
27	165	133	298	898	891	1,789	2,087
28	82	89	171	3,622	3,650	7,272	7,443
29	47	51	98	2,570	2,462	5,032	5,130
30	617	453	1,070	1,475	1,465	2,940	4,010
31	0	0	0	3,055	2,958	6,013	6,013
32	84	70	154	2,350	2,282	4,632	4,786
33	10	20	30	4,917	4,747	9,664	9,694
34	53	57	110	3,177	3,171	6,348	6,458
35	17	26	43	851	866	1,717	1,760
36	434	414	848	5,259	5,164	10,423	11,271
37	17	25	42	1,621	1,704	3,325	3,367
38	40	31	71	3,245	3,144	6,389	6,460
39	52	40	92	5,054	4,868	9,922	10,014
40	103	84	187	2,985	2,913	5,898	6,085
41	6	5	11	1,106	1,087	2,193	2,204
42	28	21	49	1,533	1,545	3,078	3,127
43	68	65	133	3,257	3,497	6,754	6,887
44	79	95	174	3,223	3,060	6,283	6,457
45	20	21	41	1,984	2,128	4,112	4,153
46	34	24	58	2,050	1,930	3,980	4,038
47	193	175	368	1,430	1,420	2,850	3,218
	4,806	4,265	9,071	114,638	113,129	227,767	236,838

was "different" from that of other children in the school system may
have been based on the studies of "retardation" in the Philadelphia
schools carried out in 1905, 1906, and 1907. Oliver Cornman, an associate superintendent, had just made a comparative study of rates of
"retardation," defined as the failure to be promoted or "the requirement
of more than a single year or term to complete the work regularly
allotted," in the public school systems of five cities.[48] The results of this
study showed that in June 1907, 65.1 percent of the elementary school
children in Philadelphia were "retarded," and that the high rate of
retardation in general was due to the large numbers of immigrant children in the public school system.[49] Thus, Superintendent Brumbaugh
believed it was necessary to make "a careful study of the mental aptitudes of several groups of children in the public schools," and he was
to commission several additional investigations during his years as
superintendent.

The argument that the growth of separate black schools in Philadelphia was supported in order to "give employment to deserving members of the colored race," in reality, touched on only a part of the contemporary controversy surrounding black teachers in the public schools.
Another part of the problem stemmed from the fact that no black
teacher was allowed to teach white children in the public school system.
Given the racist tenor of the times, most whites and some blacks did not
even question this situation, but it would cause great problems in Philadelphia in the 1920s and 1930s.[50] When a black teacher presented herself
(or himself) at the Board of Public Education in hopes of gaining a
teaching position, her name was usually placed on the "colored eligibility list." In 1908 and 1909, for example, positions on the eligibility lists
were based on residence, and black and white teachers were assigned "to
positions convenient of access from their homes. Although under such
a plan in some districts and in some cases it happens that candidates
with higher averages have to wait assignment for a brief time, in the end
this proves more satisfactory to them than would an immediate appointment with considerbale inconvenience and expense attached to it."[51]
Examinations for teaching positions were given in reading, penmanship,
and orthography, but only to those candidates who had not graduated
from high school or the city's normal school.[52] In any case, certified black
teachers were placed on the separate black eligibility list and eventually
appointed to the separate black public school nearest their home.[53]

In the early years of the twentieth century, another way for blacks
and others to obtain a teaching position in the public schools was to
"found" a school. In the era before the reorganization, if a black teacher
presented her credentials to the Board of Public Education and there

were no openings in the separate black schools, she could go into the black neighborhoods and gather together a group of children who were not already in school. After the number of children exceeded fifty or sixty, the teacher could go to the chairman of the local ward school board and request that a school be opened. The ward school board secured a building for the school, and the teacher who had found the children became the principal-teacher, and then hired other black teachers as the need arose.[54]

In the period after the reorganization of the school system (1905–36), a black school could be "created" by the district superintendent with the approval of the school board. When the percentage of black pupils in the school reached a certain point, usually about 95 percent, the white teachers at the school would be transferred en masse to other schools, and the top eight or nine teachers on the "colored eligibility list" were appointed to the school. Just before the transformation took place, the few remaining white students would take notes home to inform their parents that in a few days they were to be transferred to another school.[55]

The experiment at Martha Washington School that was mentioned by Superintendent Brumbaugh involved the teaching of black and white children in the same school building, but in separate classrooms with black and white teachers. The principal of the school was white. The experiment, however, was unsuccessful, and was not extended to other schools. By 1920 Martha Washington had been designated a "colored" school; its students and staff all were black. The expression of sympathy for the black women "who have qualified themselves to teach in our schools" but were unable to obtain appointments indicated that Superintendent Brumbaugh was aware of the situation confronting blacks desiring teaching positions in the Philadelphia public schools. And in order to gain even more information about the nature of the "Negro Problem" facing the schools, Brumbaugh commissioned a series of "scientific investigations" that began in 1908.

The study by Oliver Cornman in 1907 had revealed that the "rates of retardation" (overageness) among immigrant children were higher than those of native whites in the five school systems examined. Byron A. Phillips, an elementary school principal in Philadelphia, decided to find out if the rates of retardation were uniform throughout the public school system. Using statistics gathered in 1908, 1909, and 1910, Phillips reported that "(1) The ten [school] districts vary considerably among themselves in the amount of retardation. (2) There has been a uniform reduction in the amount of retardation during the past three years in the city as a whole, in each district, and with few exceptions in each grade. (3) Supervision is probably an important factor in the reduction of retardation."[57] He then went on to discuss the various "sociological units" in the school system that affected the rates of retardation, especially the "colored element" and the "foreign element." Phillips described the retardation rates in schools and districts with large numbers of black and immigrant children and concluded that "(1) The home conditions of the sociological units are important in retardation. (2) The negro element is out of accord with the educational system, and is an important factor in retardation. (3) The same thing is true of the foreign element, to a less extent. (4) Supervision may reduce retardation by a more liberal interpretation of the course of study."[58] Phillips also looked at "rates of acceleration," or advanced placement, and "rates of elimination," or dropping out, in the school system. His conclusions are extremely significant. Phillips believed that, "from the psychological point of view," there was a need to give more individual attention to the school work of the pupils, especially "in deciding whether it is for the best interests of the pupil to be promoted or left down, irrespective of the requirements for the average."

> From the sociological point of view, we see the need of a flexible course of study. The enrollment of the schools is made up of various sociological units, which with their varying home conditions, must be carefully scrutinized before a fixed course of study is laid down for all. In the case of the negro, it sees that the curriculum at present is entirely unfitted to his capabilities. Apparently, the solution of this problem is to be found only in organizing colored schools with a special curriculum. (Italics added.)

Phillips expressed the hope that by "recognizing the psychological and sociological factors in the problem and making adequate provision for them, supervision may reduce the amount of retardation to a minimum."[59] Thus, after looking only at the number and percentage of overage black children in the public schools, Phillips concluded that there was a need for "colored schools with a special curriculum."

The reasons for the large amount of overageness among black children were not discussed or even mentioned in the study. The possibility that poverty may have kept the black child, or any child, from entering school at age six was not explored. The recent arrival of many black children in Philadelphia from cities and towns in the South where there was little or no schooling provided for blacks was not touched upon.[60] And Phillips made no mention of the common practice of northern school officials of automatically placing black children newly arrived from the South one or two grades below the last grade they had attended. This practice would, of course, lead to high rates of "retardation" among the black pupils.[61]

Between 1910 and 1920, the newly devised and translated "intelligence tests" were introduced into the United States. These were to bring profound changes to American educational practices in the twentieth century. The first "intelligence test" was produced in 1905 by Alfred Binet and Theophile Simon in France in order to detect mentally deficient children in the public schools. These tests were revised and published in 1908. Henry H. Goddard translated Binet's "Measuring Scale for Intelligence" and published it in the United States in January 1910. The results of the testing of four hundred "feebleminded" children at Vineland Institute were reported by Goddard in September 1910. He believed that "there was no exception to be made to the grouping as determined by the Binet tests." The classifications of the mental age of the students "did work out with amazing accuracy, and I believe it is true that no one can use the tests on any fair number of children without becoming convinced that whatever defects or faults they may have, and no one can claim that they are perfect, the tests do come amazingly near what we feel to be the truth in regard to the mental status of any child tested."[62]

In the following year, Goddard reported the results of the testing of two thousand "normal" white children using the Binet scale.[63] In the report he detailed the methods used in testing the pupils, the backgrounds of the students tested, the mental and physical (chronological) ages of the children, the test items, and the range of test scores that resulted. He concluded "first, that the Binet Scale was wonderfully accurate; and second, that a child cannot learn the things that are beyond his grade of intelligence. He may be drilled upon them but can only give rote work and will fall down upon them if carefully questioned."[64] In other words, Goddard suggested at this early date and with no replication of the study, that the "intelligence tests" of Binet and Simon measured how much a child was *capable of learning* at a given chronological age.

Once Goddard had produced a range of scores for "normal" white children, comparisons began to be made with other groups of children in the United States. Thus, the "intelligence" of "normal" white children in urban areas was compared to that of "normal" white children in rural areas.[65] The test scores of native white children were compared with those of foreign-born children.[66] The possible combinations of groups that could be compared was virtually limitless. But from the outset, one of the favorite comparisons of educational researchers was between "normal" white children and "normal" black children.

With the financial backing of the Bureau of Municipal Research, a nonprofit, nongovernmental research agency in Philadelphia, Martin G. Brumbaugh, following through on his pledge of 1907, asked Howard Odum in 1910 to conduct a survey of black children in the Philadelphia public schools.[67] Odum, who had studied with educational psychologist G. Stanley Hall at Clark University, receiving a Ph.D. in 1909, had just completed his second Ph.D. in political science at Columbia University. His doctoral dissertation at Columbia on "The Social and Mental Traits of the Negro" was published that year in the prestigious Studies in History, Economics and Public Law series edited by the political science faculty at Columbia.[68]

Odum set to work on his assessment of the social background and mental capabilities of black children in the school system in the fall of 1910. In his published summary of the final report Odum presented the rationale for the study:

> That the problem of educating Negro children is not limited in its application to any community, or to the North or South, is now a well recognized fact. That it is of special importance in the study of American education; is closely related to the many problems of public policy; and bears directly upon the theory and practice of efficiency in national life, as well as upon race improvement; is not always so well recognized.[69]

The survey included "all the elementary schools of the Philadelphia public school system as organized during the months from September, 1910 to January, 1911." At that time there were 8,192 black children in the school system, 5.3 percent of the total, and they were enrolled in 238 different schools. "Approximately one-fourth (23.7 percent) were enrolled in the nine separate Negro schools, the remaining three-fourths (76.3 percent) being enrolled in 15 percent of the total schools in the city."[70]

With reference to "retardation," Odum reported that "the total Negro pupils show 71.9 percent retardation, and the white children 38.9 percent according to the accepted standard which allows one year normal age for each grade. According to a more accurate standard, allowing three years range for each grade, the Negroes show 48.6 percent retardation and the whites 18.6 percent."[71] Odum summarized the results of his questioning of teachers on the performance of black children in the classroom: "According to teachers, Negro children find most difficulty in arithmetic and studies that require compound concentration and prolonged application." In trying to account for the problems in this area, Odum suggested that many of the problems in the classroom work were due to racial and environmental influences. "The correlation of the home and social environment, together with the present racial influences, with school records will indicate the source of many difficulties which the Negro children have to face." At the same time, however, Odum believed that one of the reasons for the unsatisfactory performance in school subjects was that the black children were not doing their homework. "Lack of study is often responsible for unsatisfactory work instead of inability to succeed in their studies," wrote Odum; "especially is this true of their home study. There are few incentives to study at home, little favorable influence to promote it, and practically no facilities in the way of reading."[72]

Odum considered the high rates of "retardation" reported for black children suspect. He believed that some of these reports may be due to "the prejudice existing in the minds of white pupils and teachers. This difficulty may be understood when it is remembered that the white teachers are teaching day after day a group of children in whom the majority can see few strong points."

> The full meaning of the present situation cannot be discussed adequately until the studies of exact measurements, comparisons of Negro children in mixed and separate schools according to uniform school tests, and comparison of teaching efficiency in the white and Negro schools have been reported.[73]

The second part of the Odum study attempted to gauge the "general intelligence and mental processes" of the black child in Philadelphia. Odum began by discussing studies of the influences of environment on an individual's "mental efficiency." Unfavorable environment was said to lead to "inferior" mental abilities, while favorable environments did *not* necessarily lead to "superior" mental functioning.

> Now it has been shown that Negro children show a large proportion of inferior inefficiency [sic] in certain accepted fields according to certain accepted methods of rating. They also show a certain proportion of apparently exceptional superiority in certain processes and activities. Here again the results indicate, on the one hand, that Negro children conform to the conditions in which environment is the chief factor in determining the results; and likewise, owing to admixture of white blood, and owing to the inaccuracy of measurements, there is no evidence to show that they do not appear to furnish only mediocre native abilities at best. With only this knowledge at hand, it is absolutely impossible to say how much and of what sort are the innate differences between black and white children.[74]

What was needed, according to Odum, was "to measure with methods of scientific precision the mental and physical traits of the median group of Negro children" and to compare these results with a similar group of white children. Thus, Odum was going to measure the mental processes of the black child in Philadelphia, using the Binet and other tests, and compare the results with those found for white children who were tested by other researchers.[75]

After cautioning his audience against "dogmatic assertions and hasty recommendations," Odum reported that "this study has shown conclusively that there are distinct differences between white and Negro children in all aspects studied, environment (home conditions), school conditions and progress, and in mental and physical manifestations."[76] Odum was well aware of the seriousness of the findings; nevertheless, it is not likely that he was surprised by the results, since they generally coincided with his earlier research on southern blacks.[77]

Odum then went on to discuss the "educational implications" of his findings. He supported any educational effort to "provide education which will ultimately develop the children into their highest capabilities," but the future as well as the present situation should be provided for:

> The great majority of Negro children not only do not enter the high school but also fail to complete the elementary grades. Less than 2 per cent of the Negro children of school age reach the eighth grade. Furthermore, their training to the period of dropping out of school fits them neither for any special work in life nor for competing with the more fortunate and better fitted in society at large. . . . What then, can the school and society expect of children to whom they give neither special training for life nor equal opportunity in the struggle? Here again the basis of improvement is found in the exact definition of conditions as they are and a recognition of their significance.
>
> It follows that from the community standpoint an effort should be made not only to provide proper education and vocational guidance, but the present unfavorable conditions should be so remedied as to influence the smallest possible number of children and schools. If the lack of adaption of children to the curricula is costing the community thousands of dollars annually and is at the same time a hindrance to school efficiency and progress, and if even at this great cost the desired objects are not obtained, can there be doubt concerning the need for a more definite program?[78]

Although Odum's conclusion was more subtly presented than that of Byron Phillips, Odum was supporting the maintenance of separate black schools and the institution of a special curriculum for black children.

Howard Odum's conclusions and recommendations were consistent with those of Phillips, discussed earlier, and with his own earlier observations, as published in his dissertation of 1910. In fact, they were *too* consistent, and therein lies the reason why these and other conclusions of early educational researchers must be considered highly suspect. Over and above the fact that these early tests were very poor instruments for measuring anything, let alone "intelligence," and that the testing procedures were crude at best, there was also a real problem of bias and prejudice inherent in the entire process. Throughout the nineteenth century, so-called scientific experiments were carried out comparing the mental and physical abilities of blacks and whites.[79] The introduction of the Binet-Simon "intelligence tests" into this field of activity can thus be viewed as an attempt to measure mental differences between the races that most researchers already believed existed.[80] Indeed, this becomes apparent when one compares the pronouncements of educational researchers about the black child *before* the introduction of "intelligence tests" with the conclusions and recommendations made using the new "scientific scales of mental measurement." For example, Byron Phillips, who had made the study of "retardation" in the Philadelphia public schools in 1909, especially among black and immigrant children, went back to the black schools in 1913 and tested the students using the newly introduced Binet-Simon tests. In this second study, he drew a distinction between "pedagogical retardation," which was what he had measured in the first study, and "psychological retardation," which he was now measuring with the new "intelligence tests."[81] However, the conclusions were basically the same: "First, that the colored children are retarded to a much greater extent both pedagogically and psychologically than white children, and secondly, that the white children are accelerated to a much greater extent than colored children. If the Binet tests are at all a gauge of mentality between colored and white children, then this raises the question: Should the two groups be instructed under the same curriculum?"[82] Again his conclusions pointed toward the need for the introduction of a special curriculum for the black child.

One can also see similarities between Howard Odum's conclusions about the educability of the black child in the South and his conclusions about the educability of the black child in the Philadelphia public schools, although the former were drawn without the benefits of intelligence testing. Odum found that in spite of the large expenditures for black education in the South, the results were dubious; although "the schools for the negroes are in many cases apparently doing good work, they are not producing and have not produced results which were expected of them." Odum then tried to present the reasons for this failure, beginning with the black child. "Inherited tendency and environment of the race conditions constitute a powerful influence in the education of the negro child. Against these he must gain whatever good he is to receive and it is to help him overcome these that the best efforts and most careful study be put forth."

> Back of the child, and affecting him both directly and indirectly, are the characteristics of the race. . . . The migratory or roving tendency seems to be a natural one to him, perhaps the outcome of an easy-going indolence seeking freedom to indulge itself and seeking to avoid all circumstances which would tend to restrict its freedom. The negro shirks details and difficult tasks; he is incapable of turning his mind toward any other subject once morbid curiosity holds his attention. . . . negro children are easily susceptible to all influences brought to bear upon them. It has been observed that the negro is lacking in morals, so far as personal purity and chastity are concerned. . . . It is easily observed that these obstacles [race traits] have not been overcome, but have rather set bounds for the school's effectiveness. Because of this, the growing generation of negroes is not superior to the negroes of a generation ago, as a race, rated according to religious and moral standing, and according to their economic value to the community. The schools do not appear to have improved within the last decade nor do the results appear in so favorable a light as a few years ago.[83]

In Philadelphia, Odum had "intelligence tests," but his conclusions were the same. This consistency cannot be ignored or brushed aside as an accident. The conclusions reached and the recommendations made by these early educational researchers were more a reflection of their own and society's prejudices and opinions about blacks than an accurate assessment of the educational problems of the black child.[84] These "scientific studies" provided justifications for the further segregation of black children in the Philadelphia public school system, and for the later attempts to introduce a special industrial curriculum into the separate black public schools of the city.

The Great Migration and the Philadelphia public schools

The influx of southern blacks into southern and northern cities during the first three decades of this century caused several educational problems for these urban public school systems. Louise V. Kennedy, in her important analysis of the causes and effects of the southern and rural exodus, concluded that in most northern public school systems the black migration led to increased segregation, overcrowding, and a rise in the number of overage pupils in the elementary grades.

All of the [school] surveys which investigated the causes of retardation [overageness] among Negroes emphasized migration from the South as one of the chief factors producing this situation. Children who transferred from southern schools had been seriously handicapped by the poor educational facilities there, by the short terms and by the inadequate compulsory school laws. A large proportion of the children had been overage when they entered school and others who had been in their normal age-grades in the South had been demoted in the North because they had not received sufficient training to keep up with northern classes.[85]

In Philadelphia during this period the same conditions and practices were in effect. Dr. Daniel A. Brooks, a teacher and principal in the separate black public schools in Philadelphia throughout the years of the Great Migration, later recalled that beginning around 1916, "thousands of southern Negroes were rushing to Philadelphia to engage in war work. Their numerous children were threatening to crowd into the elementary schools where few Negroes had previously entered. The usual solution was proposed—placing them in separate schools." Brooks went on to describe the conditions of the buildings that became the new black public schools. "Old, frame buildings, gas-lighted with coal stoves in many rooms, and out-door water-closets, . . . and located in the older, poorer parts of the city were customarily given over to newly-arrived colored people. These buildings were chosen for the separate schools and the inducement was given of the appointment of colored teachers for the children." Since public school officials refused to allow black teachers to instruct white pupils, blacks obtained teaching positions primarily through the opening of additional separate public schools: "In order to gain the advantage of having teaching positions opened to colored teachers, the situation was reluctantly accepted by the colored people." Brooks also noted that with the migration, "large numbers of big, unschooled, overage southern children were in the lower grades alongside of Philadelphia-born children of normal age. Classes of 60 children were frequent, with ages 8 to 16 in one class."[86]

Dr. Brooks's observations are supported by evidence from a number of other sources. The number of separate black public schools in Philadelphia fluctuated between 1900 and 1937, when these schools were no longer officially sanctioned by the Board of Public Education.[87] As was mentioned earlier, in 1910 there were nine separate black public schools, and at no time were there more than fourteen or fifteen.[88] But the number of separate black schools did not necessarily reflect the increase in the number of black children in the school system. This was especially true in the period after 1925 as a result of the reluctance of the Board of Public Education to create "colored schools" in the face of growing black opposition to the practice.[89] Howard Odum reported that in 1910 there were 8,192 black children in the elementary schools of Philadelphia, or 5.3 percent of the total. By 1915 the number enrolled in the age group from six to fifteen had increased only to 10,609, or 5.8 percent, of the total number (179,852).[90] However, with the beginning of the Great Migration there was a steady increase in the black public school population. By 1920, of the 199,628 children enrolled in the public school system, 16,226, or 8.1 percent, were black. This 50 percent increase in the black school population in five years was due primarily to the migration of southern blacks to the city; see table 6.[91]

In 1911 the school board reported that in the entire public school system there were, on average, thirty pupils per teacher. Ten years later, this figure was raised to forty-one pupils per teacher. The average number of black pupils per teacher in the separate public schools in 1921 was thirty-eight, according to the statistics made available by the Board of Public Education.[92] However, by the mid-1920s, many of the separate black schools were extremely overcrowded, forcing the administrators to

Table 6
Enrollment in the Philadelphia public schools

Year	Total Enrollment	Total Black Enrollment	Percentage Black Enrollment
1897[a]	137,119	6,262	4.3%
1908[b]	143,570	7,559	5.0
1910[c]	145,933	8,192	5.3
1915[d]	179,852	10,609	5.6
1920[d]	199,628	16,221	8.1
1925[d]	206,154	24,286	10.5
1930[d]	202,063	32,684	13.9
1935[d]	189,338	38,134	16.8
1940[d]	188,042	48,492	20.4
1945[d]	151,963	53,587	26.0
1950[d]	143,649	63,680	30.2

Notes: a. PBPE, Annual Report, 1897 (Philadelphia, 1898), p. 32; Du Bois, The Philadelphia Negro, p. 89.
b. PBPE, Report of the Bureau of Compulsory Education, 1908 (Philadelphia, 1909), p. 12.
c. Howard W. Odum, "Negro Children in the Public Schools of Philadelphia," The Annals 49 (September 1913): 187 (elementary schools only).
d. PBPE, "Reports of the Bureau of Compulsory Education," and "Reports of the Department of Instruction," Annual Reports, 1915–1950. See also Appendix 2, tables 15 and 16.

maintain two shifts of classes each day. This led to several protests by black parents against overcrowding.[93]

Daniel Brooks's belief that the separate schools were housed in old, dilapidated buildings happens to have been widely shared, and black parents often complained about the physical conditions in the black schools. In May 1916 black parents of children attending the John Reynolds School in North Philadelphia complained to Superintendent John Garber that a new building was needed: the existing structure had been erected in 1866 and was not in very good repair. The superintendent promised to "look into the matter," but major repairs were not carried out until 1925.[94] As is suggested by table 7, many of the separate black school buildings were quite old; but old, run-down buildings were a hallmark of the Philadelphia public school system throughout the first two decades of the twentieth century.[95]

Complaints by parents and citizens about the increasing segregation in the Philadelphia public schools became more and more frequent in the period from 1912 to 1920. On 20 February 1912, a delegation of black Philadelphians met with Superintendent Brumbaugh to discuss the "increase in Jim Crow schools."[96] The meeting was one of the results of an editorial that appeared in the *Philadelphia Tribune* on 17 February 1912, condemning the superintendent for pushing for more segregation in the school system. "The general public ought to know that the

Table 7

Separate black schools in the Philadelphia public school system, 1921

School	Date of Erection	Number of Classes	Number of Students	Average Class Size
Chester Arthur	1886	17	693	42
Thomas Durham	1909	35	1,221	35
Joseph Hill	1843	12	536	45
James Logan	1883	30	1,292	43
E. M. Stanton	1870	22	653	30
John Reynolds	1866	45	1,497	33
Martha Washington	1874	17	693	41

Source: PBPE, *Annual Report, 1921* (Philadelphia, n.d.), pp. 273–93.

Note: a. The five other separate black schools in Philadelphia in 1921 were considered annexes to other schools. The only separate information reported on these schools were the dates of erection of the buildings: Pollock School, 1854; Meehan School, 1901; Roberts School, 1873; Catto School, 1913; and Wilmot School, 1874. See PBPE, *Annual Report, 1921*, pp. 273–93.

Superintendent, aided by a few sly colored men, is determined to make the colored people of our city endure the objectionable [segregated] system," warned the editor.[97] Superintendent Brumbaugh later defended himself by pointing out that black children in the Philadelphia public schools were not forced to attend the separate schools. But the committee of black citizens was not satisfied with this statement and "resolved not to let the fight cease for an open door in every school house for colored children."[98] In another editorial in the *Tribune*, on 23 March 1912, the editor reiterated, "we are opposed to the segregation of children in the schools, and because of its damning influence, we propose to fight against it."[99]

In May 1912, a proposal for a $3 million school loan was on the primary election ballot. The editor of the *Tribune* urged that "Negroes vote it down." He stated that the money would be used to build new buildings for white children, "in order to make room in the old buildings for colored children, whom they propose to 'Jim Crow.'" The measure passed, however, in spite of black opposition.[100]

When the white administrators of the public school system were questioned about the policy of segregation, they would often answer that they had opened the separate schools at the request of the

Honor students at Reynolds Public School, a separate black school in North Philadelphia, in 1916–17 (Source: TUUA)

black community. This was an important issue, and the editor of the *Tribune* admitted in March 1915 that "it is difficult to tell who is in the majority because those who favor separate schools do so 'slyly' . . . and when one asks these people they say they never did so. Our pastors and others should come from their hidings and let the public know where they stand on this question." The reason for the *Tribune*'s opposition to the practice was that "the effect of such schools on the popular mind, is the thing we have observed is the most damaging. Prejudice against color certainly grows apace with the numerical growth of the 'Jim Crow' school."[101]

In July 1915 a controversy arose over what was considered the "industrialization" of the separate black elementary schools. According to the annual reports of the Board of Public Education for 1914, 1915, and 1916, steps were being taken to introduce "manual training" into the public elementary schools of the city. In 1914 Superintendent Brumbaugh reported that in order to allow boys in the public schools to work with their hands as well as their heads, "the work of manual training has been generalized throughout our school system to the great benefit and enrichment of the curriculum."[102] Although there was some movement in that direction, the annual report for 1916 revealed that a ma-

Honor students at Durham Public School, a separate school in South Philadelphia, in 1915–16. (Source: TUUA)

jority of the public elementary schools still had no "elementary industrial arts" program, while the introduction of industrial and vocational
education classes into the separate black schools proceeded more rapidly.[103] At the Thomas Durham School, one of the newest and largest
of the separate black public schools, elementary industrial arts were
taught in all the grades, and special shop classes in carpentry and metal-
working were offered to seventh and eighth graders.[104]

There is reason to believe that Superintendent Brumbaugh was
particularly interested in introducing industrial education into the separate black schools. In 1912 he commissioned the Armstrong Association
of Philadelphia to undertake a study of the occupations and wages of
working-age black pupils in the public schools, especially in comparison
with their white counterparts. The Armstrong Association carried out
the study by comparing the wages and jobs of the working-age white
students at the Potter School with a similar group of black students at
the Durham School. Because he believed the results of the study were

*Classroom exercises at Coulter Street Public School, a separate black school
in Germantown, around 1898. (Source: PBPE)*

"far-reaching," Superintendent Brumbaugh had them reprinted by the Board of Public Education.[105] The Armstrong Association found that a higher proportion of white pupils than black pupils were able to find employment during the summer and immediately after leaving school. There was also a great difference in the types of jobs held by whites and blacks. Black males were overwhelmingly employed as domestic servants and errand boys, while white males found jobs in factories and offices. This same dichotomy existed for white and black females.[106]

With respect to wages, there was very little difference between black and white males and black and white females, since both whites and blacks were just entering the job market and thus received the lowest wages paid in their occupations. However, the difference in the types of employment of black and white youths led the Armstrong Association to conclude that a "search should be made for new lines of occupation which furnish the best and most practical opportunities for these [black] boys and girls, especially the boys, and that colored children should be thoroughly equipped to meet their new as well as their present opportunities."[107] Thus, the study supported the introduction of a more practical curriculum into the black schools in order to prepare black students for the basic realities of the local job market.[108]

In the July 1915 issue of *The Crisis*, however, W. E. B. Du Bois wrote a scathing editorial attacking the introduction of so-called practical education into the Negro colleges. "The result of limiting the education of Negroes under the mask of fitting them for work is the slow strangulation of the Negro college." The precarious financial situation of these schools, and the insistence of white philanthropists and governmental authorities forced them to introduce industrial education. "What they are really asked to do," wrote Du Bois, "is to adopt a course of study which does not conform to modern standards, which no system of education will recognize and which condemns the student who takes it to end his education in a blind alley. It is an unforgivable sin of some of the greatest so-called industrial schools that the boy who is induced to take their course is absolutely unfitted thereby from continuing his education at a recognized modern institution. This is a crime against childhood for which any nation ought to be ashamed." Du Bois then proceeded to discuss what was happening in the City of Brotherly Love.

> The latest attack on Negro education comes from Philadelphia. Very adroitly and cunningly the Negroes have been massed in segregated schools. Now "industrial training" is to be introduced *in the Negro schools.* . . .
> Do Negroes oppose this because they are ashamed of having their children trained to work? Certainly not. But they know that

if their children are compelled to cook and sew when they ought to be learning to read, write and cipher, they will not be able to enter the high school or go to college as the white children are doing. It is a deliberate despicable attempt to throttle the Negro child before he knows enough to protest. (Italics in original.)[109]

Black parents and citizens in Philadelphia agreed with Du Bois's assessment of the situation and formed a committee, headed by Dr.

Nathan F. Mossell, director of the Frederick Douglass Hospital, to meet with school officials to discuss the "industrialization" of the separate black schools. An account of a meeting held that same month was printed in the *Tribune*. The school officials disagreed with Du Bois, pointing out that "this special training is a remedy for the condition of the colored children, for there is alleged to be a retardation in the standing of the grades and that this retardation was due to the colored children." Thus, the introduction of industrial education into the separate black schools was considered by school officials to be the most efficient way of dealing with the "educational aptitudes" of black children.[110]

The committee did not pursue the issue because several pre-existing

(opposite)
Octavius V. Catto Public School, a separate black school of the nineteenth and early twentieth centuries. (Source: PBPE)

James Forten Elementary Manual Training School, a separate black public school of the nineteenth and early twentieth centuries. (Source: PBPE)

organizations working in the black community agreed to monitor educational conditions for blacks in the public schools.[111] At the same time, with the coming of World War I, industrial activity in Philadelphia increased and many blacks were hired in the industrial plants and shipyards of the city. Industrial education then came to be seen as an asset to the black youth who wanted to take advantage of new wartime employment opportunities.[112]

Certain educational practices emerge as consistent throughout the nineteenth and early twentieth centuries. The existence of separate black schools, first as the only schools black children could attend, later as the only schools where qualified black teachers could teach, caused a number of problems for the black community, aside from the stigma of

Martha Washington Public School, a predominantly black elementary school in West Philadelphia that became a separate black school after 1920. (Source: PBPE)

segregation itself. Before 1881 black children were forced to attend these schools, whether or not they were in their neighborhood or housed in safe and sanitary buildings. After 1881 the refusal of the Board of Public Education to allow black teachers to teach white children and the continual creation of new separate schools further complicated attempts by the black community at united action to push for an end to the separate schools. It would take almost two more decades (1920–37) of protest and litigation to bring an end to the official practice of segregating blacks in the Philadelphia public schools.

At the same time, the issue of the separate black schools became caught up in the new intelligence testing movement. In Philadelphia the school officials who tested black children reported not only that it was educationally "efficient" to keep blacks in separate schools, but also that they should have a special curriculum that would be better suited to their "mental aptitudes" and future occupations. Thus, industrial education, which had become associated with the uplift of socially (and mentally) backward peoples, was introduced into the separate black public schools and the public schools with large numbers of immigrant children.[113] The fact that many blacks and European immigrants also believed that industrial arts and manual training courses would be of some benefit to their children meant that the protests against their introduction into the public schools were unsustained. However, the continual creation of separate black public schools throughout the period from 1920 to 1930 was a constant source of indignation and embarrassment within the black community. During the 1920s, organized and sustained protest activities would come to replace the earlier, more sporadic attempts to effect a change in conditions for blacks in the Philadelphia public school system.

3
Politics,
the Public Schools,
and the
Black Community in the 1920s

The Great Migration, World War I, and the increase in industrial opportunities brought several important changes in the social conditions of black Philadelphians by 1920. In that year the federal census reported that there were over 134,000 blacks in the city (7.4 percent of the total population), a 58.9 percent increase since 1910. The southern black migration that accounted for the greater part of this increase continued throughout the third decade of the century, so that by 1930 there were over 200,000 blacks in Philadelphia. This was a 63.5 percent increase in the population in ten years (see table 1).[1]

W. E. B. Du Bois had reported that in 1896 the overwhelming majority of black workers were unskilled manual laborers and domestic servants.[2] By 1910 the federal census revealed that 31.7 percent of the employed black males in the city were in some kind of domestic or personal service. In 1920 only 16.0 percent of the black males were employed as "servants," but 51.0 percent were "unskilled laborers." By the same token, in 1910 only 1.9 percent of the black male workers were considered "professionals," and in 1920, 1.7 percent were in this category, with 2.7 percent classified as "proprietors, officials, and managers." Thus, the increase in the population as a result of the migration and the greater opportunities for employment in industry did not significantly alter the overall occupational distribution for black males in Philadelphia. This situation continued through the 1920s, so that in 1930 only 1.8 percent of the black males were considered "professionals"; 2.6 percent were "proprietors, officials, and managers"; and 65.1 percent were classified as "unskilled workers" (see tables 8 and 9).[3]

The main occupation of employed black females in Philadelphia during the 1890s, according to Du Bois, was "domestic service." He calculated that at least 88 percent of working black females were domestics or other service workers.[4] In 1910 the federal census reported that

92.0 percent of the employed black females were in "domestic and personal service" (see table 4). In 1920, however, only 75.0 percent of black female workers in Philadelphia were considered "servants" of any type. Though "servant" was not used as a major occupational category in 1930, the census for that year did report that 74.6 percent of the employed black females were "unskilled workers." Thus, throughout the period from 1896 to 1930, the vast majority of the employed black females in Philadelphia were either domestic or other unskilled workers. In addition, in 1910, 1.13 percent of the black females were considered "professionals," and in 1920 this figure was raised to 1.19. By 1930, however, 2.2 percent of the black female workers were considered "professionals." One of the main reasons for the increase was the large number of black females hired as teachers in the Philadelphia public schools during the 1920s (see tables 8 and 9).[5]

Southern blacks who migrated to Philadelphia in the period from 1915 to 1930 were for the most part unskilled workers looking for jobs primarily in industries that did not require special training or skills. Some of the new arrivals were able to secure employment in the city's factories, but most did not. European immigrants, who made up a much larger proportion of the city's work force, fared much better than blacks in the competition for employment in the "semiskilled occupations," which included employment in factories. In 1920 only 23.5 percent of the black male workers in Philadelphia were employed in semiskilled and clerical occupations, whereas over 33 percent of the foreign-born males were employed in these areas. The large numbers of immigrants in the craft and skilled-trades unions in 1920 meant that the largest occupational category for foreign-born males was "skilled workers," while for blacks it was "laborers." For foreign-born females the largest occupational category was "semiskilled," a classification that reflected the large numbers of these women employed in factories throughout the city (see tables 8 and 9).

To obtain information on the general employment conditions for black workers, the Armstrong Association conducted a survey of blacks in Philadelphia industries in 1927, and found that black men and women "are now being assimilated rather slowly into the border of industry. The women are being employed in the tobacco and garment industries, and as always there is yet a majority of them following domestic and personal service." The reason given for the slow assimilation was the discrimination leveled against blacks in industry and by the unions. As of August 1927, the Association reported that "there has been a decrease in general employment, [and] Negroes have suffered more in proportion than whites, especially where employed as skilled or semi-skilled workers. The percentage of Negroes unemployed in Philadelphia is about 24 percent of the total number employed. Of 65,000 employed, there are about 16,000 unemployed."[6] The survey also noted that "there is a decided upward trend in home ownership. The housing problem still constitutes a major problem, but there are improvements in the housing conditions."[7]

The Armstrong Association, the Philadelphia Housing Association (PHA), and the Whittier Centre, a community social agency, conducted several studies of black housing in the city between 1915 and 1927. In 1915 the staffs of the Whittier Centre and the Housing Association visited 1,075 black families living in South Philadelphia and found that except for the problem of high rents, "the housing problem for the race differs in no wise from that of any other race. All alike suffer from laxity of the city, the lack of a definite program for sanitary improvements, the burden of a reactionary city council that knows no energy save to defeat or delay that which is for the good of the people." The researchers also pointed out that a large number of black families were forced to take in lodgers, which added to the overcrowding. The need for more single-family homes in the sections of the city where blacks lived and were employed was also stressed.[8]

Table 8
Occupational distribution of Philadelphia workers, 1920

Occupations	Males		Females	
	Foreign-born	Black	Foreign-born	Black
Proprietors, officials, managers	13.6	2.4	6.7	1.6
Clerks and kindred workers	7.3	3.8	15.7	1.7
Skilled workers	28.2	8.0	1.1	0.1
Semiskilled workers	25.7	15.4	46.2	18.7
Laborers	18.0	51.1	1.0	1.0
Servants	3.4	16.0	25.5	75.0
Public officials	0.1	—[a]	—	—
Semiofficial public employees	1.4	1.8	—[a]	—
Professionals	2.3	1.7	3.8	1.9
Total	100.0	100.0	100.0	100.0

Source: Dean Dutcher, The Negro in Industrial Society (Lancaster, Pa., 1930), Tables 20 and 23, pp. 96, 97, 106.
Note: a. Less than one-tenth of 1 percent.

In the 1921 annual report of the Philadelphia Housing Association, the organization's officials noted that the survey of homes carried out for that year showed that only 10 percent of black homes, as opposed to 28 percent of those of whites, were fully equipped for "sanitation, convenience, and comfort." The number of persons per hundred rooms for blacks was found to be seventy-eight, while the rate for whites in the same section of the city was ninety-four persons per hundred rooms.[9] In another survey of housing conditions, the Armstrong Association found that in 1922 there was little overcrowding among blacks, but many of the houses blacks lived in were "old, dilapidated and unsanitary."[10] The association also reported that blacks were often the victims of "rent-profiteering." For example, they noted that "early in 1920, real estate operators began a campaign to encourage former renters to buy homes. In many cases notices were served on tenants to buy or move. Having nowhere to go many undertook the task of buying homes at highly inflated prices." The Armstrong Association recommended the formation of a city housing agency, "whose purpose would be buying or taking on long time improvement leases of the old, dilapidated houses, and converting them into houses of comfort and respectability."[11] This recommendation, however, was not carried out.

The most comprehensive study of housing for black Philadelphians during the 1920s was the survey conducted by Thomas J. Woofter and Madge Priest in 1927 for the Institute of Social and Religious Research and the Interracial Commission of Philadelphia.[12] Woofter and Priest

Table 9
Occupational distribution of Philadelphia workers, 1930

Occupations	Males			Females		
	All	Foreign-born[a]	Black	All	Foreign-born[a]	Black
Proprietors, officials, managers	10.9	18.5	2.6	1.9	9.0	0.6
Clerks and kindred workers	18.7	5.5	4.3	32.5	11.9	1.6
Skilled workers	23.2	22.0	9.0	1.3	0.8	0.2
Semiskilled workers	24.4	22.5	16.6	32.6	25.8	20.8
Unskilled workers	18.2	29.0	65.7	21.8	42.3	74.6
Professionals	4.6	2.5	1.8	9.9	10.6	2.2
Total	100.0	100.0	100.0	100.0	100.0	100.0

Source: United States Natural Resources Committee, *Population Data: State Level* (Washington, D.C., 1937), pp. 93, 103–7.
Note: a. Figures are for foreign-born workers in the state of Pennsylvania.

described the various black neighborhoods and contrasted the better sections with the areas of "bad housing." Health conditions in tenements
and houses were also discussed. The high density rates (per acre) in
wards with large numbers of blacks were said to have been "responsible
for the fact that the tuberculosis death rate is so much higher than the
average for all cities in the registration area. The infant mortality rate
approximates the general city average largely because of the efficiency of
child health agencies. . . . The general Negro birth rate in Philadelphia
is 25.7 and the general death rate 22.1, making a small annual excess of ·
births over deaths."[13]

After brief mention of the sanitary conditions in the houses and
tenements, Woofter and Priest concluded that hope for improvement
lay in the constant movement toward greater home ownership among
blacks and in the continuing efforts by social agencies, such as the
Philadelphia Housing Association, the Whittier Centre, and the Octavia
Hill Association, to attack housing problems through the education of
tenants.[14] Some solace was derived from the observation that blacks were
beginning to move out of the south central section of the city into less
congested areas of North and West Philadelphia.[15]

Another "social problem" that was laid at the doorstep of the Great
Migration was the high crime rate among blacks in Philadelphia during
the 1920s. In a survey of crime based on arrests from 1 January 1924 to
30 June 1924, Anne B. Thompson reported that 24.4 percent of total
arrests for the period were of blacks. The overall rate of white arrests in
proportion to the white population was .007, or seven arrests for every
one thousand persons. For blacks the rate was .029. Although some of
the police statistics were viewed with suspicion by the researcher, it was
suggested that there was a need for vocational training and education
for blacks in Philadelphia similar to that provided at Hampton and
Tuskegee Institutes. It was also recommended that more recreational
facilities be made available to blacks, especially black juveniles.[16] Though
it was not mentioned in the report, discrimination in employment was
very likely as important as lack of training in accounting for the high
crime rates. The 20 percent unemployment rate and the inability to
obtain employment in areas other than those paying the lowest wages,
such as manual labor and domestic service, meant that some blacks were
forced into criminal activities in order to sustain themselves and their
families.[17]

Between 1920 and 1930, the increase in the percentage of blacks in
the city was not as large as the increase of black children in the public
schools. In 1920 blacks were 7.4 percent of the city population and 7.7
percent of the elementary school population. By 1930, however, blacks

were 11.3 percent of the city population, but 15.4 percent of the elementary school pupils.[18] The annual reports of the Department of School Superintendence did not note this significant increase until after 1925: in the period between 1915 and 1925, the public school administrators seem to have been more concerned about the large numbers of immigrant children in the school system. In 1915 it was reported that 92.3 percent of the children in the city between the ages of six and sixteen were born in the United States, but 46 percent had fathers who were foreign-born. In 1925, 97.1 percent of the children in Philadelphia were born in the United States, and 43.2 percent had fathers who were born outside this country. After 1925, and the change in the United States immigration laws, the number of children in the city foreign-born and with foreign-born parents began to decline, so that by 1930, although 41.4 percent of the children between six and sixteen had fathers who were foreign-born, 98.2 percent of the children of school age in the city were born in the United States.[19]

Beginning in 1917, the Board of Public Education began offering

Despite the existence of separate black public schools, most black children were enrolled in desegrated public schools and were instructed in mixed classrooms, such as this kindergarten class of the early 1930s. (Source: PBPE)

special English classes for children who were "handicapped by a foreign language, but who were capable, under special training, of placement in regular grades suited to their physical and mental development."[20] There were never large numbers of students enrolled in these English classes throughout the period from 1917 to 1930, although there were large numbers of foreign-born school-age children in the city. Many of the foreign-born students did not begin school until after they had learned to understand English, and many attended Catholic schools, where instruction was sometimes conducted in their native languages.[21]

After 1925 the increasing number of black children in the school system began to be a subject of concern for school officials. The Bureau of Compulsory Education's report for 1928 noted that between 1917 and 1928, the number of black children of school age in the city had increased by 108 percent, while the white school-age population had increased by only 4.6 percent.[22] Between 1917 and 1930, the white school-age group increased by 4.17 percent, while the black school-age population increased by 131.63 percent, and the greater part of this increase was absorbed by the public schools.[23] (See table 6.) Although the majority of black children in the public schools of Philadelphia were enrolled in racially mixed schools throughout the 1920s, the continual

Racially mixed junior high school shop class in the 1920s.

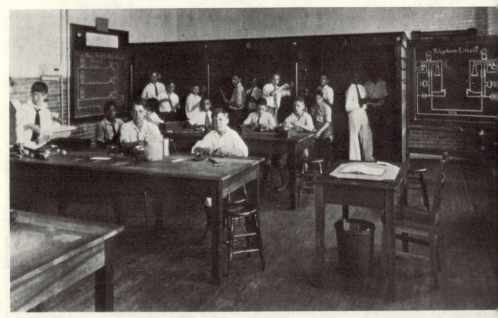

creation of separate black public schools led to an organized effort by black leaders in the city to end the official practice of segregation in the public school system.[24]

Black leaders and the struggle for the equal rights law

Black Philadelphia during the nineteenth century had a large number of gifted and talented leaders. As the community entered the twentieth century, however, many of these leaders passed from the scene. Robert Purvis, the former abolitionist and civil rights advocate, died in 1898; Robert Adger, civic leader and founder of the American Negro Historical Society, and Jacob C. White, principal of the Vaux School and a leading spokesman for the black community in the last quarter of the nineteenth century, both died in 1902. Several other important leaders of the old guard expired in the next two decades. Fannie Jackson Coppin, educational leader and principal of the Institute for Colored Youth, passed away in 1913, and William C. Bolivar, Philadelphia banker and for twenty years columnist for the *Philadelphia Tribune*, died in 1914. The founder and editor of the *Tribune*, Chris J. Perry, and Rev. William

Racially mixed special education class in the Philadelphia public schools in the early 1930s. (Source: PBPE)

Creditt, pastor of the First African Baptist Church and principal of Downingtown Industrial School, both died in 1921. G. Grant Williams, Perry's successor as editor of the *Tribune* and a militant black leader, passed away in 1922. Thus, by the end of the third decade of this century, Dr. Nathan F. Mossell, director of Frederick Douglass Hospital, and Dr. J. Max Barber, former editor of the *Voice of the Negro* and onetime president of the local branch of the NAACP, were the only surviving members of the old black leadership class still active in community affairs.[25]

A somewhat younger group of black leaders in Philadelphia were involved in city politics and the local NAACP during the twenties. These men and women tended to be rather conservative in outlook and worked primarily through the established political structures in the city. The undisputed leader of this "middle group" of black leaders was Edward W. Henry, president of the Citizens Republican Club, the leading black political organization in the city. Henry's success in rallying the black vote for the Republican party during the early 1920s led to his appointment as magistrate in the municipal court system in 1925.[26] The conservative leader of the Philadelphia branch of the NAACP throughout the 1920s, Isadore Martin, a prominent real estate broker, set the tone for the low profile that organization was to assume with regard to many of the important political demands of blacks in the city.[27]

Several writers have characterized the black political scene during the 1920s as one of "declining interest in local problems. . . . The Philadelphia Negro group was quiet, conservative, and more interested in education and religion than local politics."[28] However, this is not the impression one gets from perusing the *Philadelphia Tribune* and other sources for the period. Two important issues dominated the political activities of the black community: the struggle for the passage of a state equal rights bill, and the movement to end segregation in the Philadelphia public school system. The former struggle was led by the "middle group" of black leaders in the city; the latter, by a group of young black lawyers, including E. Washington Rhodes, Raymond Pace Alexander, and Herbert Millen.[29] The failure to achieve either of these important political objectives during the 1920s has generally been attributed to a lack of interest in local politics. There was a great deal of political activity, however, but the lack of black political power during the decade meant that these important community issues would not be resolved until the late 1930s.

"It is a far cry from the little, dingy, poorly ventilated, badly lighted converted storeroom," recalled the reporter for the *North American*, "to the splendid new theater devoted exclusively to 'cinema art,' as it is called these days, but it has been accomplished." The opening of the $2 million Stanley Theater at Nineteenth and Chestnut Streets on 28 January 1921 was a major social and political event of the season. Samuel and Jules Mastbaum, the major investors and promoters of the project, invited a potpourri of film personalities, socialites, and civic leaders, including the governor of Pennsylvania, William Sproul; the mayor, J. Hampton Moore; and all the city councilmen and state legislators. "The Stanley Company has a different idea about the amusement business. We believe we belong to the public, and not that the public belongs to us," Samuel Mastbaum assured the first-night audience; "we have tried to do everything we could, and if the public wants us as badly as we want them, we will go ahead and do greater things."[30]

John C. Asbury, the newly elected member of the state house of representatives from Philadelphia's predominantly black thirtieth ward, did not get to hear Mastbaum's pledges to the "public." When he arrived at the theater, rather than showing him to a seat with the other political dignitaries, an usher told him to go to the balcony; there, another usher told him to go up to the gallery. "Mr. Asbury, wishing to see just what the management would do, followed the usher until he reached the very last row in the gallery and was told, 'This is your seat.' Mr. Asbury looked at the situation of the seat, and realizing just what was meant, left the building." G. Grant Williams, the *Philadelphia Tribune's* managing editor, who reported the incident, also described the vicious attack upon his own wife in April 1917 at the old Stanley Theater at Sixteenth and Market Streets, where the ticket agent had refused to sell her a ticket. Williams reprinted Stanley Mastbaum's letter of 9 April 1917 in which he promised to "investigate the matter and assure you if the occurrence you spoke of took place, that it was without the slightest knowledge on our part." The managing editor concluded his report by noting that Representative Asbury had recently (February 1921) introduced an equal rights bill into the state legislature, and suggested that this latest insult may "perhaps give him more inspiration to push it."[31]

An abortive attempt to gain the passage of a state equal rights law had been made once before, in 1915. A bill successfully made its way through both houses of the legislature, only to be vetoed by Governor Martin G. Brumbaugh on what was termed a "technicality."[32] In the May 1920 Republican primary, several blacks ran for nominations to the state house of representatives from the predominantly black seventh and thirtieth wards in South Philadelphia. In the November election two black candidates were victorious: attorney John Asbury, a former city solicitor; and Andrew F. Stevens, a partner in one of the leading black insurance and brokerage firms in the city. These men were the first blacks from Philadelphia to be elected to the Pennsylvania General Assembly. Representative Asbury introduced his equal rights bill during the early days of the session, and from the outset the measure met with strong opposition. Initially the bill had the support of two powerful Republican bosses in the commonwealth, Boies Penrose, the U.S. senator, and State Senator Edwin H. Vare of the First District in Philadelphia. Hotel owners and restaurateurs throughout the state, however, began to lobby against the measure because it called for "the protection of all persons in their equal rights regardless of race, color or creed in places of public accommodations, entertainment or amusement and providing for the violation of the same." The hotel and restaurant owners argued that if blacks were allowed into their establishments, they would drive away paying white customers.[33]

On 12 March 1921, it was reported that the Asbury equal rights bill had been tabled by the Judiciary General Committee of the house. A second effort was launched in support of the bill by prominent black and white citizens led by Senator Edwin Vare. Several rallies were held in Philadelphia, and NAACP executive officials James Weldon Johnson and Robert Bagnall urged blacks to continue to lobby for the bill's passage.[34] On 29 March 1921, the measure successfully passed the house of representatives, but when it reached the state senate, a formidable attack was launched by Senator Cadwallader W. Barr of Allegheny County.[35] Hearings were held by the senate's Law and Order Committee. The opponents of the measure were ultimately successful, and the bill was not voted out of committee. It was later reported that one reason for the failure was the abandonment of the bill by Senator Boies Penrose in the face of the strong hotel and restaurant owners' lobby.[36]

In November 1922 John Asbury and Andrew Stevens were re-elected to the state house of representatives, and Representative Asbury again introduced the equal rights bill.[37] This time the measure was sent to the Judiciary General Committee, but no hearings were held and there was no floor debate; it was merely tabled by the committee and was not taken up again during that session of the assembly.[38]

When the time came for the announcement of candidacies for the state elections in 1924, to the surprise of the entire Philadelphia black community, Representatives John Asbury and Andrew Stevens announced that they were not going to run for re-election.[39] The reasons they gave for their decision were somewhat vague, but it was later reported that the Republican City Committee had decided not to support them for another term because of their advocacy of the passage of the equal rights bill.[40] In the Republican primary and general elections for 1924, William Fuller and Samuel Hart, supported by the Republican City Committee, were elected to the House seats vacated by Asbury and Stevens.[41] William Fuller, a graduate of Howard Law School, practiced law in the city. Samuel Hart was an inspector in the Department of Health and Charities and a clerk in the office of John A. Sparks, a prominent black Philadelphia attorney. Once in the legislature, these new black legislators did not introduce an equal rights measure throughout the remainder of the decade. It was not until the mid-1930s that a new group of black legislators was successful in gaining the passage of a state equal rights law.[42]

The problem of separate public schools, 1920–30

Throughout the 1920s, black Philadelphians were daily confronted by official and unofficial segregation. Racial barriers were erected in housing, employment, public accommodations, schooling, and other areas. Although restrictive covenants made it almost legal to discriminate in housing, and union membership regulations kept blacks out of most of the skilled trades, many blacks hoped that the passage of an equal rights bill would end discrimination at theaters, movie houses, hotels, restaurants, and other public places.[43] As was noted, black and white citizens worked for the passage of the Asbury bill during the 1920s, but without success. In the area of public education, however, there was already legislation prohibiting the forcing of black children to attend segregated schools. That is, opening public schools for blacks was not illegal, but forcing black students to attend them was. Moreover, when these schools were opened, black teachers gained jobs. The fact that some blacks benefited from their existence and continuation meant that during the 1920s the separate schools issue was a divisive one in the black community.

The situation surrounding the Cheyney Training School for Teachers during the early twenties graphically illustrates the conflicts that segregated schooling generated among black Philadelphians. Formerly the Institute for Colored Youth, the school had been supported primarily by the Society of Friends since 1837 as a secondary and teacher-training institution for blacks. Throughout most of its history the Institute for Colored Youth was located in Philadelphia and served many of the social, economic, and educational needs of the black community. In 1903, however, the school moved to Cheyney, Pennsylvania, twenty-five miles outside of the city, and in 1913 it became the "Cheyney Training School for Teachers."[44] At various times, beginning in 1914, the principal of the school, Leslie Pinckney Hill, tried to get state funds for the institution and certification as a state normal school.[45] Finally, in 1920, state officials designated Cheyney as a state teacher-training institution.[46]

Initially, blacks in Philadelphia were pleased with the announcement.[47] But in 1923, when Cheyney was about to receive its annual appropriation, several black citizens began to question the advisability of a state normal school "for Negroes" in Pennsylvania, and the motives of Principal Hill and others in seeking support for the "Jim Crow" institution. Hill was obliged to make his position clear. Writing in the April 1923 issue of *The Crisis*, the official magazine of the NAACP, Hill addressed the issue of increasing segregation in schools and other public places in the North. "This discussion, notably in Ohio, Pennsylvania, and New Jersey, is dividing colored people into bitter camps and factions. The arguments revolve around the fundamental question of segregation." With regard to his administration at Cheyney, Hill declared, "First I believe in no kind of enforced segregation, and in no kind of Jim-Crowism. On the contrary, the whole weight of this school has been exerted against these evils." However, Hill fully supported voluntary segregation by blacks themselves for mutual benefit and advancement. "I believe completely in the right of any group of Negroes to organize by themselves alone, or in cooperation with white friends, for any proper ends which they themselves may voluntarily choose to further. This right of self-determination is of the very essence of democracy. . . . When others will not help us, we will help ourselves." For Hill, Cheyney was "not a school set up by white state officials and forced upon Negroes, but a voluntary undertaking developed from within by the finest type of inter-racial cooperation. The State did not create Cheyney, on the contrary it represents the basic principle of voluntary group endeavor."[48]

Hill went on to oppose what he considered "the general hue and cry about segregation," each time a black teacher or student was allegedly the victim of discrimination. "The effective method is to treat each case specifically, locally, and directly. . . . My own limited experience in Pennsylvania teaches that whenever two or three colored men of personality, clear mind and good judgment, careful of the meaning of words, confer directly with officials about these local embarrassments, they almost invariably get a hearing and clear up the muddle." Hill saw little value in rallies and forums to educate the black community about these problems and the ways of dealing with them. "Indignation mass meetings, appeals to the passions of the crowd, general condemnation of the whole white race, bad manners and violent language turn back the wheels of progress." Hill concluded by pledging that he would "continue to develop this school primarily in the interest of my people, to keep its doors open at the same time to all qualified youth of any other race, to broaden the whole scope of its teaching and to work for the highest professional recognition."[49]

In the May 1923 issue of *The Crisis*, however, Philadelphia attorney G. Edward Dickerson and the Reverend William Lloyd Imes, chairman of the local NAACP's committee on public education, completely disagreed with Principal Hill's presentation of the situation. They pointed out that although state laws prohibited segregation in the public schools, the designation of Cheyney as a state normal school for blacks in effect meant that the state was supporting a *dual* teacher-training system. Hill had asserted that although Cheyney was ostensibly "for Negroes," with the receipt of state funds it had to open its doors to "any qualified student without regard to race, color or creed." Imes and Dickerson viewed this as a sham: if the school's catalogue stated that it prepared "Negro teachers," why should any white student wish to attend, especially since the predominantly white normal school for the area was only six miles from Cheyney? The writers also described incidents that supported their claim that after the certification of Cheyney, black students were less welcome at "white" normal schools than before, and the victims of greater mistreatment there, now that they did not have to attend them. The final criticism was especially significant: they suggested that the designation of Cheyney as the "separate" state normal school was only the prelude to the development of a separate public higher educational system for blacks in the state. "The next step will be to again legalize what has been illegally done; and we will have in law, as well as in act, a completely segregated school system in the entire state."[50]

W. E. B. Du Bois, in a speech at Cheyney in July 1923, reprinted in *The Crisis* under the title "The Tragedy of 'Jim Crow,'" decried the increasing segregation in the North and outlined the activities of the NAACP in opposing its spread. He went on to discuss the paradox of having to oppose segregation in the public schools, and, at the same time, honor and appreciate black teachers and black schools. "How can we follow this almost self-contradictory program? Small wonder that Negro communities have been torn in sunder by deep and passionate differences of opinion arising from this pitiable dilemma." Du Bois stated unequivocally that "first and foremost and more important than anything else, Negro children must not be allowed to grow up in ignorance. This is worse than segregation, worse than anything we could contemplate."

"Race feeling" among white southerners, Du Bois noted, made it very unlikely that segregation would soon end in the South. Thus, blacks must do the best they can to educate their children within the segregated system. But in the mixed schools of the North it was necessary to give encouragement and inspiration to black students, many of whom were discriminated against in these schools. He mentioned a program in New York City where parents and teachers were involved in supervising the courses of the black children in mixed schools: "We are seeking to guide them there and to help them at home; we try to discover and oppose prejudiced teachers; we encourage their enrollment in high schools." Then he touched upon the situation in Philadelphia. Du Bois believed that black Philadelphians had been allowing the number of separate schools to grow for several years without protesting, but on this occasion were upset over the designation of Cheyney as a state normal school. He believed there was no evidence that Hill and his faculty were interested in "forcing" segregation on blacks in the state; they merely wanted to train more black teachers. Thus, protests should be leveled not against the black teachers, but against those persons, black and white, who sought to saddle a program of permanent "Jim Crow" upon the state system of higher education. Du Bois concluded with some suggestions as to how blacks in Philadelphia could work to halt the growing segregation in the city schools.[51]

Later events, however, showed that black Philadelphians were correct in their belief that the support of Cheyney by the state could lead to further attempts at segregation in public higher education. In February 1925 State Senator Albert MacDade of Delaware County, in which Cheyney was located, introduced a bill that would have taken the school out of the state system of public normal schools and made it a separate technical and industrial institute for blacks under the direction of an administrative board within the state Department of Public Instruction.[52] This would have made Cheyney a separate state college that would not only offer teacher-training courses, but would also provide technical and industrial education. Thus, Cheyney Training School for Teachers would become the "Pennsylvania State Industrial Institute for Negroes." Opposition to the measure immediately sprang up in Philadelphia, and when the bill was read in the house in April 1925, Representative William Fuller of Philadelphia led the attack that returned the measure to the Committee on Education. There the bill was tabled and not taken up again.[53] In this instance, black politicians were able to thwart the efforts of some state legislators to create a publicly supported industrial institute for blacks in Pennsylvania.

The Philadelphia Board of Public Education, however, was much more successful in its efforts to create separate black public schools than were the members of the Pennsylvania General Assembly. In Philadelphia the increase in the black school population led not only to the transformation of old schools from predominantly white or mixed to all-black, but also to the construction and opening of new schools for black pupils only. The continual creation by the school board of all-black public schools during the first two decades of this century led to the formation in 1922 of the Committee on Public Schools and Race Relations within the local branch of the NAACP. In June of that year the committee launched a protest campaign against the practice of segregation in the public schools and presented a program to public school officials for the integration of both the faculties and students in the public school system.[54] At a conference between the NAACP representatives and the Elementary Schools Committee of the Board of Public Education in July 1922, the school officials promised to consider the NAACP's recommendations.[55]

Later that year, the NAACP Committee on Public Schools received a letter from a Mrs. Raymond MacDevitt (a white woman), who protested against the "dangerous physical conditions" at the E. M. Stanton Public School, an all-black institution created in 1920.[56] The school building was well over fifty years old, and she believed it was a hazard to the safety of the pupils. Rev. William Lloyd Imes, chairman of the Public Schools Committee, wrote a letter of protest to the school board, asking to be kept informed of any action it decided to take with respect to the Stanton School.[57] Although there is no evidence that the school board kept the local NAACP "informed" of its efforts to improve conditions, the E. M. Stanton School was rebuilt in 1925.[58]

At the membership drives and rallies held by the Philadelphia NAACP in 1923 and 1924, the situation in the city's public schools was often an important topic of discussion. At a rally held on 13 May 1923 at Central Presbyterian Church, segregation in public schools in Philadelphia and throughout the North was the subject of a speech by Robert Bagnall, then national director of branches of the NAACP.[59] The ninth annual convention of the association was held in Philadelphia in June 1924, and several sessions were devoted to the issue of segregation in the public school systems of the North.[60] W. E. B. Du Bois, Rev. William Imes, and several others discussed various strategies, including litigation against school officials, to bring about a change in the policies and practices of these school systems.[61]

During the 1924–25 school year, blacks in Philadelphia decried the continued existence of separate schools in the city as new incidents occurred stemming from the "Jim Crow" system. In September 1924 Daniel Brooks, then principal of the Reynolds Public School, predicted that the school board would be creating as many as four more separate schools during the 1925–26 school year.[62] In January 1925 several recent black graduates of Philadelphia High School for Girls were humiliated when they were forced to sit at a separate table at a luncheon at the Bellevue-Stratford Hotel.[63] In February 1925 the Board of Public Education attempted to transfer the black students from the newly renovated Joseph Hill Public School to another old building in order to allow white students to use the remodeled building. Black parents immediately protested against the move and sent a petition with fifteen pages of signatures to the school board. A few days later the board decided to rescind the transfer order.[64] As a result of these incidents and other problems, the local NAACP's Committee on Public Schools sent

E. M. Stanton Public School, a predominantly black elementary school in South Philadelphia that became a separate black school in 1920. (Source: PBPE)

another protest letter to the Board of Education, asking to meet with them about the school situation.[65] This request, too, was ignored.

The school board's failure to respond to the NAACP's petitions, protests, and requests for meetings could not be attributed entirely to the insensitivity of the board members to black concerns. For while the *Philadelphia Tribune* and the NAACP were quite open in expressing their indignation at the increasing school segregation, there were other, less vocal members of the Philadelphia black community, most notably the black public school teachers, who favored the creation of separate black public schools. During the early twenties, the school system was saddled with the problem of a shortage of qualified teachers, primarily due to World War I. As a result, school officials decided to increase the number of students admitted to the Philadelphia Normal School, the major supplier of elementary school teachers for the city's system.[66] By 1924, however, the policy had been so effective that the school board announced that it would begin to cut back the number of entrants.[67] At the same time, while the number of white students entering the elementary schools was declining, the number of black elementary school pupils was increasing. Thus, if the Board of Public Education continued its practice of creating separate black schools with all-black faculties, there would be jobs for black teachers at a time when the total number of teaching positions available in the system was decreasing.[68]

In May 1925 the Pennsylvania Association of Teachers of Colored Children (PATCC) held its tenth annual meeting at the Cheyney Normal School. The membership of the organization was made up mainly of black teachers from Philadelphia and the surrounding suburbs. Thus, during the 1925 convention the major questions discussed were: "Are Colored Schools Necessary? When is a Colored School Improperly Constituted? What are the Dangers of Colored Schools? What Is the Effect of Colored Schools on Attendance, Retardation and Scholarship?"[69] At the height of the campaign against the increase in the number of separate public schools in Philadelphia, the PATCC passed a resolution in favor of the continuance of segregation in public education in the state. The PATCC argued that the separate institutions were an aid to "race development." The leadership pointed out that a large number of black children had problems in mixed schools with prejudiced teachers, administrators, and students. They also argued that although many blacks attended mixed schools throughout the state, few graduated. Thus, PATCC resolved that separate schools did provide some benefits to black Pennsylvanians.[70]

The resolution was published in its entirety in the *Philadelphia Tribune* without editorial comment. Indeed, the statement by the teacher's association did serve to bring some balance to the controversy over the separate public schools. In the process of condemning the increasing segregation of black children in city schools, the opponents also sometimes condemned the black teachers, who may have been trying to provide the best possible education for the pupils under their instruction. But it is clear that the resolution reflected to a great extent the self-interest of black teachers, and that it could have given added encouragement to those persons seeking to increase the number of Jim Crow schools in Philadelphia.

Although it is unlikely that the Board of Public Education was influenced by the resolution of the PATCC, it did proceed with its policy of creating separate schools at the opening of the 1925–26 school year. In September 1925, the newly constructed Walter George Smith

Walter George Smith Public School, opened in South Philadelphia in 1925 as a separate black school. (Source: PBPE)

Public School was opened in School District 2 in South Philadelphia. The school board decided not only that the school would be all-black, but also that black pupils enrolled at the nearby Childs, Nichols, and Landreth (mixed) schools would be transferred to the new Smith School. The parents of the children who were to be transferred from their neighborhood schools to the new, separate school immediately protested against the policy to school officials. It was reported that the District 2 superintendent, Armand J. Gerson, gave as the reason for the policy the "overcrowding" in the mixed schools and "the desire of Negroes for separate schools."[71] It was also reported that Italian and Jewish parents in the neighborhood of the Smith School were upset by the refusal of the principal, George Lyle, to allow their children to enroll in the "brand-new" school.[72]

A protest meeting was held in South Philadelphia on 9 September 1925 in St. Simon's Parish House, and Robert Bagnall from the national office of the NAACP and Isadore Martin, president of the Philadelphia branch, pledged the support of that organization in a legal battle. Up to this point the Board of Public Education had not violated the school law of 1881, which prohibited the forcing of black students to attend separate schools. However, the transfer of only black students from their neighborhood mixed school to a new, separate school was considered by many lawyers a clear violation of the school code.[73] A second protest meeting was held on 13 September at Simmons Baptist Church, and a third took place on 15 September, again at St. Simon's. At the last meeting it was announced that Superintendent of Public Schools Edwin Broome had let it be known that black children would be allowed to attend the Landreth School since it was quite a distance from the new Smith School, but "the ban would not be let down at the others."[74]

The Legal Aid Committee of the local NAACP, led by Herbert Millen, an attorney, had been exploring "what grounds we have to base legal action upon and also against whom the proceedings shall be initiated."[75] The school board probably could legally transfer black students from the Nichols and Childs schools to Smith because all three were in the same neighborhood. In the case of Landreth, however, the Board of Public Education had refused to admit black pupils to their neighborhood school, and a suit could be filed. But when the school board realized this and decided to rescind the transfer order, the Legal Aid Committee decided it lacked grounds for litigation.[76]

In the ensuing months, as the NAACP lawyers wrestled with the issue of the possible infractions of the school code committed by the Board of Education, other individuals made suggestions as to how the black community should deal with the separate schools. A. Philip Ran-

*Herbert Millen, attorney and later judge in the municipal courts of Phila-
delphia. (Courtesy of the Philadelphia Tribune)*

dolph, then leader of the Brotherhood of Sleeping Car Porters, suggested
that blacks in Philadelphia boycott the separate schools as black parents
and students had done in Dayton, Ohio, in order to end segregation in
the public schools.[77] The inability of blacks to organize such a school
boycott in Philadelphia was indicative of the lack of unity on this issue.
At the Emancipation Day Celebration on 1 January 1926, Hallie Q.
Brown, former president of the National Association of Colored Women,
urged that blacks in Philadelphia work to get a black on the school

board who would represent the educational interests of the black community.[78] This was not a new suggestion, for the *Philadelphia Tribune* had been urging the nomination of Rev. William Lloyd Imes to the school board since 1924.[79]

In January 1926 the Board of Public Education created another separate black school, this time in North Philadelphia. The Singerly Public School, which had had a predominantly black student body and an all-white faculty, was transformed into a school with all-black pupils and teachers.[80] On 6 February 1926, the Philadelphia NAACP again wrote to the school board and complained that "a number of times we have asked for a conference and as many times you have ignored our request. . . . Self-respecting Negroes of Philadelphia do not feel that they are receiving a square deal from the Board of Education. Nearly 200,000 citizens have no voice in the management or anything connected with the schools their children attend. This is not fair or just and we respectfully ask that you think this matter over seriously and then arrange for a conference with a small committee of our group to the end that the present feeling of bitterness in the hearts of many be brought to an end."[81]

Again there was no response from the school board, and the Philadelphia NAACP held another series of rallies on "The Evils of the Separate School System and the Remedies for the Situation." At these meetings, in February and March 1926, the major topic of discussion was how blacks who opposed the creation of separate public schools could bring litigation to end the practice. The problem of the black teacher in the separate school was also a subject of concern. Local NAACP President Isadore Martin summed up the issue by pointing out that "there was no feeling against the colored teachers except where the teacher justifies or advocates the creation of Jim Crow schools to provide places for Jim Crow teachers." The many opponents of the separate public schools agreed that if segregation went unprotested in one area of city life where it was illegal, this would be the signal to begin segregation in others.[82]

In May 1926 blacks in Philadelphia finally received some indication of the opinion of school officials about the separate schools from a speech delivered by Superintendent Edwin Broome at the annual meeting of the PATCC. The *Philadelphia Tribune* reported that Superintendent Broome believed that "the mere fact that Negroes in Philadelphia were opposed to a separate school system was no basis upon which the policy of the Board of Education was decided."

> The question of education is general—neither white nor colored. No one wants segregated schools but this in itself is no basis upon which

we decide as to the advisability of separate schools. If colored people are more happy together, trained by their own teachers, and ask for a hearing on an educational basis—they will be listened to. We will, I assure you, fight against poor school houses and poor equipment in South Philadelphia.

Superintendent Broome went on to point out that a school would stay white if the "white element" predominated, but "whenever the colored element was in predominance it was deemed wise to transfer all of the white students and faculty members and install a colored faculty."[83] The superintendent's remarks informed the black community that school administrators would continue to create separate public schools. And those persons interested in ending the practice of segregation knew that they would have to find some legal grounds to force a change in the policies and practices of the school board.

To raise money for litigation and to inform more members of the community of the issues surrounding the separate schools, the *Philadelphia Tribune* announced on 17 April 1926 the formation of the *Tribune* Defense Fund Committee to hold meetings and collect funds for litigation against the school board. The goal of the Defense Fund was to raise $1,000, which would be turned over to any group involved in a suit to bring about an end to segregation in the Philadelphia public school system.[84] The *Tribune* solicited funds through the columns of the newspaper, and contributions were kept on deposit in a local black bank.[85]

During the summer of 1926 the Sesquicentennial Celebration of the United States was held in Philadelphia. Black residents were successful in their lobbying efforts against the practice of segregation at the exposition.[86] The festivities extended into September 1926, after the opening of the public schools for the 1926–27 school year. Thus, the segregation practiced by the public school system became much more blatant and offensive, especially in light of the municipal government's ban on the practice during the Sesquicentennial. In an editorial in the *Tribune* on 9 October 1926, E. Washington Rhodes, editor and chairman of the Defense Fund Committee, voiced his concern over the apathy of many black leaders in pursuing the litigation against the school board. He went on to state that the *Tribune*'s pleas for public support in bringing an end to separate public schools seemed to have "fallen on deaf ears."[87] The following week a letter from State Representative Samuel Hart appeared in the newspaper. Hart disagreed with the editor's statement about the lack of interest of black leaders in the school issue, and asked that a special public meeting be held in the interest of the

Defense Fund where the various community and political leaders could make their positions clear.[88]

Later that month an incident occurred that might have allowed the local NAACP's Legal Aid Committee to take the school board to court for practicing segregation. It was reported that when Roscoe P. Douglas tried to enroll his son at the Keyser Public School in the Germantown section of the city, the principal refused to allow the child to be registered. When Mr. Douglas went to discuss the problem with Louis Nusbaum, the district superintendent, he was told that he should send his child to the Meehan Public School, a separate black school four blocks away, because "there had never been a colored child at this school." Mr. Douglas had his lawyer, Henry P. Cheatham, file a writ of mandamus to allow his son to attend his "neighborhood school." At that point the district superintendent still refused to allow the child to be enrolled at the Keyser School, but now claimed the reason was "overcrowding."[89] At the public meeting in support of the *Tribune* Defense Fund at the Gibson Theater on 5 December 1926, the Legal Aid Committee of the NAACP pledged to assist Mr. Douglas and attorney Cheatham in their suit against the Board of Public Education.[90]

In answer to the petition for the writ of mandamus, the school board argued that it did not have to send pupils to the school nearest their homes, especially if the nearest school was overcrowded. The court agreed with the Board, and the petition for the writ was denied.[91] The Legal Aid Committee found that this was not the case that could challenge the board's practice of creating separate black public schools; in fact, no case that involved the admission or nonadmission of pupils to a school would get at the problem of segregation as practiced in the Philadelphia public school system. For the real problem was not the twelve or fourteen separate schools where only black children were enrolled, but the fact that these were the only schools in the system where black teachers were allowed to teach.[92] And it was not until the mid-1930s, when opponents of segregation in the schools shifted their emphasis from the creation of separate black public schools to the policy of "Jim Crowing" black teachers, that some change was made in the practice of segregation in the Philadelphia public schools.

Through the numerous rallies sponsored by the *Tribune* Defense Fund Committee and the articles and editorials that appeared in the newspaper, the issue of the separate schools was kept before citizens in the community.[93] At the 16 October 1927 rally at the Royal Theater, which featured Kelly Miller, dean of Howard University, and V. F. Calverton, literary critic and editor of *The Modern Quarterly*, it was announced that the Defense Fund had passed the $1,000 mark.[94] On 7 November 1927, a letter was sent by the Defense Fund Committee to Julian St. George White, secretary of the Philadelphia NAACP, to inform the organization that the money collected would be available to help defray the costs of litigation against the Board of Education.[95] However, because the Legal Aid Committee was unable to find a suitable case, the money remained on deposit in the bank. Finally, on 11 July 1929, after more than a year without a response from the local NAACP, an editorial appeared in the *Tribune* entitled "The NAACP Needed." The editor, E. Washington Rhodes, congratulated the national organization on its twentieth anniversary and praised the work the NAACP had accomplished nationally for black Americans. Then Rhodes went on to discuss the local branch.

> Philadelphia needs the N.A.A.C.P. badly. Conditions here are just a little better than they are in Georgia. It would not be a bad idea for the association to begin operation in this city. Philadelphians have contributed to the national fund. We are not selfish. We are interested, intensely so, in our brothers in the South. We would not have the work lag there. We are willing to contribute our full quota to the cause of securing for them the right of franchise and the abolishment [sic] of segregation. But on the other hand, segregation is taking a death hold on the Negroes of Philadelphia. We have jim crow schools springing up like mushrooms. Theaters, cafes and hotels humiliate and bar us. City and state officials persecute us. We realize the value of the association. We, therefore, beseech those who are at the head to come over and help us.
>
> A campaign of intense activity is needed to arouse those who have become indifferent because of so much suffering. The old fighting spirit has died down. It needs to be reawakened. While we have been dreaming of other fields to conquer the enemy has slipped in and defeated us. The local situation is serious. There is need for new blood, clearer vision and a will to fight.[96]

Though there was no official response to the statement, in a letter to Walter White, then assistant secretary of the NAACP, Isadore Martin, president of the Philadelphia branch, commented on some of the charges in the editorial. Martin claimed that Rhodes was "narrow and selfish" and "a little 'sore' because the local officials would not cater to his selfish plans in connection with a small fund raised here to fight segregation in our schools." He then described the origin and activities of the *Tribune* Defense Fund Committee. Martin stated that the reason the Legal Aid Committee would not accept the funds was that the *Tribune* committee was trying to "dictate to us what we should do."

He said he had informed the committee that any action would have to be planned and coordinated through the national office of the NAACP, and implied that Rhodes, who was also an attorney, resented the insistence that the NAACP choose the lawyers to fight the school segregation cases. Martin asked that the national office not publicize the editorial, and ended by asserting that "if after more than two years a paper like the *Tribune* can raise only $1,000 to fight public school segregation, you can easily see how much the people of this city want to do away with segregation."[97]

This last statement provides more insight into the attitudes of the local NAACP officials than those of black Philadelphians in general. When Rev. William Lloyd Imes was chairman of the Committee on Public Schools, he led the local NAACP in trying to combat the growing number of separate public schools in the city. However, after Imes's departure from Philadelphia, the organization became less and less involved in the struggle. After 1925 Rhodes and the *Philadelphia Tribune* assumed leadership of the fight and succeeded in maintaining interest in the issue long after it appeared that the local NAACP had given up.[98] There is very little evidence that black Philadelphians were indifferent to segregation in public schools, and a great deal of evidence, especially in the form of large attendances at the Defense Fund rallies, that they wanted the practice ended.[99] It should also be noted that it took a year and six months (not over two years) to raise $1,000 largely because the Defense Fund had to compete with various other worthy causes to which blacks were asked to contribute during the period, including the Philadelphia branch of the NAACP.[100]

The failure of the leadership in the Philadelphia black community to bring about a change in the policies of the school board with regard to the separate schools should not be blamed entirely upon the conservatism of the local NAACP, nor on the alleged apathy of the black community. The problem of segregation in the public schools was a political issue that could best be dealt with through the utilization of political power to force the school officials to change their policies. Most black Philadelphians were well aware of the great social and economic advances being made by blacks in other northern cities, especially Chicago, through the mobilization of black voters and participation in municipal politics.[101] A few blacks participated in Philadelphia politics during the twenties, but because the black vote was considered to be in the hip pocket of the Republican bosses, few concessions were made to black demands by the Republican machine. The dearth of prominent black politicians in the ranks of the city's Republican Party made it even less likely that black demands for an equal rights law or an end to school segregation would be supported (or even acknowledged) by Republican city officials. It was only with the challenge of a black defection to the Democratic Party in the early thirties that Republican politicians began to move on black political demands.

Thus, after almost three decades of protests, petitions, conferences, and rallies, black teachers and children were more segregated in the Philadelphia public school system in 1929 than they were in 1899. The migration of southern blacks that began before the outbreak of World War I and continued throughout the 1920s brought large numbers of black children into the Philadelphia public schools. But the major response of school officials to this situation was the creation of more separate black public schools.

4
Community Education in Black Philadelphia, 1900–1930

The families and individuals that made up the black community of Philadelphia had a great deal in common with the other residents of the city. They all read the same daily newspapers and followed the win-loss records of the local sports teams. Increases in taxes and municipal corruption were deplored by honest, hard-working Philadelphians in the local Italian, Jewish, Polish, or Afro-American communities. W. C. Fields's epitaph, "I'd rather be here than in Philadelphia," and the numerous other "Philadelphia jokes" gave black and white, rich and poor, religious and irreligious residents at least a twinge of embarrassment, especially if they believed the stories had some basis in truth. These and other social events and local traditions were part of the Philadelphia experience, and families and individuals shared in this experience because they were living in the Quaker City during the same era.

The similarities and commonalities of experiences for Africans living in colonial Philadelphia were necessary in developing a sense of community among them, but these were not sufficient. In order for free blacks to organize and deal effectively with problems and issues as a group, there had to be a collective awareness or "consciousness" of their common interests and a willingness to act on the basis of shared group experience. Thus, when Richard Allen arrived in Philadelphia in 1786, there were many pressing social problems and little sense of community among African families and individuals. Allen, Absalom Jones, Samuel Batson, Cato Freeman, Caesar Chanchall, William White, and others knew that most of the free blacks were religious, and so tried to organize a community around their common social and religious experiences. Initially the attempt failed. Though virtually all of the Africans in the city were Christians, they were also Roman Catholics, Episcopalians, Methodists, Quakers, or members of a number of other Christian denominations active in colonial Philadelphia. Christianity was common to most free blacks in the city, as was racial discrimination, but it was consciousness of the group or racial basis of oppression, and the willingness of Allen, Jones, and the other founders of the Free African Society to act to further group—as opposed to individual—interests, that signaled the real beginning of the black community in Philadelphia.[1]

Once the community was organized, it had to be kept informed of the issues and problems facing its members. This led to the development of community education programs that allowed individuals and organizations within the group to communicate with one another. As was the case with many other racial, cultural, and religious minority groups, the community education programs were only a part, though a significant part, of the total educational process for the Philadelphia black community. Black Philadelphians were informed and educated by the public schools, the local media, including books, magazines, newspapers, lectures, forums, conferences, and later radio and television (several decades after 1930), as well as a myriad of other educational activities available in a large urban center. In this chapter, however, we will examine the programs sponsored between 1900 and 1930 by the more important black social organizations to educate the members of the community about those things that they should know as Afro-Americans living in a city that was only slightly north of the Mason-Dixon line.

During the last decade of the eighteenth century, a community education program was sponsored in the free black community by the Pennsylvania Abolition Society. The Committee to Visit Coloured People came to the black church congregations every two or three months and read "memorials and dissertations" on public conduct, citizenship, and morality.[2] During the same period, the Free African Society and the black churches sponsored activities to educate free blacks in the essentials of "mutual protection" and "social advancement." In antebellum Philadelphia, a wide variety of black social and literary societies sponsored community-wide educational activities. Historian and archivist Dorothy Porter has examined black literary and debating societies, library companies, and social improvement societies in Philadelphia, New York, Washington, D.C., and other cities and found that these groups were active in presenting public lectures, publishing and distributing antislavery newsletters, tracts, and pamphlets, and providing reading materials.[3] In Philadelphia the most important social organizations providing community-wide educational programs during this era were the Female Literary Society, the Library Company of Coloured Persons, and the Association for the Moral and Mental Improvement of People of Colour. Although the primary function of these organizations was not necessarily the sponsoring of educational programs, their members believed that providing community-wide educational activities was an effective way of serving the community. These social groups viewed "community service" as an important aspect of their overall program of activities.[4]

As the number of blacks in Philadelphia increased between 1870 and 1900, there was a proliferation of social organizations and institutions in the black community. W. E. B. Du Bois described the activities of many social, secret, and cooperative associations in *The Philadelphia Negro*—the benevolent and fraternal organizations, the literary societies, and political clubs—but he virtually ignored the "community service" and community education programs sponsored by these groups. Many of the organizations active during the first three decades of the twentieth century had their origins in the late nineteenth century. These organizations sponsored hundreds of lectures, exhibitions, conferences, and public meetings on a wide variety of topics and issues of community interest.[5] Between 1900 and 1930 the educational activities tend to fall into three overlapping areas of concern: education in the black heritage, education for individual and community development, and education for black social and political advancement. Through an examination of the educational activities of black social organizations, we are able to determine just how black Philadelphia educated itself during the early decades of the twentieth century.

Education in the black heritage

Many of the black social institutions and organizations to be discussed were active in the discovery and rediscovery of black history. Since the accomplishments of blacks and their contributions to the development of the nation were often not integrated into American history, it became necessary for black Americans to preserve and document their own history in the United States. Just as the black newspaper filled a specific need of the black community, the rise of historical societies and organizations can be seen as an attempt to fill a gap in the black community's knowledge of itself.[6]

The earliest black historical organization in Philadelphia was the Reading Room Society, founded in March 1828. This was followed by the Benjamin Banneker Institute in 1854. Both of these societies were primarily involved with providing reading materials for the "mental improvement" of black Philadelphians.[7] The most ambitious and important historical undertaking of blacks in Philadelphia in the late nineteenth and early twentieth centuries was the formation of the American Negro Historical Society in October 1897. Meeting at the Church of the Crucifixion, Robert Adger, Rev. Matthew Anderson, Rev. Henry L. Phillips, and several other prominent persons started the society in order to "collect relics, literature and historical facts in connection with the African Race, illustrative of their progress and development."[8] Coming together on the fourth Tuesday of every month, the members discussed historical materials unearthed by the individuals in the group. On 28 December 1897, a committee on the celebration of the Emancipation Proclamation reported on the preparations for the first public lecture to be sponsored by the society. It took place on 3 January 1898 at Allen Chapel, on Lombard Street above Nineteenth. Rev. J. C. Brock, a member of the group, spoke on "The Dawning of Liberty"; Rev. Matthew Anderson discussed "The Achievements of the Colored People in 25 Years of Liberty"; and Mr. William Baugh related the exploits of "The Colored Soldier."[9]

The public lectures of the American Negro Historical Society were an important forum for the education of Philadelphians in the black heritage from 1898 to 1923, when the society ceased its activity. During that period such illustrious black Philadelphians as Bishop Levi J. Coppin, John C. Asbury, Jessie Fauset, and William C. Bolivar were to lecture on historical and contemporary topics under the society's auspices.[10]

Several church and literary societies in black Philadelphia also sponsored free lectures on historical topics. The largest and most active of these groups were listed in the Philadelphia "colored directories" for 1908, 1910, and 1913.[11] These literary societies were usually made up of interested communicants from the various black churches; for example, the J. C. Price Literary Society was organized by the members of the Wesley A. M. E. Zion Church in Philadelphia.[12] Other groups were not directly connected with churches, as was the case with the Paul Lawrence Dunbar Literary Society and the Phillis Wheatley Literary Society, which was founded by Rev. Richard Robert Wright, Jr., for many years editor of the *Christian Recorder*, an official publication of the African Methodist Episcopal Church.[13]

One can gauge the amount and type of activities of these societies through a perusal of the *Philadelphia Tribune*, which usually published information on the groups in its religious columns.[14] One of the most active of the church literary societies during the period from 1920 to 1928 was the Pinn Memorial Literary Society. This organization not only sponsored lectures by its membership and other Philadelphians, but also worked with other groups to bring speakers to the city to give free public lectures, especially for celebrations of the black heritage.[15] Beginning with Emancipation Day, 1 January, speeches and lectures at these commemorative celebrations informed the black community of its heritage and made clear the relationship between the past event and contemporary conditions. In the period from 1920 to 1930, the Citizens' Committee of Allied Organizations arranged for audiences of five hundred to five thousand to assemble at the Philadelphia Academy of Music or Tindley Temple on Emancipation Day to hear such prominent speakers and musicians as Carl Diton (1920), James Weldon Johnson (1921), Emmett J. Scott (1924), Marian Anderson (1925), and Hallie Q. Brown (1926).[16]

The month of February was particularly eventful because of the celebrations of the birthdays of Abraham Lincoln (the twelfth) and Frederick Douglass (the fourteenth). Activities included public lectures and speeches throughout the city dealing with the contributions of these two men to the nation.[17] Beginning in 1926, Negro History Week subsumed both dates under a more general celebration of black history. With the formation of the Philadelphia chapter of the Association for the Study of Negro Life and History in 1927, a coordinated program of lectures and exhibits on black history and culture was available to Philadelphians in the public schools and other locales during the second week of February.[18]

Longer celebrations of the black American heritage took place in Philadelphia in 1913 and 1926. In 1913 the entire month of September was designated as a time to commemorate the "Fifty Years of Progress" of black Americans. A very successful exposition was mounted emphasizing the religious, economic, political, and artistic achievements of blacks since the signing of the Emancipation Proclamation. Thousands of persons took part in the festivities, which were planned and coordinated by blacks from throughout the state.[19]

As part of the celebration of the Sesquicentennial of the United States, which dominated Philadelphia during the summer of 1926, blacks played an active role in the planning and development of exhibits and educational programs that described the contributions of blacks to the United States. Despite the threat of segregation at exhibits and facilities and the lack of sufficient state and local funding, on the whole, Philadelphia blacks were pleased with the recognition they and all black Americans received through participation in this important exposition.[20]

The 1920s also witnessed a resurgence or renaissance in black cultural and literary expression. Centered in Harlem, young black writers and artists plumbed black historical and cultural traditions in order to reveal the unique "black aesthetic." Black Philadelphians participated in the "New Negro" creative mood of the decade in both New York and Philadelphia, and in 1927 published their own literary journal *Black Opals.* Through this magazine and other popular journals of the era, blacks in Philadelphia were exposed to the latest cultural expressions of Afro-American artists.[21]

Education for individual and community development

While the historical and literary societies concentrated on the general historical development of black Philadelphia and black America, the black social, religious, and fraternal institutions in Philadelphia were primarily involved in providing educational activities for self-improvement and individual and community development. Women's clubs and organizations not only sponsored lectures on such topics as "The Accomplishments of Negro Womanhood" and "The Industrial Labor Problems of Colored Women," but also worked closely with the various social welfare agencies in the black community.[22] The Colored Women's Society for Organized Charity, the Allied Social Agencies Aid, and the most important group, the City Federation of Colored Women's Clubs, were intimately involved in the improvement of social and recreational conditions for blacks, especially black youth, in Philadelphia through educational and charitable works.[23]

Many of the members of the women's clubs worked with the community centers and settlement houses in the city. The Eighth Ward Settlement House, the St. Simon Settlement, and later the Wharton Settlement House sponsored community development activities as well as educational and recreational programs for children and adults in the black community.[24] Though most of these centers were financed by the municipal government or philanthropic agencies in the city, the staffs were often made up of blacks with the knowledge and experience to formulate a meaningful program of activities.[25]

The Sunday schools of the black churches passed on the religious traditions of the various denominations to the children in their congregations; the teachers usually had special training in religious instruction. We have a relatively complete account of the activities of these schools from the *Philadelphia Tribune* for the period from 1912 to 1930. In its columns on "Churches and Their Pastors," the *Tribune* published information provided usually by the teachers or the pastors of the churches.[26] Beginning in June 1924, the *Tribune* began publishing a weekly "Sunday School Lesson" prepared by Arthur Huff Fauset, then principal of the Singerly Public School. This lesson usually consisted of a Bible story, followed by a short religious commentary.[27] Special events that involved the Sunday schools, such as the Annual Sunday School Congress, were often reported in the religious section of the *Tribune*.[28]

The most thoroughly reported educational activities of the black religious community of Philadelphia, however, were those of the Young Men's Christian Association (YMCA) and the Young Women's Christian Association (YWCA). The YMCA movement, which began in England in 1844, was imported into the United States in 1852. The first Association for Negroes was started in Washington, D.C. in 1853. In the early years, the activities of the organization centered on evangelism (preaching and sermons), Bible classes, and other religious observances for young adults. After 1885 the YMCA developed a fourfold purpose: to improve the physical, intellectual, social, and religious life of young men and boys.[29]

The earliest YMCAs for blacks sponsored mostly social and religious gatherings because they had no separate buildings and were usually confined to the space offered by churches in the various communities. Beginning in 1912, however, several northern cities began to plan the building of "colored YMCAs," aided in this endeavor by generous contributions from the Rosenwald Fund. As a result, by 1938 there were forty-six separate black branches of the association, of two basic types: YMCAs with buildings, and "nonequipment" YMCAs, which carried on activities in local churches. Besides the recreational and physical education programs of the YMCAs, they also had extensive programs in adult education, crafts, black heritage clubs, Bible schools, art classes, and glee clubs. Many Negro YMCAs had important "extension programs" to provide activities for young men and boys who lived far away from the main black branch.[30]

In Philadelphia the colored YMCA began functioning in 1889. By 1898, however, the disadvantages of operating without a separate building had become apparent. W. E. B. Du Bois found that the "Y.M.C.A. has been virtually an attempt to add another church to the numberless colored churches in the city, with endless prayer-meetings and loud gospel hymns in dingy and uninviting quarters. Consequently the institution is now temporarily suspended. It had accomplished some good work by its night schools and social meetings."[31]

The campaign to erect a building for the colored YMCA was carried out during the first decade of this century. With assistance from the Rosenwald Fund, Rev. Henry L. Phillips and others were able to purchase a lot in South Philadelphia, and construction of the building began in April 1912.[32] Completed by January 1914, the Southwest Branch (Christian Street) YMCA not only provided much-needed recreational

and educational activities for the large black community of South Philadelphia, but also served as social center and meeting place for black organizations from all over the city.[33] Under the leadership of Rev. Henry
Porter, the Christian Street YMCA was one of the most important educational agencies in the black community throughout the period from
1914 to 1930 and afterward.[34]

The history of the Young Women's Christian Association (YWCA)
to a great extent parallels that of the YMCA. Established in England in
1855, the YWCA began operation in the United States in 1858 in New
York City. By 1900 there were hundreds of associations throughout the
country, and a national organization was formed in 1906. The first
"colored YWCA" was opened in Dayton, Ohio, in 1893. After the formation of the national organization, a "colored" secretary was appointed
in 1913. The YWCAs also sponsored a number of activities to promote
interracial understanding and cooperation.[35]

In Philadelphia the work of the YWCA among blacks began in
1902. Within a few years the organization had acquired a building on
Fifteenth Street in South Philadelphia.[36] The Southwest YWCA provided educational and recreational activities for women, and offered
classes in industrial and domestic arts, including dressmaking, millinery,
crocheting, and knitting.[37] Soon after, the Southwest YWCA acquired
a building for the lodging of single women and became active in seeking
employment for its membership.[38] The main branch in the city (the
Metropolitan branch) exercised a good deal of financial control over
the Southwest YWCA, and on several occasions conflicts arose.[39] After
1921, however, the Southwest branch launched campaigns to raise funds
to allow it to remain relatively independent. Like the YMCA, the Southwest YWCA served as a social and convention center for the Philadelphia black community. It sponsored numerous lectures and exhibits on
black womanhood, religious traditions, artistic achievements, and many
other popular topics.[40]

Secret and fraternal organizations also played a significant role in
providing educational activities as part of their general community service programs. The Knights of Pythias, the Odd Fellows, and most importantly, the Improved Benevolent and Protective Order of Elks of the
World (the Elks), sponsored public lectures and debates, not merely
for their membership, but for the black community at large.[41] In August
1925 the Grand Lodge Session of the Elks passed a resolution "to provide scholarships for deserving Negro youths in the various Schools of
Higher and Secondary Education. . . . In order to provide the funds
necessary to granting of these scholarships . . . every subordinate lodge
shall pay annually into the Educational Fund twenty-five cents for every

member carried on its rolls."[42] These Elks scholarships were an important source of financial aid for many black students down to the present day.[43]

Beginning in 1925, the Elks sponsored "Educational Weeks" in which meetings were held and programs presented in the Elks lodges throughout the country to encourage black youths to stay in school. At the second annual Educational Week in 1927, the Elks inaugurated the National Oratorical Contest, in which cash prizes and scholarships were given to young black men and women who presented the best orations on the topic "The Constitution of the United States."[44] The Elks lodges in Philadelphia participated in the local and regional oratorical competitions and received enthusiastic support from the rest of the black community. Philadelphians were particularly pleased when a local boy, William Harvey III, triumphed over representatives from the entire nation in the oratorical contest for 1929.[45]

Delta Sigma Theta sorority and Alpha Phi Alpha fraternity were also active in promoting the schooling of black youth and providing educational activities for the Philadelphia black community. The Deltas brought speakers to the city for free lectures and sponsored an annual Education Week similar to that of the Elks.[46] The annual "Go to High School—Go to College" campaign of Alpha Phi Alpha fraternity was supported by the organization's national and local membership. The campaign in Philadelphia usually consisted of a week of activities for children and their parents stressing the benefits of secondary and higher education. Such prominent persons as A. Philip Randolph, Carter G. Woodson, Raymond Pace Alexander, and W. E. B. Du Bois spoke in the city during these educational campaigns.[47] There were, of course, many other social, religious, and fraternal groups that sponsored educational activities for the black community between 1900 and 1930; however, this sampling of activities and organizations indicates not only the commitment of these groups to informing black youth about the need to improve themselves through education, but also their general efforts to improve the black community through community-wide educational activities.

Education for black social and political advancement

There were a number of social organizations in black Philadelphia between 1900 and 1930 whose primary function was to work for the general improvement of the social, economic, and political conditions for blacks in the city. As part of their general activities, these organizations usually sponsored public meetings, conferences, and lectures to inform black citizens of the important social and political issues of the day. As was discussed in chapter 3, the *Tribune* Defense Fund Committee was formed by the staff of the *Philadelphia Tribune* to raise funds for litigation against the local school board. Through rallies and public meetings, the Defense Fund Committee attempted to raise the political consciousness of black Philadelphians about the problem of the segregated public schools. Between 200 and 2,000 persons attended these meetings, whose programs were often described in detail in the weekly black newspapers. The lack of black political power in the city meant that the Republican city leaders did not believe it was necessary to support black demands for an end to public school segregation, but the Defense Fund Committee was successful in raising funds and educating large numbers of blacks about the issue of the separate schools.

The Philadelphia Association for the Protection of Colored Women, organized in 1905, worked with newly arrived southern black women in need of housing and employment in the city. Although the primary objective of the association was to protect these women from the "immoral influences" of the city, it also provided information to women intending to leave the South about such matters as the industrial conditions, wages, opportunities, and competition that they would meet in Philadelphia and other northern cities.[48] Thus, education was one of the specific goals of this organization for social improvement. The community at large was informed, almost on a monthly basis, of the activities of the organization through the *Tribune*, and rallies were held throughout the city to raise funds for its endeavors.[49] At these meetings, speakers from all over the nation would describe efforts of this and similar groups to assist black migrants to northern cities during the Great Migration.[50]

The Armstrong Association of Philadelphia, an interracial organization concerned primarily with the industrial and employment conditions for blacks in the city, often sponsored activities that not only informed the community of its work and progress, but also educated Philadelphians about the general industrial conditions of the nation.[51] In 1912, for example, the Armstrong Association participated in a number of public meetings with the Legal Aid Society, Children's Aid Society, and several black churches, and sponsored a series of rallies to raise funds for the Tuskegee Institute that brought Booker T. Washington to the city.[52]

In 1926 the association organized classes in trade education at the Christian Street YMCA to prepare blacks for jobs in the skilled trades and construction industry, and sponsored Negro in Industry Week, which was a drive to open up industries in the city to blacks.[53] The association also worked as a liaison between the municipal court and black youths who were in trouble with the law, and cooperated with social workers in dealing with many of the problems facing blacks in the city.[54] As the National Urban League affiliate in Philadelphia, the Armstrong Association planned and coordinated the national convention of that organization when it was held in the city in 1928. Thus, Philadelphians participated in the national efforts to inform Americans of the industrial conditions for the black population.[55]

As was discussed earlier, the Philadelphia branch of the NAACP, through its annual membership drives and special lectures and conferences, was one of the most important agencies for the education of the Philadelphia community, especially the black community, in the contemporary legal, political, and social conditions of black Americans. Organized in 1913, the Philadelphia branch brought many speakers to the city to address audiences assembled at the Southwest YWCA, the Christian Street YMCA, and various black churches throughout the period from 1913 to 1930.[56] Although it was not politically active before 1920, the local NAACP participated in efforts to protect the civil rights of black citizens and worked to bring an end to discrimination against blacks in the public schools, hotels, and other public places during the 1920s.[57] In conjunction with the Citizens Republican Club, the Armstrong Association, and other organizations, the Philadelphia NAACP sponsored many public meetings and educational conferences.[58]

The separate public and Catholic schools for blacks in Philadelphia, in spite of their many inadequacies, did benefit the black community by serving as social centers and meeting places for black organizations. The Durham Public School and St. Peter Claver Catholic School in South Philadelphia and the Reynolds Public School in North Philadelphia opened their doors to a wide range of activities for community improvement.[59] One of the most successful annual events sponsored in the black public schools was Negro Health Week. Exhibits set up in the schools stressed the benefits of a nutritious diet and dental hygiene, mothers were advised about the care of their families and their homes, and, most importantly, doctors were available in the schools to give free checkups for tuberculosis and other diseases.[60] Parent-teacher organizations in the black schools and the Citizens Committee for Regular School Attendance sponsored an annual Friendship Week, which fostered interracial cooperation in the schools and community. In the first annual celebration in 1925, George Washington Carver came to Philadelphia and discussed his famous agricultural experiments at the Tuskegee Institute.[61]

A great part of the above discussion of the educational activities of the black social institutions and organizations in Philadelphia is based on reports in the *Tribune*, the most important black newspaper in the city during the period. The newspapers in general and the *Tribune* in particular were important educational agencies for the black community. Under the leadership of Chris J. Perry, the founder and publisher, G. Grant Williams, managing editor, and later E. Washington Rhodes, editor, the *Tribune* actively participated in campaigns to improve social, political, and educational conditions within the black community. The newspaper announced public meetings and disseminated information on what occurred at them through editorials, articles, and special features. It published columns on "Negro History and Heroes," "School and Community News," "Health Problems," and other topics relevant to black social advancement, and supported and publicized the candidacies of black politicians in Philadelphia. The *Tribune* was usually at the forefront of the various campaigns for the social and political advancement of black Philadelphians.[62]

It is clear that there was a wide variety of social organizations and institutions active in providing community education programs in black Philadelphia between 1900 and 1930. Thus, it is likely that most blacks in the city came into contact with these educational programs, either as members of a sponsoring organization, or as participants in educational programs. Although some of the organizations had small memberships, the activities they sponsored often reached a much larger audience. Thus, the fifteen black members of the committee on the "Fifty Years of Progress" were instrumental in the planning and coordinating of an exposition attended by thousands of persons, blacks and white. The committees and organizations that promoted the adjustment of southern blacks to the city did not have many members, but there is evidence that their work affected large numbers of black migrants in need of housing and employment during the Great Migration.[63]

In previous examinations of social organizations in urban black communities, researchers have discussed only certain aspects of the functioning of these groups. Thus, literary and debating societies and historical associations are viewed as middle-class organizations that served as little more than social clubs for enhancing the status of the members. These organizations were then contrasted with race betterment or "race conscious" organizations, which were primarily interested in the advancement of blacks as a group—the National Urban League, the NAACP, the Universal Negro Improvement Association, for example.[64] This dichotomization of black social organizations may provide some important information on the differences among the various groups, but it has also tended to obscure their similarities. In black Philadelphia between 1900 and 1930, both race conscious and status conscious organizations were involved in sponsoring community-wide educational programs that were not aimed solely at the "middle-class" members of these organizations, but generally focused on issues affecting the entire Afro-American community. Thus, the public meetings, newspaper articles, and conferences on the separate public schools dealt with an issue that had ramifications for a large proportion of blacks in the city. The numerous celebrations of the black heritage served to educate both upper- and lower-status blacks about their history in this country and throughout the world.[64]

As an oppressed racial and cultural minority, Afro-Americans were the victims of discrimination in many areas of city life, including housing, employment, public accommodations, and schooling. Before the Civil War, this discriminatory treatment was sanctioned by law as well as tradition. Thus, one of the major purposes of organized black educational activities was to educate the dominant white society and themselves about the need to change the laws that undergirded the tradition of black enslavement in this country. Gradually, through education and actions, the laws that denied personal freedom and citizenship to Afro-Americans were repealed.

Following the Civil War, the thrust of educational activities within the black community shifted, and there was more emphasis on black social advancement. The need for blacks to learn skilled trades and advanced industrial techniques associated with the rise of the industrial city inspired Fannie Jackson Coppin's Industrial Crusade of the 1870s. Increasing discrimination against blacks in their traditional areas of employment—catering, barbering, personal and domestic service—led to an organized campaign to improve the opportunities for blacks in the skilled trades and advanced technical education in Philadelphia. Mrs. Coppin, principal of the Institute for Colored Youth, led the community education program that culminated in December 1879 in a "World's Fair" that displayed the creative and artistic talents of black Americans in handicrafts, art works, inventions, and many other areas. As one black newspaper reported, "Nothing like this Bazaar has been held in Philadelphia within the memory of the present generation." The establishment in January 1889 of an industrial department within the Institute for Colored Youth to provide training in carpentry, shoemaking, dressmaking, and later plastering, tailoring, stenography, and typing was another important outgrowth of the Industrial Crusade.[65]

Throughout the industrial education campaign, the entire community of blacks in the city was informed about the economic progress that would result from advanced technical training. Unfortunately, with the rise of the trade and industrial union movements, blacks in Philadelphia found themselves the victims of discriminatory treatment by the

European immigrant minorities who controlled the labor movement, and thus were barred from employment in many of the new industries. In the competition with white immigrants for the limited employment opportunities in industry, blacks generally fared poorly, but not because they were unskilled or uneducated—many of the immigrants who managed to obtain positions were also unskilled and often did not even speak English. Blacks in Philadelphia and many other cities lost out in the factories, on the docks, and in service areas initially because white immigrant workers were willing to work for wages lower than those previously paid, and later because industrial and trade union organizers appealed to racial prejudices to exclude blacks and maintain white control. The exclusion of black workers from the labor unions and industries, and the association of industrial education with the uplift of "backward peoples" following the rise of Booker T. Washington at the turn of the century, dampened the enthusiasm of many black Philadelphians for Industrial Crusades.

As we have seen, between 1900 and 1930 the dominant thrust of community education programs was still black social advancement. But there was also increasing concern about the need to preserve and pass on Afro-American cultural beliefs and traditions. Increased "racial consciousness" was a sign of the times, and Afro-Americans were generally considered mentally (if not physically) inferior to whites, and were thought to have contributed little that was positive to American civilization. Through documenting, preserving, and celebrating the African heritage in this country, black Philadelphians instilled in themselves group pride and informed the larger society of black contributions to American culture.

Educational programs usually reflected contemporary needs and the issues facing the black community. While southern migrants had to be educated about life in the big city, the "old Philadelphians" were reminded that they should set a proper example for the new arrivals. Given the discrimination against blacks in skilled and semiskilled employment, black youths had to be informed of the need to remain in school in order to be "qualified" for even the most menial positions. The "Fifty Years of Progress" exhibition, the Afro-American contribution to the Sesquicentennial Exposition, Negro History Week, the "Go to High School—Go to College" campaigns, Negro in Industry Week, NAACP membership drives, the *Tribune* Defense Fund rallies, and the numerous other educational programs and activities reflected the dual concern for racial pride and black social advancement.

The Great Depression, New Deal, and Second World War not only greatly affected the social, political, and economic conditions of black Philadelphians, but also brought about changes in the public school system and in the thrust of community education programs. While the Depression highlighted the interconnections between the status of black workers and the national economy, the need for greater interracial cooperation was dramatized by the much-publicized racial conflicts on the homefront during the war. In Philadelphia, the re-emergence of the Democratic party on the heels of the Roosevelt victories in 1932 and 1936 led to increased competition for black votes. Among the political concessions won by the black community was the official desegregation of the public school system. And calls for improvements in race relations in the public schools and the city at large during the 1930s and 1940s brought an increase in interracial educational activities and an important shift in the community education of black Philadelphia.

Part Two / 1930 to 1950

5
Depression,
New Deal,
and the
Black Community

The Great Depression of the 1930s had a devastating effect upon many citizens of Philadelphia. One of the reasons why Philadelphians suffered so greatly, especially in the early years, was that the so-called Roaring 20s were a period of economic recession in the city. Although Philadelphia was primarily a manufacturing and industrial city, its economic condition did not always reflect the boom and bust cycles of the national economy. During the 1920s, when the country at large was experiencing huge expansions in business and industry, many of Philadelphia's more important industries, such as textiles and metal production, were trying to recover from the post–World War I recessions. As early as 1919, declines were registered in the number of wage earners employed in local industries. Even in the construction industry, there was a sharp decline in activity, and by the end of the decade some residents had begun to question Philadelphia's reputation as a "city of homes."

In a survey of local unemployment conducted by the University of Pennsylvania's Department of Industrial Research in April 1929 for the Federal Bureau of Labor Statistics, it was reported that "one out of every ten wage earners in 31,551 families interviewed by the Bureau of Compulsory Education was found to have been unemployed during the latter part of April, 1929."[2] From that date the unemployment rate climbed until April 1930, when a second study revealed that 15.0 percent of the persons surveyed who were usually employed found themselves jobless.[3] From 1931 to 1938, statistics were compiled on the rates of unemployment and part-time employment on several blocks in Philadelphia. These studies revealed that in 1933, 46.0 percent of the employable persons were unemployed, and by 1938 this figure had dropped only to 32.5 percent (see table 10). With the outbreak of World War II in Europe in 1939 and the advent of defense production in many of the industries

Table 10
Employment status of employable persons in Philadelphia, unemployment census sample, 1929–38

Year	Number of households enumerated	Total		Employable Persons							
				Employed				Unemployed	
				Full-time		Part-time			
		Number	Percentage	Number	Percentage	Number	Percentage	Number	Percentage
1929	31,551	58,866	100.0	52,756	89.6	—[a]	—[a]	6,110	10.4
1930	36,665	69,884	100.0	55,788	79.8	3,648	5.2	10,448	15.0
1931	36,410	67,150	100.0	40,766	60.7	9,243	13.8	17,141	25.5
1932	35,471	66,854	100.0	24,782	37.1	13,887	20.8	28,185	42.1
1933	35,820	66,454	100.0	22,630	34.1	13,256	19.9	30,568	46.0
1934	40,931	78,121	100.0	38,420	49.2	11,437	14.6	28,264	36.2
1935	43,997	78,524	100.0	41,489	52.8	11,125	14.2	25,910	33.0
1936	44,817	79,822	100.0	48,669	61.0	7,066	8.1	24,067	30.1
1937	45,928	79,610	100.0	56,150	70.5	4,007	5.1	19,453	24.4
1938	45,715	75,402	100.0	46,231	61.3	4,641	6.2	24,530	32.5

Source: "Unemployment in Philadelphia, 1938," Monthly Labor Review 49 (1939): 838.
Note: a. Figures for part-time employment not available.

of Philadelphia, the rate of unemployment dropped to 19.4 percent in March 1940.[4]

The statistics compiled by the University of Pennsylvania as well as those of the Department of Research of the Pennsylvania State Emergency Relief Board in the period 1931–37 also provided data on the race and nativity of unemployed workers. For example, in the survey conducted by the State Emergency Relief Board in February 1934, it was revealed that of the total number of unemployed workers in Philadelphia at the time, 15.7 percent were foreign-born and 20.2 percent were black. Of the foreign-born employables in the city, 71.6 percent were employed and 28.4 percent were unemployed and seeking jobs. Within the black employable population, 52.1 percent were employed and 47.9 were unemployed. The figures for the native white population were 69.4 percent and 30.6 percent respectively.[5]

In a survey of 31,159 applicants to the State Employment Office in 1932 and 1933, Gladys Palmer found that there was no conclusive relationship between the amount of schooling and unemployment in Philadelphia. "There seems to be no evidence that those who have gone further in school have any particular advantage in an unemployment situation like the present. The employment office applicants in Philadelphia appear to have a better educational background than similar groups in other places or than other unemployed groups in the city. Over one-half of the applicants had more than a grammar school education."[6]

As the Depression wore on, the problem of long-term or hard-core unemployment became a topic of concern for government researchers. In a study of the conditions of Philadelphia's hard-core unemployed in 1935, it was found that the chief wage earners among the long-term unemployed in the city resembled all other chief wage earners who were on relief with respect to sex, race, and general occupational distribution. "As compared with other unemployed workers, however, they included relatively fewer women and many more Negroes."

> The hard core had relatively greater numbers of unskilled workers, and fewer skilled, semiskilled, and clerical or professional workers. The chief wage earners in the long term unemployed were also older, on the average, than other unemployed workers for whom comparable data were available. There was an especially heavy concentration in the age group 30 to 55 years among the first priority workers in this study.[7]

At the outset of the economic crisis, Philadelphians believed that the tried and true methods of dealing with unemployment would be sufficient. Voluntary relief organizations immediately swung into action, but the magnitude of the economic crisis soon revealed the inadequacy of private relief. The Committee for Unemployment Relief, chaired by Horatio Gates Lloyd, a prominent banker, was formed by Mayor Harry Mackey in November 1930 to carry out the city's "comprehensive program of private relief." The committee members, believing that the economic distress would be temporary, proceeded to conduct a campaign for private donations with the goal of raising $4 million. Meanwhile, the Philadelphia City Council was authorized by the Pennsylvania General Assembly to borrow $3 million for relief, and formed a separate Bureau of Unemployment within the Municipal Department of Public Welfare. The new relief funds were immediately placed under the control of the Committee for Unemployment Relief.[8]

Initially, the Lloyd Committee distributed limited amounts of money and food to unemployed workers, set up an Emergency Work Bureau that offered "made-work" jobs to the unemployed, and made arrangements for the issuance of loans to needy families. The committee also established shelters in various parts of the city for "homeless men." The entire program was considered very efficient and well-coordinated, and a model for other cities to imitate.[9] In November 1931 the Lloyd Committee joined with the Federation of Jewish Charities and the Welfare Federation and launched the "United Campaign," which had as its goal the raising of $9 million. The campaign surpassed its goal and raised over $10 million by March 1932. With its $5 million share of the collection, the Lloyd Committee again proceeded to distribute relief assistance throughout the city. But there were so many unemployed workers in Philadelphia during the winter of 1931–32 that the money lasted less than four months.[10]

At this point the committee turned to the state for appropriations. The Talbot Act, which passed the General Assembly in December 1931 and provided for relief funds to be distributed throughout the state, was being challenged in the state courts. Finally, on 7 April 1932, the Pennsylvania supreme court ruled that the state appropriation of funds "for persons without ability or means to sustain themselves" was legal. Again the Lloyd Committee began distributing relief, having received $2.5 million from the state appropriation. These funds, however, lasted only two months. Rather than maintain an illusion of activity, the Lloyd Committee disbanded on 20 June 1932. Upon dissolution, the committee offered this advice to government officials:

> It must be obvious to everyone, as it is to the committee, that the situation today is quite different from what it appeared to be when the committee was first formed. The duration of the depression, the vast and increasing numbers of unemployed, and the gen-

eral economic condition are such that it requires no argument for realization of the fact that the situation has progressed far beyond any possibility of relief from sources of private philanthropy, even for the most primitive necessities of life.

The present need is on a scale that calls not for mere charity but for governmental action to save the health and indeed the lives of a large proportion of the citizenry.[11]

The statement ended with the request that the governor call a special session of the General Assembly to deal with the mounting problems of unemployment and relief.[12]

Pennsylvania Governor Gifford Pinchot agreed to call a special session of the state legislature for the summer of 1932, and three acts were passed that brought into existence the Pennsylvania State Emergency Relief Board. It began operation on 1 September 1932, and in the period from September 1932 to October 1933, the board spent over $16 million on relief in Philadelphia, most of which was used for food for unemployed workers.[13] With the establishment of the federal Civil Works Administration in Pennsylvania on 15 November 1933, headed by Eric H. Biddle, the executive director of the State Emergency Relief Board, these state and federal agencies began to administer a coordinated program of food and work relief for unemployed citizens throughout the state.[14]

The lack of adequate relief funds in Philadelphia in general between 1930 and 1933 meant that many blacks would suffer. Throughout those early years, the percentage of black families on relief far exceeded their percentage in the city population; it was estimated that in April 1933 approximately 35.7 percent of the families requesting relief were black, at a time when blacks were no more than 12 percent of the total population of Philadelphia.[15] High unemployment rates had plagued the black community since the late 1920s. As was discussed in chapter 3, the Armstrong Association survey of August 1927 had revealed that one out of every five employable blacks questioned was unemployed.[16] A survey of employable persons on sixteen Philadelphia streets inhabited by blacks found that 14.6 percent were unemployed in 1930. Records were kept of the employment conditions for individuals on these blocks from 1930 to 1938, and by the latter date it was reported that among black males and females the unemployment rate was over 51 percent (see table 11).[17]

In reports on Philadelphia's unemployment rate by the Industrial Research Department of the Wharton School of Finance of the University of Pennsylvania between 1929 and 1933, a great deal of information was presented on the impact of the Depression upon black Philadel-

Table 11
Race and nationality of employable persons in Philadelphia sample,
by sex and employment status, summer of 1938

Sex, Race, and Nativity	Total[a]		Employed		Unemployed[b]	
	Number	Percent-age	Number	Percent-age	Number	Percent-age
Males	54,004	100.0%	37,171	68.8%	16,833	31.2%
Native-born white	35,601	100.0	25,074	70.4	10,527	29.6
Foreign-born white	11,451	100.0	8,691	75.9	2,760	24.1
Black and all other	6,952	100.0	3,406	49.0	3,546	51.0
Females	21,397	100.0	13,701	64.0	7,696	36.0
Native-born white	15,476	100.0	10,288	66.5	5,188	33.5
Foreign-born white	1,859	100.0	1,439	77.4	420	22.6
Black and all other	4,062	100.0	1,974	48.6	2,088	51.4

Source: "Unemployment in Philadelphia, 1938," *Monthly Labor Review* 49 (1939): 840.
Notes: a. Excludes one man who did not report nativity.
　　　b. Includes persons employed on Emergency Works Program projects.

phians. Joseph H. Willits, the director of the Wharton School, discussed these findings in an article that appeared in *Opportunity* in July 1933. Willits pointed out that since many blacks were recent migrants to Philadelphia from the South, the vast majority of black workers were in unskilled occupations, which were the first positions to be eliminated.[18] The 1930 census had revealed that many black males employed in "manufacturing and industries" in the city were in reality "unskilled laborers," and those supposedly employed in "trade, transportation, and communication" were also primarily unskilled workers.[19] Willits also noted that at least 30 percent of all black females employed in the city were in "domestic and personal services," but almost 75 percent of the employed black females were in some form of unskilled work.[20]

Seventeen percent of the applicants to the state employment offices surveyed were black, while "Negro workers constituted almost half (44.7 percent) of applicants coming from domestic and public service pursuits, 35.2 percent from unskilled trades, and 8 percent from other occupations." Blacks were also 28.8 percent of the "made-work" employees, those workers whose "need in the judgment of the investigators was greatest," though black wage earners were only 13.5 percent of the city's work force in April 1932. In each age group, unemployment among blacks was higher than that among native whites, but the survey of made-work employees did reveal that there was very little difference between white and black workers with respect to duration of unemployment.[21]

Previous earnings of black workers were also lower than those of whites among these made-work employees. The largest group of blacks averaged $20.00 to $24.00 per week, whereas the largest group of white workers had received $25.00 to $29.00, with many receiving $30.00 to $34.00 per week. This income difference during periods of employment meant that blacks had much smaller savings reserves from which to draw during periods of unemployment. All of these statistics were important in determining the overall standard of living of the families of unemployed workers. According to Willits, researchers estimated that "white families with savings and credit could have continued operations on the old scale for about three months. Negro families, with reserves much lower, could have continued six weeks before resources would have been exhausted." This situation helped to account for the earlier statistic that 35.7 percent of the families receiving relief in April 1933 were black. Willits concluded, "undoubtedly the Negroes of Philadelphia have suffered much distress, and relatively more severely than the whites," mainly because of differences in "occupational and economic status." Though no details were presented, Willits believed that "prejudice against Negroes in certain occupations has also undoubtedly played its part."[22]

Other assessments of the effect of the Depression on the black population of Philadelphia tended to complement the findings of the Industrial Research Department.[23] Studies of the urban black population in Pennsylvania during the period from 1928 to 1936 revealed a generally precarious economic situation for blacks throughout the state.[24]

Blacks and the New Deal in Philadelphia

With the inauguration of Franklin Delano Roosevelt in March 1933, and the establishment of the various "alphabet agencies," the president and Congress attempted to follow through on the Democratic campaign pledges to relieve the suffering caused by the Depression and to end the downward trend in the national economy. Thus, the Federal Emergency Relief Administration (FERA) sought to subsidize the relief payments made by the states, while the Civil Works Administration (CWA) provided relief work for the unemployed in federal and state projects during the winter of 1933–34. With the Agricultural Adjustment Administration (AAA), the federal government attempted to restore the purchasing power of American farmers through government subsidies, while the National Industrial Recovery Administration (NIRA) and the raising of the minimum hourly wage in certain industries worked to improve the purchasing power of producers and consumers through the imposition of new standards of production and wage schedules. Other pieces of New Deal legislation were geared toward improving the general functioning of various sectors of the national economy in order to avoid another Great Depression and to ameliorate the effects on American workers of fluctuations in the economy. The Federal Deposit Insurance Corporation (FDIC) would insure the savings deposited in member banks up to $1,500. The large number of bank failures in the early years of the Depression had destroyed many Americans' faith in the national banking system; the FDIC was an attempt to restore that faith. The Social Security Administration, which regulated workmen's unemployment compensation and retirement benefits, proved to be one of the most important legacies of the New Deal.[25]

Some of the New Deal agencies were geared to assist specific groups, such as youth (the National Youth Administration (NYA) and the Civilian Conservation Corps (CCC)), while others, such as the Tennessee Valley Authority (TVA), tried to improve the long-term conditions in a specific region of the country. For blacks in general and black Philadelphians in particular, two important New Deal programs were the NYA, with Mary McLeod Bethune as secretary for Negro Affairs and Rufus Watson as supervisor of the Negro Program in Pennsylvania, and the Works Progress Administration, later the Works Projects Administration (WPA).[26]

The WPA was created by President Roosevelt in 1935 under the terms of the Emergency Relief Appropriations Act. It replaced the FERA, which was ruled unconstitutional in 1935, and had as its major purpose "to get able-bodied unemployed persons off the dole and back to work on government projects."[27] The period of greatest activity for the WPA in Philadelphia and throughout Pennsylvania was between 1935 and 1940, though it continued in operation until 1943. *Philadelphia: A Guide to the Nation's Birthplace* was completed in 1937 by the WPA's Federal Writers' Project in Pennsylvania. This was part of the "American Guide" series compiled by unemployed writers on various regions, states, and cities in the United States.[28] The Research and Survey Division of the WPA in Pennsylvania produced an important report on the causes and consequences of juvenile delinquency, especially in the larger cities. This survey proved helpful in later efforts to reduce delinquency among black and white youth in Philadelphia.[29] A history of blacks in Philadelphia was also undertaken by the WPA Writers' Project, under the directorship of Helen Lee Pinkett. Ten black researchers gathered information on the social, economic, educational, and political conditions of blacks in Philadelphia from the eighteenth century to the 1930s.[30] This was one of the few "Negro projects" of the WPA in the city; generally blacks were supposed to be hired on various projects operating in Philadelphia along with white workers. However, few blacks were hired, and many protests were made against the alleged discriminatory employment practices of the WPA and other New Deal programs in the city.[31]

The most ambitious and significant undertakings of the WPA in Philadelphia were the Real Property Survey and the Real Property Inventory. The survey was begun in October 1934 as a project of the Pennsylvania State Emergency Relief Program, under the directorship of Ralph W. Smith, and was taken over by the WPA in 1935 under Arthur Siegrist. It was completed in 1937. The Philadelphia Real Property Inventory was sponsored by the Philadelphia Housing Authority in 1939 and completed in 1940, with John T. Ross as project director. These surveys, the first comprehensive investigations of housing conditions throughout the city, provided detailed information for subsequent campaigns for better housing.[32]

The housing boom associated with the New Deal was represented in Philadelphia solely by two Public Works Administration (PWA) housing projects: the Carl Mackley homes (1936) and the Hill Creek homes (1938), both for white middle-income, rather than lower-income, families. Before 1938 the major reasons for the scarcity of publicly financed low-income housing were the limited federal funds available and local Republican opposition to the implementation of "experimental" New Deal programs in Philadelphia.[33] The findings of the Real Property Survey, however, spurred the efforts of several black social improvement organizations to call attention to the completely inadequate housing available to the masses of blacks in the city. Beginning in February 1935, the *Philadelphia Tribune* and the *Philadelphia Independent*, a black tabloid that began publication in 1932, ran a number of articles and special features on housing. In 1934, following the receipt of PWA funds for slum clearance and housing construction, the Philadelphia Advisory Committee on Housing was formed, but no black was appointed to it. After federal officials and black leaders objected, Crystal Bird Fauset, then president of the Colored Women's Democratic League, and Major R. R. Wright, Sr., president of the Citizens and Southern Bank and Trust Company in South Philadelphia, were appointed to the committee, but the lack of federal funds and its subsequent inactivity led in 1936 to renewed campaigns and demands for better housing for blacks under the leadership of the Philadelphia chapter of the National Negro Congress.[34]

The collapse on 19 December 1936 of the ramshackle home of Mrs. Alberta Richardson in North Philadelphia, which killed seven persons, including four children, increased the volume of complaints, letters, editorials, and mass meetings for better housing. The Tenants' League of Philadelphia, which was formed in 1937 following one of the community forums on housing, took the lead in fomenting tenants' protest meetings and rent strikes, but was no more successful than the black press and the National Negro Congress chapter in bringing about an increase in decent housing for black Philadelphians. It was not until the passage of the Wagner-Steagall Act and the allocation of $20 million for housing construction in Philadelphia that some relief was forthcoming. In October 1940 the federally sponsored James Weldon Johnson Housing Project was opened in North Philadelphia at a cost of $3 million, providing spare, though decent, housing for over 1,800 persons. Initially, most of the residents were middle-income, as was the case in the white housing projects, but gradually many lower-income black residents found their way into the complex. The New Deal–sponsored housing projects that opened in the early 1940s were segregated, but most black Philadelphians accepted them because they represented the first decent housing made available to large numbers of the city's blacks in this century.[35]

The pattern of excluding significant numbers of blacks from projects and programs, except those specifically designated as "Negro projects," extended into other areas. The National Recovery Act (also disparagingly referred to as the "Negro Removal Act") was viewed with particular disdain by many black Philadelphians. The National Industrial Recovery Administration (NIRA) was charged with the task of recommending suitable wage schedules for various positions in industries. However, since the wages to be paid for specific jobs were set by the NIRA, many employers refused to hire blacks because they believed the wages set were too high to be paid to Negroes. The NIRA was therefore viewed as another barrier to the entrance of more blacks into private industry. And even in programs completely funded by the federal government, blacks in Philadelphia complained of discrimination. In January and February 1934 a controversy over the lack of black workers in New Deal–sponsored programs arose between Wayne Hopkins, executive secretary of the Armstrong Association, and Franklin G. Connor, director of the state employment offices in the city. When asked by black reporters why there were so few blacks employed on the various Civil Works Administration (CWA) projects throughout the city, Connor said it was because Wayne Hopkins had not submitted proposals for funding projects that could employ blacks. However, Hopkins produced a file on projects that he had suggested to Connor, many of which could have utilized black workers, and pointed out that he was not a CWA employee and therefore could not and was not expected to submit projects for approval. Connor subsequently denied that he was to blame for the small number of blacks working on CWA projects, but there is little evidence of any attempts to improve this situation.[37]

Other controversies arose over local institutions that ran federally sponsored programs but admitted very few blacks. This was the case with many of the training programs sponsored by the WPA and NYA and administered by the Philadelphia Board of Public Education. Numerous complaints are found in the *Philadelphia Tribune* against what was considered the discriminatory admissions practices of school officials, and it was not until large appropriations were made for national defense and vocational training programs in the late 1930s and 1940s that blacks were enrolled in representative numbers in these programs.[38]

Another very real problem for blacks in Philadelphia centered on the alleged discrimination practiced by the local branches of the Pennsylvania State Employment Office. In the late 1930s this problem became acute as more and more federally sponsored programs were being phased out or declared unconstitutional, and blacks were virtually forced to seek employment in private industry. When blacks appeared at the state employment offices, they were only considered for what were termed "Negro jobs" no matter what qualifications they might have. At the same time, even if a job was not labeled "for whites only," employers would often refuse to hire black applicants.[39] It was not until national defense jobs became available in large numbers that blacks began to be hired in representative numbers by private industries in Philadelphia.[40]

The outbreak of war in Europe in 1939 led to a build-up of the defense resources in the United States. The Office of Production Management (OPM) in Washington, the major governmental agency in charge of the mobilization of American manpower and industrial resources, pledged itself from the outset to a policy of "justice for Negro Americans in the program of national defense."[41] If the United States was to prepare itself for war, it would require a total commitment of its human and material resources. Philadelphia, one of the major industrial centers on the east coast, received a large number of government contracts for the production of military material and equipment. Black workers were hopeful that they would not again be the victims of discriminatory hiring practices in Philadelphia industries, especially since many of these industries were receiving government contracts.[42]

The precedent of the New Deal was none too favorable, however, and from the beginning of the defense mobilization, blacks expressed fears about the possibility of job discrimination.[43] Again we find references in the black press to the problem of factory and navy yard employers specifying to personnel and state employment offices that certain jobs were for whites only.[44] Blacks were particularly chagrined by what they termed the "hiring of aliens rather than American citizens" on defense jobs.[45] And many times when blacks were hired by private industries with defense contracts, they were relegated to the worst-paid positions.[46]

Investigations were made by OPM officials of alleged discriminatory practices, and conferences were held on "Negroes and the National Defense."[47] In Philadelphia it was reported that when employers were questioned about their not hiring blacks, they would often reply that white workers on the jobs would refuse to work with blacks, or that they could not find "qualified" blacks for the positions.[48] Although the former rationale was usually an assumption on the employers' part, the latter contention—that blacks were unqualified—was one to which members of the black community addressed themselves. Throughout the period from 1939 to 1942, the *Tribune* and other newspapers published editorials and special features on the need for more skilled black workers.[49] Since blacks had not been hired in most skilled areas before 1939 and were still not allowed in most skilled trades unions, there was not a large pool of black workers from which to draw. The solution suggested by the editors of the *Tribune* and others was for blacks to enroll in the trade and defense training courses being offered throughout the city.[50] During the defense build-up, the WPA and NYA helped finance special classes in various vocational educational areas at public and private schools in the city, and blacks were urged to take these courses in order to become qualified for the new skilled and semiskilled positions opening up in private industry.[51]

The problem of discrimination against blacks in defense industries was a national issue that spurred the organization of the March on Washington Movement (MOWM) led by A. Philip Randolph. Formed in 1940 and 1941, the movement planned a massive march and rally at the nation's capital for 1 July 1941, but the march was called off following President Roosevelt's issuance of Executive Order 8802, which prohibited discrimination in hiring in defense industries. The order also created a Fair Employment Practices Commission (FEPC) to investigate complaints of discrimination in hiring.[52] In Philadelphia, the Mayor's Council on Defense preceded the executive order and investigated complaints against industries in the city, but had no power to make adjustments in the discriminatory practices of employers. As a result, alleged incidents of discrimination that occurred after October 1942 were investigated by the Philadelphia office of the FEPC.[53]

Throughout the World War II period, incidents of racial discrimination and violence occurred in Philadelphia, the most notorious being the Philadelphia Transportation Company (PTC) strike in August 1944. This strike, which brought almost all public transportation in the city to a halt because of the hiring of black workers, demonstrated among other things that the struggle against job discrimination was only mitigated, not solved, by the need for national defense and wartime mobilization in the City of Brotherly Love.[54]

Black self-help during the Depression

It was quite apparent that the Philadelphia black community was economically weak on the eve of the Great Depression. The large numbers of unskilled migrants, the lack of large-scale businesses, and the high pre-Depression unemployment rate placed the community in a very insecure position from which to launch a campaign to deal with the economic crisis of the 1930s. As things went from bad to worse, the major objective for many blacks was survival, almost on a day-to-day basis. Despite these conditions, however, efforts were made by members of the black community to relieve the suffering among their brothers and sisters. These relief efforts were not large individually, but they did represent a long-term commitment by blacks to aid each other during the decade of economic depression.

The first major type of assistance was the provision of food and clothing for persons in need. Several churches had their members donate what they could in the form of material goods, which were then distributed to needy families in the congregation or in the neighborhood.[55] The students and teachers in the separate black schools in the community also took up collections for destitute families. In February and March 1933, the teachers at the Reynolds and Arnold public schools organized relief activities among their pupils for the families of pupils in the schools and for poor families in the surrounding neighborhoods.[56] In April and May 1933, the North Philadelphia Relief Society, a predominantly black organization, collected and distributed food and clothing to the needy in that section of the city.[57] Another group active in providing relief for the impoverished was the Improved Benevolent and Protective Order of Elks of the World (the Elks). Several Philadelphia chapters organized relief efforts and worked in conjunction with other social agencies and organizations to distribute baskets of food to the needy, especially during the Christmas season.[58]

Another important type of black self-help activity was the contribution that blacks made to the United Campaign and the various welfare agencies working in the black community. The welfare organizations were active in soliciting funds from the black community, and many blacks were responsive because they knew that several black social welfare organizations received funds from these campaigns. In the United Campaign for 1931, for example, blacks were urged to contribute as much as they could because, of the 125 agencies supported by the campaign, 15 were black. Thus, in helping the United Campaign to reach its goal, blacks were in effect helping themselves.[59]

The Depression caused great financial hardship for social welfare agencies functioning in the black community. To reduce operating expenses, the board of directors of the YWCA in Philadelphia merged the Belmont Center and the Southwest Branch in May 1933. As a result, only one campaign would be needed to raise funds for the two predominantly black branches of the organization in Philadelphia.[60] In the early years of the Depression, the YMCA and the YWCA had trouble raising enough funds for their activities and were forced to make significant cutbacks in staff and programs. But in 1935 both organizations succeeded in raising sufficient contributions for a return to the full program.[61]

The Frederick Douglass Hospital was denied state appropriations in 1931 because of the opposition of the State Department of Welfare and Governor Gifford Pinchot to some of the policies and practices of the director and board of trustees of the hospital.[62] The controversy continued until 1933, when the founder and director, Dr. Nathan J. Mossell, resigned because of age.[63] The hospital received sufficient contributions, primarily from blacks, to continue operations until February 1934, when the hospital again began to receive state funds.[64] Other organizations, such as the Philadelphia branch of the NAACP and the Armstrong Association, also found it difficult to raise funds through contributions during the worst days of the Depression. But many managed to weather the storm through cutbacks in personnel and programs. In the years after 1938, those organizations that survived found that the improving economic conditions brought contributions from the black community that were even larger than those of the pre-Depression era.[65]

The most important and successful black self-help activities during the Great Depression, however, were the campaigns and movements to gain jobs for blacks in Philadelphia. Beginning with the Crusade for Jobs and the "Don't Buy Where You Can't Work" campaigns in 1930, various temporary and permanent organizations were formed in the black community to bring pressure on public and private employers to hire black workers.[66] The two most important black newspapers in the city during the period, the *Philadelphia Tribune* and *Philadelphia Independent*, conducted some of the campaigns and publicized the activities of many organizations.[67] The Armstrong Association had long been the major organization engaged in finding employment for blacks, but the gravity of the situation during the 1930s generated a widespread movement against job discrimination.[68] The Educational Equality League, a citizens' group concerned primarily with public school issues, was successful in its campaign to increase the number of black workers employed at the new administration building of the Board of Public Education, which was opened in 1932.[69] But the league failed in its attempt to persuade the Free Library of Philadelphia to hire black librarians.[70]

The Ministers' Council on Economic Affairs, composed primarily of black clergymen from several denominations and organized in October 1935, rallied the support of black church congregations in the campaigns for jobs.[71] The Ministers' Council supported the strike in November 1935 by black film operators protesting against the existence of a double wage standard for black and white employees of the Union Theater in West Philadelphia. The strike was successful, and black workers began to receive the same wages as whites doing the same jobs.[72] In December 1936 the Ministers' Council joined with the Better Business Council of Philadelphia and other organizations in working to improve the overall employment status of black workers, and in February 1937 launched a successful campaign to gain jobs for blacks at the Philadelphia Gas Company.[73] The National Negro Congress was organized in

Arthur Huff Fauset, former principal of the Joseph Singerly Public School and president of the Philadelphia branch of the National Negro Congress in the 1930s. (Courtesy of the Philadelphia Tribune)

Washington, D.C., in 1936 to monitor the overall employment conditions for Afro-Americans under the New Deal. The Philadelphia chapter exposed not only poor housing conditions, but also the discrimination leveled against blacks by the Pennsylvania state employment offices and later by local defense industries. The congress was also successful in its campaign in 1938 to gain employment for blacks at the Philadelphia Electric Company.[74]

A number of black civic leagues and neighborhood improvement organizations sprang up in several sections of Philadelphia in 1936 and 1937. Although the major objective of the these groups was community and neighborhood improvement, they were also aggressive in seeking employment for blacks in grocery and department stores in predominantly black areas of North and West Philadelphia. Sam Evans, president of the North Philadelphia Youth Movement, an offshoot of the North Philadelphia Civic League, led these two groups in the picketing of stores on Columbia Avenue whose owners refused to hire black workers. Initially, Evans and members of the organizations met with representatives of the Columbia Avenue Businessmen's Association to try to persuade store owners to hire blacks as clerks. This effort failed, however, and in August 1937 pickets were set up in front of several stores. Leon Steinburg, president of the Businessmen's Association, had warrants issued for the arrest of the protesters, charging them with "disorderly conduct." Sam Evans, however, was charged with "breach of the peace and inciting to riot," and was held on four hundred dollars' bail.[75] At the hearings before Magistrate Vincent Girard later that month, despite the fact that the merchants who testified against Evans were unable to explain just what was "disorderly" or "threatening" about his behavior, Evans was held for trial because Magistrate Girard had visited the scene of the action and believed he "knew what it was all about." "There are more colored people working today than ever before," he declared, "I have the records of the WPA and I know."[76] In subsequent court appearances, however, the lawyers for the Youth Movement, E. Washington Rhodes and Carlyle Tucker, succeeded in having the charges dropped. Eventually, the North and West Philadelphia Civic Leagues were able to convince many local merchants that hiring black workers was good for business.[77]

Between 1930 and 1940, the depressed economic conditions in Philadelphia served as a motivating force for the black community to launch a concerted effort to end job discrimination in the city. Almost everyone suffered during those years, but it is likely that black Philadelphians suffered more than others. When attempts were made to alleviate the conditions through "made-work," relief work, and New Deal public works programs, black Philadelphians again found themselves the victims of discriminatory hiring practices. As a result, blacks not only began a number of activities to help themselves, but also launched campaigns to confront public and private employers with their demands for equitable treatment. As consumers, blacks could request that stores and businesses return some of the profits they received from the black community to individual members of the community in the form of jobs. If these requests were ignored they could (and did) organize boycotts against these stores. As citizens, blacks could request that public officials treat them with the same respect and justice that they showed other law-abiding citizens. But it was in their role as voters that black Philadelphians could best influence those institutions and agencies they believed were most important in meeting their needs and those of their children.[78]

Black politics in Philadelphia in the 1930s

The shift of the black vote in Philadelphia from almost completely Republican to overwhelmingly Democratic in the period from 1932 to 1936 has been termed astonishing by political scientists.[79] But what was also amazing about this occurrence was the fact that this shift did not bring with it any significant increase in black political power in the city. One reason for this was that while the black vote in the city became more and more Democratic the city government remained under the control of the Republican Party.[80]

In the early 1930s the Republican Party in Pennsylvania was being challenged not merely by a resurgence of the Democratic Party, but also by a large-scale "Independent" movement within its own ranks. Gifford Pinchot, former governor and leader of the Independent movement, succeeded in winning the gubernatorial race in 1930 on a reform, anti-machine platform.[81] Pinchot had the support of the *Philadelphia Tribune* and many black Republicans in the city, but machine control of the black wards kept Pinchot from receiving a large number of black votes.[82] In that year three black Republicans were elected to the state house of representatives: Samuel Hart and William Fuller from Philadelphia and Walter L. Tucker from Pittsburgh.[83]

In 1931 Representative William Fuller introduced and ushered through the legislature an equal rights bill similar to the one that had failed to get out of committee in 1923 and 1925.[84] At the same time, Representative Samuel Hart guided a bill through the legislature that called for the creation of two black battalions of the National Guard, one in Philadelphia and another in Pittsburgh.[85] Both bills, however, were vetoed by Governor Pinchot in July 1931; he claimed that the equal rights measure was "too harsh on employees of theaters," and that the bill for the two black battalions was "class legislation."[86] These and other actions by the governor were denounced by E. Washington Rhodes of the *Tribune*, the former chairman of the "Pinchot for Governor" campaign among blacks in the state.[87]

By the elections of 1932, the black vote was beginning to shift into the Democratic columns. It was estimated that Roosevelt received about 27 percent of the vote in Philadelphia's predominantly black wards.[88] In the gubernatorial race of 1934, however, the shift was more apparent. William Schnader, the Republican candidate, received a majority of the votes in the black wards, but George H. Earle, the victorious Democratic candidate, received over 38 percent of the vote there.[89] That year five blacks were elected to the state house of representatives. Of the four who were elected from Philadelphia, one was a Democrat, demonstrating that by 1934 the Democratic Party had begun to make significant inroads into the previously Republican black wards of the city.[90]

The period from 1934 to 1937 witnessed the height of black political influence in Philadelphia during the decade. By March 1934 both parties had begun openly to solicit the black vote. Several important black political appointments were made during these years. In December 1934 Joseph Rainey, a Democratic politician from Philadelphia, was appointed by Governor George Earle to the State Athletic Commission. Attorney J. Austin Norris was appointed deputy-assistant attorney general of the state in February 1935. Not to be outdone, the Republican city government made Walter Gay an assistant district attorney and supported the candidacy of James H. Irvin for the City Council in 1935. Irvin became the first black to be elected to the council in Philadelphia since 1919.[91] And, most importantly, in 1935 the Republican-dominated General Assembly finally passed the equal rights bill introduced by Republican Representative Hobson Reynolds, and the Hart Bill for the creation of two black battalions of the National Guard.[92] However, these two Republican accomplishments had to be shared with the Democrats, since it was Democratic Governor George Earle who signed the two measures. It was during this same period that Dr. John P. Turner became the first black to be elected to the Philadelphia Board of Public Education by the Republican judges of the Court of Common Pleas, and subsequently the school board ended its policy of segregating black teachers in the system.[93]

The election of 1936 demonstrated the extent of the defection of black voters in Philadelphia to the Democratic Party. Six blacks were elected to the state house of representatives, all members of the Demo-

Hobson Reynolds, local politician and leader of the Improved Benevolent and Protective Order of Elks of the World, and sponsor of the Pennsylvania Equal Rights Law of 1935. (Courtesy of the Philadelphia Tribune)

cratic Party. This was the largest number of blacks to serve at one time in the Pennsylvania legislature to that date.[94] And in the presidential election of 1936, over 60 percent of the vote from the majority black wards in the city went to Franklin D. Roosevelt.[95] This achievement could have been the beginning of the formation of a black "sub-machine" within the Democratic Party in the city; however, as early as February 1937, splits began to occur within the black Democratic ranks. The successful bill for the reapportionment of districts for the election of representatives to the state legislature caused a fissure among the black legislators. Representative Marshall Shepard, pastor of Mt. Olivet Taber-

Rev. Marshall Shepard, pastor of Mount Olivet Tabernacle Baptist Church and Democratic politician. (Courtesy of the Philadelphia Tribune)

nacle Baptist Church and chairman of the House Reapportionment Committee, supported the bill, while the five other Representatives opposed it, believing that blacks would lose seats as a result of the reapportionment and that the bill would decrease the likelihood of the election of a black state senator in the near future.[96] Another controversy arose over the selection of Democratic committeemen in the black wards of Philadelphia.[97] The real obstacle to gaining the support of the white Democratic leadership in the city, however, was not the disunity within the ranks of black Democrats, but the seeming lack of commitment of some black leaders to the Democratic Party.

Most black Democratic politicians in Philadelphia during the 1930s were recent converts from the Republican Party. Rev. Marshall Shepard, who had been denied Republican support for a seat in the Pennsylvania General Assembly in 1932, became a Democrat in 1933 and was elected to the state house of representatives in November 1934. Hobson R. Reynolds, Republican representative and sponsor of the equal rights bill that became law in 1935, became a Democrat in 1936. Magistrate Edward Henry, former president of the Citizens Republican Club, became a Democrat in 1935, but when Jay Cooke and the Republican City Committee offered to support him as the Republican candidate from the Second Congressional District of Pennsylvania, he returned to the Republican fold. Henry won in the primary, and tried to gain the support of black Democratic leaders in his election bid, believing that black Democratic and Republican voters would support him in order to have a black congressman from Philadelphia. He was mistaken, however, and the predominantly black wards of the Second Congressional District went Democratic, mainly because the Democratic Party was considered responsible for many of the relief programs that seemed to be assisting black citizens' survival during the worst years of the Depression.[98]

In the election for the state house of representatives in 1938, six blacks were again victorious, five Democrats and one Republican.[99] E. Washington Rhodes, publisher of the *Tribune*, was able to win a seat as a Republican primarily because of the support he had generated for the party in the seventh ward in the campaign for the election of Edward Henry. It was also in that year that Crystal Bird Fauset was elected state representative from the Eighteenth District in Philadelphia. She was the first black woman to serve in a state legislature.[100]

In 1940 six black Democrats were again elected to the Pennsylvania General Assembly, carried in on the Roosevelt-Democratic majorities in the black wards of Philadelphia and Pittsburgh.[101] Between 1938 and 1949, while most blacks were moving into the ranks of the Democratic Party, the city government and the Pennsylvania General Assembly remained under the control of the Republicans.[102] Thus, the defection of black Philadelphians to the Democratic Party did not bring a significant increase in black political power within the city and state governments. It was only during the period from 1934 to 1937, when both political parties were actively competing for black votes, that some attempt was made to move on black political demands. And it was during those years that the greatest changes were made in the policies of the Philadelphia Board of Public Education with regard to the segregation of blacks in the public school system.

(opposite left)
E. Washington Rhodes, attorney, editor and publisher of the Philadelphia Tribune, and leader of the Philadelphia black community from the 1920s through the 1950s. (Courtesy of the Philadelphia Tribune)

(opposite right)
Eustace Gay, reporter and later editor of the Philadelphia Tribune. (Courtesy of the Philadelphia Tribune)

(below left)
Raymond Pace Alexander, attorney and later judge in the municipal courts of Philadelphia. In the 1930s he worked with the Educational Equality League on various cases to bring about the desegregation of the public school systems in the Philadelphia area. (Courtesy of the Philadelphia Tribune)

(below right)
Crystal Bird Fauset, Democratic politician and civic leader, and the first black woman elected to a state legislature in the United States. She was elected to the Pennsylvania house of representatives in November 1938. (Courtesy of the Philadelphia Tribune)

The Campaign to End Public School Segregation, 1930–1940

The movement to end official segregation in the Philadelphia public school system was a long struggle, related to a number of other political activities and campaigns taking place during the first four decades of this century. The desegregation of the public schools was part of the ongoing effort to improve social and economic conditions for blacks in Philadelphia, and one of the major political objectives of the city's newly mobilized black electorate. But the campaign in Philadelphia was also part of the growing national movement for the improvement of black public education. In order to comprehend fully why blacks were successful during the 1930s in bringing about a change in school board policies and practices, we must first examine the contemporary controversies over segregation in public education and American society in general.

Afro-Americans had long opposed the existence of segregation in public education because although the public schooling provided blacks was usually separate, it was rarely equal. In one of the early volumes in the famous Atlanta University series, "Studies in Negro Life" (1896–1911), W. E. B. Du Bois examined the expenditures per year for the public education of black and white children in thirteen southern states and the District of Columbia between 1870 and 1899. He documented what was generally known in 1900: that the expenditures for black and white pupils were unequal.[1] But Du Bois was also able to demonstrate that the taxes paid by black residents in these areas between 1870 and 1899 were greater than the total amount expended on black public schools during the period. This was quite contrary to contemporary suggestions that the white South exclusively had been paying for the public education of southern blacks.[2] Although the gap between expenditures for black and white public schooling in the South narrowed during the first three decades of this century, as late as 1930 blacks received from one-half to one-third the amount expended on the public schooling for whites in most southern states. Horace Mann Bond published in 1933 his lengthy reanalysis of the financing of the "dual system" of public education in the South and concluded that "as compared to the Nation at large, it may be said categorically that Southern states are not able to support systems for the two races comparing favorably with national norms of achievement. The result is that Negro children are discriminated against universally in states with a heavy Negro population, all available funds being devoted as far as possible to the needs of white school children."[3]

Investigations of private and public secondary and higher education for blacks also revealed extreme financial problems. Private schools for blacks received a great part of their funds from private sources, such as churches and private foundations, including the Slater Fund, the Southern Education Board, and the General Education Board. These schools thus flourished or fell into desuetude depending on the ability of these agencies to provide monies, grants, and gifts.[4] As was the case with elementary education, publicly supported institutions of secondary and higher education for blacks were victimized by discriminatory funding policies and practices. All of the major surveys of black higher education sponsored by the federal government discussed the tenuous financial arrangements that existed between black schools and state funding agencies.[5] Even with the allotment of federal funds for public higher education, black colleges could not depend on adequate or even equitable funding. In the official report of President Herbert Hoover's National Advisory Committee on Education, issued in December 1931, the majority of the committee members concluded that private donations had done more for black secondary and higher education than had federal aid, and recommended that the federal government refrain from making grants directly to black public schools, since funds could be distributed through the various state funding agencies that handled federal aid.[6] The conclusion and recommendation, however, were completely at variance with the economic realities of black public colleges in the South. As a result, the three black members of the committee, Presidents R. R. Moton of Tuskegee Institute, Mordecai Johnson of Howard University, and John W. Davis of West Virginia State College, made the heretofore unprecedented decision to file a minority report.[7] In their statement the black educators pointed out that the existence of the separate school systems in the South meant that "the normal processes of public opinion and public functioning which operate to secure a fairly equal educational opportunity for all children of the advantaged majority, therefore, do not effectively operate to secure this result for children of this disadvantaged minority." As a consequence, "in many states this separate school system receives an abnormally low proportion of the state monies appropriated for education. While serving the children of more than one-fourth, this racial minority received in 1930 an average appropriation of only 10.7 percent of public funds. The facts will show that as a rule they also received an abnormally low proportion of all federal grants made in aid of education within the states." The black college presidents recommended that the federal government continue to provide grants-in-aid earmarked for black education until the U.S. Office of Education made a thorough investigation of the financing schemes in the southern states for black and white public educational institutions.[8]

The constant discrepancy between the public educational facilities provided for blacks as compared with those for whites in the South led many black leaders and educators in the 1930s to launch a concerted effort to end *de jure* segregation in public education. But these leaders had not only to determine the optimal strategy for ending public school segregation, but also to deal with the ideology behind "Jim Crow."

The problem of segregation in American society

In attempting to come to grips with the practice of segregation in the United States, many black and white leaders and educators first had to confront the geographical peculiarities of the custom. In the North in the 1930s, many blacks were primarily concerned with ending segregation through legislative action and preventing its spread to other aspects of social and public life. Thus, while some blacks and whites in Pennsylvania fought for the passage of a state equal rights law that would prohibit discrimination in public accommodations, black Philadelphians organized and lobbied for a change in school board policies that supported the segregation of black teachers in the public school system.

In the southern states, however, most black leaders believed that the time was not yet ripe for launching a broad campaign to repeal Jim Crow legislation. White southern politicians would have been very reluctant to introduce or support antisegregation measures. Thus, the opponents of Jim Crow "down South" had as their initial goal the creation of truly separate but equal public schools and other accommodations for southern blacks. However, the ultimate goal remained the creation of a truly desegregated American society, where blacks and other oppressed minorities would have access to all public institutions. The early strategy of the NAACP in fighting public school segregation, beginning with *Murray v. Maryland* (1936), was to bring suit for the admission of blacks to white public law and professional schools in states where no publicly financed legal and professional education was provided for blacks. The NAACP lawyers were ultimately able, in 1954, to get the U.S. Supreme Court to declare official segregation in public education unconstitutional.[9]

But even more significant than the slight geographical variations was the ideology behind racial segregation in American society. The belief in black mental and cultural inferiority permeated almost every aspect of black-white relations and served as adequate justification for most whites for continued racial segregation. The ideology of racism had achieved a reality of its own by the 1930s, independent of the numerous pseudoscientific experiments carried out to demonstrate the inferiority of blacks. Whereas in the early nineteenth century some white Americans believed that blacks were inferior as a result of their enslaved conditions, in the latter part of the century, with the articulation of Social Darwinism, most whites came to believe that blacks were inferior because they belonged to an inferior race that was losing the struggle for survival.[10] By the late 1930s, however, with the revelations about Nazi activities and atrocities in Germany and Eastern Europe, the insidiousness of racist ideologies was becoming apparent.[11]

At the same time, white and black scholars were challenging systematically the idea that one race or cultural group is innately inferior to another. Franz Boas of Columbia University suggested in the early 1900s that there was no difference in the mental capacities of so-called primitive and civilized men.[12] By the late 1930s, when the threat to humanity presented by Nazi propaganda was becoming obvious, several British geneticists re-examined the evidence on the benefits and disadvantages of "race crossing" and reported that there was no conclusive information on the effects of race mixture. Until evidence was forthcoming, these scientists concluded, there was no reason to accept the Nazi's demands for greater "race purity."[13]

In the United States, during the first three decades of this century, several psychologists and educators used the newly developed "intelligence tests" to try to demonstrate the mental inferiority of one group to another. As was discussed in chapter 2, in the case of black students in the Philadelphia public schools, "intelligence test" results were used to justify the creation and maintenance of separate black public schools. These tests became another touchstone for demonstrating the inferiority of blacks, and indirectly supplied a new rationale for the perpetuation of segregation in American society.

Beginning in the early 1920s, however, black scholars began to challenge the findings and pronouncements of intelligence testers. In March 1923 Howard H. Long of Paine College re-examined the findings of the psychologists who had developed and administered the Alpha and Beta Army Tests during World War I. The psychologist Lewis Terman of Stanford University, in commenting on the army test results, had stated that "Army mental tests have shown that not more than 15 percent of American Negroes equal or exceed in intelligence the average of our white population, and that the intelligence of the average Negro is vastly inferior to that of the average white man."[14] Long, however, pointed out that in these army test scores, "greater differences were found between Southern whites and a selected group of whites, than between Southern whites and Northern blacks. . . . In other words, the situation in the field of mental testing agrees with the general findings in anthropology that variation of individuals and groups within races is greater than the variation between the races as major groups."[15] Long went on to discuss the findings of both black and white researchers and psychologists who had found that environment was a much greater influence on intelligence or mental ability than was heredity.[16]

In July 1925 Horace Mann Bond published a re-examination of the Alpha Army Test scores in response to the interpretation of these test results suggested by Carl Brigham in *A Study of American Intelligence* (1923).[17] In that work Brigham had ascribed the differences in Army test scores between northern and southern blacks to his belief that "the most energetic and progressive Negroes migrated northward, leaving their duller and less accomplished fellows in the South."[18] Bond showed that black migrants must have left their "duller and less accomplished *white* fellows in the South" as well, since the average scores of blacks in several northern states were higher than those for whites in many southern states. Bond concluded that the Army test scores reflected the social and educational environment of the individuals who took the tests rather than their innate intellectual abilities.[19]

Throughout the 1920s and 1930s, Long, Bond, Charles Thompson, Doxey Wilkerson, and many other black and white social scientists challenged the findings and statements of the intelligence testers with respect to racial differences in test results.[20] In several cases these researchers demonstrated that when children were taught how to take the various I.Q. and mental tests, their scores could be raised fifteen or twenty points. This was considered another demonstration that intelligence test scores could be influenced by environmental conditions and were not necessarily measuring innate mental abilities. In July 1939 Martin D. Jenkins, a black psychologist at Howard University, published a comprehensive examination of the major studies that were supposed to have compared the mental abilities of blacks and whites in the United States. Among other things, Jenkins concluded that "differences within the two groups are greater than the differences between the two groups." He reported that "intelligence test scores reflect both environmental and hereditary factors; but differences between the average test scores of white and Negro groups may be attributable, either in the whole or in part, to the environmental factor."[21]

The unanimity within the ranks of black psychologists and educators in challenging the pronouncements of the mental testers was not found among black leaders in general. Differences of opinion existed throughout the 1920s and 1930s over the issue of "voluntary segregation." Some blacks believed that segregation had allowed separate black churches, schools, and other social institutions to flourish. These individuals would ask the opponents of segregation: what would happen to black institutions and culture in a desegregated American society?[22]

Throughout the 1920s black leaders debated the optimal strategy for the achievement of black economic and political equality in the United States. The challenge presented by Marcus Garvey's Universal Negro Improvement Association (UNIA) and its demand for separate black economic development forced several mainstream black spokespersons to reiterate their commitment to a desegregated society.[23] The Depression and the New Deal presented new challenges to black leaders and the movement to bring an end to legal discrimination against blacks in the United States. A full-scale debate on the economic disadvantages and advantages of segregation took place within the pages of *The Crisis*, the official publication of the NAACP, in 1934 between W. E. B. Du Bois, the magazine's editor, and Walter White, executive secretary of the association.

Dr. Du Bois, disturbed by the NAACP's lack of a definite economic program for black people during the Great Depression, began to criticize openly the organization's officials. He agreed that the organization should work for the desegregation of American society; however, it had supported segregation when necessary, and Du Bois believed that in light of the economic crisis, "colored people should come forward, should organize and conduct enterprise, and their only insistence should be that the same provisions be made for the success of their enterprise as that being made for the success of any other enterprise. It must be remembered that in the last quarter of a century, the advance of the colored people has been mainly in the lines where they themselves working by and for themselves, have accomplished the greatest advance."[24]

Du Bois was advocating that blacks use their segregated institutions as a political and economic base for launching further attacks on social and economic discrimination in the larger society.

Walter White argued that, on the contrary, "to accept the status of separateness, which almost invariably in the case of submerged, exploited and marginal groups means inferior accommodations and a distinctly inferior position in the national and communal life, means spiritual atrophy for the group segregated." This idea was echoed in the writings of many other opponents of the voluntary segregation of blacks for social and economic advancement.[25]

The debate over the benefits and disadvantages of segregated public schools also found its way into the pages of the *Journal of Negro Education*, which began publishing in 1932. In the first yearbook issue (July 1932), several educators and administrators examined the financial support, general administration and control, physical equipment, and teaching staffs of the black public elementary schools in twenty-six states. The existence of segregation in black elementary education, the writers concluded, was not the immediate problem; the "removal of financial shortages" and "stopping the spread of segregation" were more important. In the southern states, many black leaders believed that gaining equity in funding was primary. They made it clear, however, that "segregation should be regarded by Negroes as a means to an end rather than an end in itself."[26]

In May 1934 a conference on the "Fundamental Problems in the Education of Negroes," sponsored by the U.S. Office of Education, addressed the issue of school segregation, but only in a broad and general manner. The participants in the conference recommended that "A. The objectives of elementary education should be the same for all American citizens. B. Adaptations to unfavorable conditions and practices [e.g., segregation] should not serve to perpetuate these conditions and practices."[27] The 1935 yearbook issue of the *Journal of Negro Education* (July 1935), however, directly confronted the problem of school segregation in its consideration of the topic "The Courts and the Negro Schools." Despite W. E. B. Du Bois's now-classic explication of the benefits of the separate school in the development and maintenance of the black social, cultural, and intellectual heritage, the majority of writers in the yearbook opposed the extension of segregated schooling. The contributors suggested several legal strategies that could be utilized to bring an end to Jim Crow in public education, and many of these recommendations were followed by the NAACP lawyers who eventually succeeded in getting the U.S. Supreme Court to outlaw legal segregation in American public education.[28]

The consensus of the majority of authors in the *JNE* yearbook in many ways symbolized the more general consensus among black leaders on the issue of public school segregation. Most agreed that the spread of separate schools, especially in the North, should be openly protested, and that a concerted effort, primarily through litigation, should be launched to end legal public school segregation where it existed.[29] The situation in Philadelphia was an issue in the 1934 debate between W. E. B. Du Bois and Walter White. Du Bois believed that "in the city of Philadelphia a partial system of elementary Negro schools was developed with no definite action on the part of the NAACP." Du Bois was, of course, referring to the inactivity of the Philadelphia NAACP between 1926 and 1934 with regard to the issue of the separate schools. Walter White responded, however, that "the failure of the citizens of Philadelphia to resist more persistently, intelligently and militantly the establishment of a partial system of elementary Negro schools is [not] necessarily approval of the segregation which has been established. This opening wedge will undoubtedly result in more segregation in schools and other public institutions unless aggressively fought. Like cancer, segregation grows and must be, in my opinion, resisted wherever it shows its head."[30] Many black Philadelphians agreed with Du Bois's observation about the inactivity of the local NAACP, as well as White's assessment of the potential danger of allowing public school segregation to continue unchallenged. Black citizens and parents formed new organizations that would fight aggressively during the 1930s and 1940s to end discrimination against blacks in the Philadelphia public school system.

The struggle against school segregation in Philadelphia, 1930–40

The onset of the Great Depression brought new and even greater financial hardships to the Philadelphia public schools. Cutbacks had to be made each year, and no new employees were hired to replace those who left or retired. The annual reports of the Philadelphia Board of Public Education in the 1930s chronicle the increasingly distressful financial situation of the school system. In 1931, for example, the school board was being pressured by the City Council to reduce teachers' salaries, and to dismiss married female teachers and nonresidents of the city. The board, however, found that it could not move on any of these issues under the existing school code of the Commonwealth of Pennsylvania.[31]

The movement of many families to the suburbs meant that there were fewer pupils entering the elementary grades. At the same time, the Depression forced many children to remain in school longer, which meant that there were more and more pupils in the higher grades, where the costs of providing adequate schooling were relatively greater than in the elementary schools.[32] The president of the school board in 1933, Joseph Catherine, reported that the major source of school funds in the city was the assessed valuation of real estate property. The economic depression led to an increase in the rate of delinquency in tax payments from a low of 4.7 percent in 1923 to a high of 26.0 percent in 1933. As a result, "no new appointments to teaching, supervisory or clerical positions have been made during the year."[33] In fact, in 1933 the public school system discontinued 19 junior high school, 123 grade school, 2 kindergarten, and 7 special education positions.[34]

The conditions for black teachers in the public schools worsened with the declining financial condition of the system. In 1918 school officials introduced the "6-3-3 format" with the opening of public junior high schools throughout the city: students would attend the elementary schools for the first six grades, the junior high schools for the next three, and the senior high schools for the last three.[35] This change was carried out gradually during the 1920s, and in 1931 it was announced that there were sufficient junior high schools to allow all the elementary schools to comprise only grades one through six. Many of the separate black public schools, however, included grades one through eight. Thus, under the board's new policy many black teachers would lose their positions. The fact that the school board was not hiring or even replacing elementary school teachers meant that there was little likelihood that these teachers would be transferred to other separate black schools in the city. And since no black teachers were allowed to teach in the mixed secondary schools, there was no possibility that they would be transferred to junior or senior high schools.[36]

The black community was informed of the plight of the black teacher in the public schools through the black press and community meetings. Several rallies and public debates were held in the black churches on such topics as "The Treatment of the Black Teacher" and "Segregated Schools, Yes or No?"[37] In an open letter to the school board in October 1931, E. Washington Rhodes, editor of the Tribune, even suggested that the board "begin quietly to place a few Negro teachers" in the junior high schools and thus desegregate the secondary schools with very little trouble. The school board, however, did not respond to this suggestion.[38]

Then, in December 1931 and January 1932, another issue emerged that would provide the first important victory of the newly organized black minority in its struggles with the Board of Education. E. Washington Rhodes and Floyd L. Logan, a U.S. Customs Office employee and contributor to the *Tribune*, began informing the black community of the "slanderous statements" against blacks found in *Problems in American Democracy* by Harry R. Burch and Dean Patterson, a textbook used in the public junior high schools throughout the city.[39] In a letter to William Rowen, president of the school board, Logan declared that "its chapter on the American race problem which deals with the Negro race is in most part derogatory."

> For instance, the statement that the Negro's ignorance and superstition are proverbial and his uncleanliness exacts a terrible toll is extremely misleading. It leaves one to think that such is true of the entire race.

The chapter also seemed to suggest that the reason blacks did not vote in the South was "not because of race, but by reason of illiteracy." Logan noted that this "is not confirmed by any actual survey of the conditions in the southern part of the country. It is the dissemination of such propaganda . . . that has not only poisoned the minds of white people against us, but in addition thereto has brought about misunderstandings of the Negro and the consequent mistreatment of him in every department of American social and economic life." Logan also announced the formation of a citizens' committee that was willing to meet with school board members. The Committee of 15, made up of the leaders of several black social, religious, and fraternal organizations, later met with several school officials.[40]

The entire front page of the 14 January 1932 edition of the *Tribune* was devoted to the "textbook issue." It was reported that Superintendent Edwin Broome had declared that school officials "would not tolerate such a book," and that "action would be taken if the facts warrant."[41] Then, on 28 January 1932, Floyd Logan announced that Superintendent Broome had recommended that the *Problems in American Democracy* text no longer be used in the public schools.[42]

Another important outcome of the mobilization to remove the textbook was the formation of the Educational Equality League of Philadelphia in January 1932, with Floyd Logan as president and E. Washington Rhodes as vice-president. This organization was to take the lead in the struggle to end school segregation in Philadelphia in the 1930s. But the League's first victory came in Berwyn, a suburb adjacent to Philadelphia. After months of litigation and a two-year boycott of the separate black public school in the area, black parents and citizens from the local community and from Philadelphia were able to bring about a change in the segregatory policies of the two suburban public school districts.

Philadelphia Tribune, front page for 14 January 1932, containing charges against the Problems in American Democracy textbook used in the public schools. (Photo by Jack T. Franklin)

The Berwyn School Case, as it came to be known, began in March 1932 with a protest by the parents of black children attending the elementary grades in Easttown and Tredyffrin townships (Berwyn), school districts in Chester County. All of the black children in the two districts were placed in a separate one-room schoolhouse, with one black teacher instructing grades one through six. A new elementary school had recently been opened in the Easttown School District, but black children were not allowed to attend it. Shortly afterward, the Bryn Mawr branch of the NAACP and the Educational Equality League in Philadelphia committed themselves to legal and financial support of the efforts of the black parents to desegregate the school districts.[43]

At the beginning of the 1932–33 school year, black children were refused admission to any but the separate black school. A black parent brought suit against the Easttown School District in October 1932.[44]

Floyd L. Logan, president of the Educational Equality League of Philadelphia. 1932–78. (Courtesy of the Philadelphia Tribune)

However, this first round of litigation was lost in December 1932 on the grounds that an individual could not file a suit to change the practices of a school district; it would be necessary for the state attorney general's office to file a class-action suit against the Easttown school board.[45] At that point, rather than allow their children to remain in the inadequate separate school, the parents began a boycott that was to last almost two years.[46]

In the ensuing months, the lawyers for the parents' group, Raymond Pace Alexander and Maceo Hubbard of Philadelphia, tried unsuccessfully to persuade State Attorney General William Schnader to bring suit against the Easttown School District for violating the state's school code.[47] In May 1933 several rallies and public meetings were held in Philadelphia to raise funds for the litigation, sponsored by the Educational Equality League.[48] At these gatherings, the local branch of the NAACP was soundly criticized for not taking an active part in the case. Later, officials in the national office of the organization also expressed their dismay at the lack of activity. In the correspondence between the national office and the Philadelphia branch during the 1930s, national officials often commented that the branch leadership had been "notoriously inactive in taking up cases of any description and as a result it is being sharply criticized."[49] Many blacks in Philadelphia believed that the Berwyn parents should be supported, since a favorable decision in that case could serve as a legal precedent for future litigation by black parents against the practice of segregation in the city's public schools.

In April 1933 several of the Berwyn parents who had been educating their children in makeshift classrooms were arrested and fined for violation of the state compulsory school attendance laws. The parents refused to pay the fines, and the charges were later dropped.[50] Throughout the spring and summer of 1933 more rallies were held in Philadelphia and in the nearby suburbs to keep the black communities in the area informed of the school situation.[51]

With the opening of the public schools for the 1933–34 school year, the problem that faced the black parents in Berwyn was whether or not to continue the boycott into a second year. Spurred by the positive support of the Philadelphia and other black communities, the Berwyn parents decided to continue their struggle. At a rally of over seven hundred persons, sponsored by the Educational Equality League at the Bellevue-Stratford Hotel in Philadelphia on 20 September 1933, the International Legal Defense (ILD) organization, which received support from the Communist Party of the United States, the American Civil Liberties Union (ACLU), as well as the Bryn Mawr NAACP, pledged to continue to back the Berwyn parents.[52] In October 1933 the Easttown school board again swore out warrants and had several parents arrested for violating the compulsory school law. Initially the parents refused to pay the fines and went to jail, but later they were released on bond. Several more rallies were held in Philadelphia to raise funds for the case; it was estimated that over 4,000 persons attended the one held at Bethel A.M.E. Church on 10 October 1933.[53] Then, on 19 October, it was announced that the national office of the NAACP had agreed to give its full support to the prosecution of the case.[54]

In early November, Attorney General Schnader again refused to bring charges against the Easttown school board for violation of the Pennsylvania school laws. The reason given this time was a report that school officials had already allowed two black children to attend white schools in the district. At this juncture Governor Gifford Pinchot made known his opposition to the discriminatory practices of the two school boards, in a statement issued in December 1933.[55]

During the first two months of 1934, several more rallies were held in support of the boycott. The attorney general announced in March that he would begin prosecution of the Easttown school board for violating the state's school code, and appointed two black attorneys, Herbert Millen and Henry Cheatham, to represent the state. Finally, in May 1934, the Easttown and Tredyffrin township school boards issued a joint statement declaring that no children would be forced to attend a separate public school because of their race. This decision was viewed as a major victory for the black parents of Berwyn and the Educational Equality League of Philadelphia.[56]

It should be noted, however, that the decision of Attorney General Schnader to prosecute the Easttown school board for practicing segregation and to appoint two black lawyers to handle the case was very likely spurred by the political reality that he would be needing the support of the Philadelphia black community in his bid for the office of governor of Pennsylvania in November 1934. In that election, however, Schnader received little support from black Republicans in the city, and he lost the race to Democrat George Earle.[57]

The victory in the Berwyn case provided momentum to the ongoing attempts of blacks in Philadelphia to desegregate the public schools. From its formation, the Educational Equality League had pushed for the achievement of three objectives in Philadelphia: the appointment of a black to the school board, the appointment of black teachers to the public secondary schools, and the abolition of the dual lists (black and white) for the appointment of teachers in the public elementary schools. In the period from 1932 to 1937, the League achieved all three goals, thus ending the official practice of segregation in the Philadelphia public school system.[58]

By the end of the 1920s, most black and some white leaders in the city had agreed to support the nomination of Dr. John P. Turner, a prominent physician and police surgeon, as the first black on the school board. Appointments to the Board of Public Education during this period were made after the nominee had received a majority of the votes of the fifteen judges of the Court of Common Pleas.[59] These judges were elected, and thus school board appointments were often made on a partisan basis. The fact that the Republican Party had been in control of the city government since the 1890s meant that fourteen of the fifteen Common Pleas judges were Republicans.[60] Traditionally, school board appointments were made in order to satisfy a particular constituency of the Republican Party in the city; thus, there was the Catholic appointee, the Italian appointee, the representative of the Main Line "aristocracy," and so on. It was only when the black minority became a constituency whose demands for representation on the board had to be satisfied that the Republican judges supported the appointment of a black nominee.[61]

In 1928 Dr. Turner was nominated for appointment to the school board by various groups, but only one judge voted for his appointment. Judge Henry McDevitt fully supported Turner for the school board and urged Philadelphians, especially blacks, to send cards and letters to the other judges in support of Turner's appointment each time an opening appeared on the fifteen-member board.[62] In the early 1930s, other Common Pleas judges made public statements supporting Turner's appointment. Judge Raymond MacNeille endorsed Dr. Turner in November 1932, and Judge Edwin O. Lewis in September 1933 urged blacks to vote only for those judges who supported the appointment of a black to the school board.[63]

The *Philadelphia Tribune* had been calling for Turner's appointment since 1927. Each time a vacancy appeared on the board, the newspaper editorialized on the need for a more "Democratic Board of Education" in Philadelphia or simply asked "Why Not A Negro Now?"[64] With the formation of the Educational Equality League in January 1932, the black community had a strong organization for coordinating its activities. The league led the community in the unsuccessful attempt to gain Dr. Turner's appointment in August 1933.[65] After that defeat, most blacks openly stated that race prejudice was the major reason for the judges' refusal to elect him.[66]

With the primary elections of May 1934, the newly emerged Democratic Party in Philadelphia, under the leadership of John B. Kelly, began to slate black candidates for elective offices. John Summers won the Democratic nomination in the Seventh District (thirtieth ward), and Rev. Marshall Shepard won in the Eighteenth District (seventh ward), both for the state house of representatives. In the November elections, Shepard won a seat in the legislature as a result of a Democratic sweep in his district.[67] The Democratic Party also picked up a great deal of support in the black community with the appointment of J. Austin Norris, an influential lawyer, to the state attorney general's office in February 1935. The Republicans had made no major black appointment since 1926, when *Tribune* editor E. Washington Rhodes was appointed an assistant U.S. attorney for the Eastern District of Pennsylvania.[68]

In March 1935 another vacancy appeared on the school board. The Educational Equality League and the *Tribune* immediately swung into action, contacting the judges and urging Turner's appointment. Finally, in May 1935, a majority of the Common Pleas judges voted to appoint Dr. Turner. Thus, after over seven years of active campaigning by the *Philadelphia Tribune*, the Educational Equality League, and other black groups and individuals, a representative of the black minority was appointed to the Philadelphia Board of Public Education.[69]

With its first objective accomplished, the Educational Equality League soon became preoccupied with the second: the appointment of black teachers to the public secondary schools. The 1931 decision to limit the elementary schools to the first six grades united many of the

Dr. John P. Turner, police surgeon and first black elected to the Philadelphia Board of Public Education. (Courtesy of the Philadelphia Tribune)

disparate opponents of the school board's policies. The league had been urging black teachers to take the examinations for appointment to the junior high schools, but often black teachers who had filled out the application to take the exams would receive a note from John Christopher, the director of examinations, stating that "we wish to call your attention to the fact that at the present time we have no segregated junior high schools."[70] With the Depression and the freeze on hiring, it became virtually impossible for qualified black teachers to get positions in the public elementary schools. Finally, in June 1934, even the Pennsylvania Association of Teachers of Colored Children (PATCC) resolved to support the efforts being made by the Educational Equality League to gain the appointment of black teachers in the public secondary schools.[71]

The Educational Equality League continued to protest against the policies of the school board between 1932 and 1935, indirectly through its attempts to find ways of bringing the issue of the separate eligibility lists into the courts, and directly through its appearances before school board meetings. At the board meeting held on 12 June 1934, for example, John Francis Williams, an attorney and a member of the league, pointed out that the practice of not allowing blacks to teach in the junior and senior high schools "is working a hardship and is discouraging some of our group from going to college. Others who hold college degrees and are equipped to teach in the higher schools are not permitted to do so. For that reason I am going to acquaint you with some of the facts."

> We have 34 young men and women holding college degrees who are eligible to teach in junior and senior high schools, 57 young men and women who are working and studying for their degrees, 23 young men and women who have passed the tests for junior and senior high schools and who are not permitted to teach in these schools. We have 14 who have qualified for teaching in the junior and senior high schools, two for physical education, one for industrial art, one for music, etc.

Williams went on to describe the problems caused by the school board's discriminatory hiring practices in nonteaching areas.[72]

The members of the school board did not respond immediately to the Educational Equality League's presentation of "the facts," and as a result the league and other opponents of the school board's policies continued to protest.[73] Then, on 4 October 1935, five months after the appointment of Dr. John P. Turner to the board, it was announced that Mrs. Beatrice Clare Overton had been appointed an art teacher at Sulzberger Junior High, a predominantly black school in West Philadelphia.[74]

Though the ice had been broken with the appointment of a black teacher to teach white children in a junior high school, it took another year and a half before the two eligibility lists for teacher appointments in the public elementary schools were merged. Blacks did not stop petitioning the school board after the appointment of Mrs. Overton, but there was less urgency in their demands. Probably many believed that with Dr. Turner on the school board the interests of the black community would be represented, and that Turner would work to bring an end to the dual eligibility lists, just as he had assisted in gaining the appointment of the first black in the junior high schools.[75]

Moreover, after 1934 there were other jobs available for unemployed black teachers in the city. The large number of blacks attending the public evening schools brought jobs to black teachers, if only on a part-time basis.[76] There were three public evening schools with all-black staffs offering classes in basic literacy skills in the 1930s: Barratt, Reynolds, and Sulzberger. When the school board threatened to close these schools for financial reasons in December 1937, many blacks, especially

All-black evening class in basic literacy training sponsored by the Philadelphia Board of Public Education in the 1920s. (Source: PBPE)

black students, protested, and funds were appropriated by the state to keep the schools open.[77] The Works Projects Administration (WPA) and the National Youth Administration (NYA) educational and recreational classes in black neighborhoods also employed a large number of black teachers.[78] And the improving financial condition of the public school system in the second half of the decade led to the appointment of two new teachers in the separate black public schools at the beginning of the 1935–36 school year, and two more in 1936–37.[79]

The Educational Equality League and others persisted, however, in their efforts to have the separate eligibility lists merged. Finally, in March 1937, the school board announced that the separate lists had been merged because the majority of members were finally convinced that the dual eligibility lists were opposed to the "spirit" of the Pennsylvania school code.[80] But even before the shouts of victory died down, it had become apparent that some individuals were not satisfied with the way things had worked out. As was mentioned above, the teacher surplus in Philadelphia at the end of the 1920s and in the early 1930s had led to a cutback in the number of students admitted to the Philadelphia Normal School and an increase in the requirements for certification for public school teaching.[81] The fact that for several years no elementary school teachers and very few secondary teachers were appointed meant that in 1937 there were well over a thousand names on the list of whites eligible for appointment to the elementary schools and over one hundred on the list of blacks. When these two lists were merged, the black teachers dropped precipitously in their standings for appointment. For example, the black teacher who was first on the black eligibility list dropped to number 390 on the merged list; the one who was number 5 dropped to number 470; the one who was number 11 dropped to number 577. This virtually precluded the possibility that a black teacher would be appointed to a position in the public elementary schools in the near (or distant) future.[82]

Protest meetings were held by the disgruntled black teachers and their supporters in April 1937, and the PATCC issued a series of "objectives" that it believed would rectify the situation for the black teachers. The teachers' organization concluded that "Negroes should be appointed immediately to the Board of Examiners, the Rating Board, and the Department of Superintendence" of the public school system, and that "Negro teachers should be allotted the following number of positions in the Philadelphia schools: Elementary, up to 450; Junior High, 75; Senior High, 74; Normal School, 2; Practical School, 2 each; other schools, 25." The PATCC presented its objectives to the school board in May 1937.[83]

The school board made no official response, but in July 1937 it announced the names of the principal and teachers who had received appointments to the newly constructed Roberts Vaux Junior High School, which was to be opened in a predominantly black neighborhood in North Philadelphia in September 1937. There were no black teachers appointed to the school at that time. The committee that had been formed to support the black teachers on the merged eligibility list conducted several meetings and debates during the summer of 1937 and voiced its disapproval of the Vaux Junior High appointments to school officials.[84] Meanwhile, it sought the support of the Educational Equality League and other organizations.[85]

In late July 1937, Floyd Logan of the Educational Equality League issued a statement to clarify the organization's position on the problems of the black teachers. Logan pointed out that when the league was successful in getting the school board to appoint a black teacher to the junior high schools, the teacher's organization (PATCC) was pleased; after the merging of the elementary school appointment lists, the league was criticized. "The contention was that before asking for such a merger, the League should have requested the Board to make some adjustments in order to compensate for inequalities suffered by colored teachers under the dual lists." Logan reminded the PATCC that for years it had *not* protested against the "inequalities suffered by colored teachers" and labeled its objectives "absurd." The entire program of the PATCC "seems in the opinion of the League a trick program for the perpetuation of segregation in the schools." Logan concluded that the league would not support the PATCC objectives but would continue to work for the achievement of "educational equality" in the Philadelphia public schools.[86]

The conditions at the Vaux Junior High School during the 1937–38 school year became a much greater concern of the Educational Equality League than the PATCC objectives, and without league support the issue soon faded. Vaux had opened in September 1937 with an 85 percent black enrollment, but there was only one black teacher, Marjorie Tucker, who had been appointed as the "faculty counselor" at the school. The league and most black Philadelphians were disappointed that black elementary school administrators were not allowed to compete for the principalship.[87] Moreover, the white educator chosen to head the new school, Margaret Maguire, appeared insensitive to the racially volatile conditions that developed and was accused of overt racial prejudice by several students and teachers. The league entered the picture in the spring of 1938 after black parents began to express complaints about the principal's attitudes and practices. John Francis Williams and Walter Gay, the league lawyers, worked with attorney Sadie T. M. Alexander in gathering affidavits from individuals who had specific incidents to report, and in May 1938 a meeting was held with a special board committee, which included Francis Biddle, Mrs. John Frederick Lewis, and Gilbert Spruance. Among the incidents investigated was the charge of Mrs. Estelle Scroggins, a music teacher, that Miss Maguire was "racially prejudiced." Mrs. Scroggins claimed that she had heard the principal shout at a student, "Get off these steps, you black tramp. You are not fit to be in a school like this, you dirty black sucker." A black student charged that after slapping his face, the principal repeatedly called him "a damned black tramp, a damned dirty louse." Similar complaints were presented, and later Francis Biddle admitted that, based on the evidence, "it appears that Miss Maguire had a prejudiced attitude on the basis of race and color." In July 1938 the league reported that individual board members had promised that Miss Maguire would be replaced.[88]

Black elementary school principals were to take the examination for appointments in the secondary schools in September 1938, and Dr. John P. Turner interviewed several black principals eligible for secondary school appointments. During the week of 7 September 1938 Miss Maguire was transferred to the Vare Junior High school in South Philadelphia, and Dr. Turner pledged, "I am going to insist both in season and out of season for the appointment of a colored principal in the junior high school." Meanwhile, the parents of some three hundred white students at Vaux petitioned the school board for transfers to other schools because the "racial tensions" were affecting their children's health. "Boys as well as girls are suffering from nervous conditions caused by mistreatment, threats, and fear of fellow classmates." No specific incidents were mentioned in the petition, but the parents refused to send their children to Vaux, and by October 1938 school officials were threatening to swear out warrants for the parents of 130 students who could not be placed in other schools and therefore were still on strike. The petition and protests of white groups led to the appointment of Dr. Willard Zahn as principal of Vaux at the beginning of the month, even before the black principals were eligible; and Zahn was eventually successful in calming racial tensions at the school. Alexander J. Stoddard, formerly superintendent of the Denver public schools, became the head of the Philadelphia system in October 1938. He arrived in the city in 1939 pledging himself to a policy of fairness in dealing with the black community, and in many ways followed through on this pledge in the early 1940s.[89]

The abolition of the dual eligibility lists for appointments in the elementary schools and the opening of positions in the secondary schools to blacks signaled the end of official segregation in the public school system. With Dr. Turner on the school board and other school officials, including board member Francis Biddle and Superintendent Stoddard, pledging to adjust discriminatory practices, many black Philadelphians began to believe that they would get a fair deal in the public schools.[90] Unfortunately, only some school officials worked for the desegregation of faculties and student bodies in the 1940s, and with the large increase in the black enrollment during the decade, the degree of racial segregation also increased.

This is not to say, however, that the appointment of Dr. Turner to the school board, the abolition of the dual eligibility lists, and the appointment of blacks to the public secondary schools were unimportant or insignificant achievements. Indeed, they must be viewed as three of the most important political victories for the Philadelphia black community in the first half of the twentieth century. And they were *political* victories. The black community mobilized its political resources to bring about a change in school board policies in ways that were quite similar to its activities for the appointment of Dr. Turner and the passage of the equal rights law. The key was not the sudden awareness of the majority of the school board's members that many of its policies and practices were contrary to the "spirit" of the Pennsylvania school code, but the realization that some black leaders were in contact with Democratic politicians in the city and state who were willing to support the black community in its demand for the official desegregation of the public school system. Several black and white Democratic leaders realized that supporting the black community on the issue of the separate schools could mean more black votes for Democratic candidates on election day.[92]

The increased political power of the black community during the 1930s helps explain why tactics that failed in the 1920s were successful in changing school board policies in the 1930s. Ad hoc organizations, mass protest rallies and debates, and petitions had all been utilized in the 1920s, without any real success. It was only when blacks began to leave the Republican Party in unprecedented numbers, and black leaders began to seek out the support of Democratic politicians who wanted black votes, that Republican leaders and school officials began to move on black demands.

At the same time, an important change was beginning in the attitudes of many black and white Americans about the practice of racial segregation. In the 1920s very few whites or blacks seriously contemplated the demise of Jim Crow in American society. Most blacks opposed legal segregation not for idealistic reasons, but because it usually meant separate and unequal rather than separate but equal. By the mid-1930s, however, many blacks and some whites had come to believe that legal segregation had to be opposed in the North and the South, because it essentially prohibited black advancement in many important political, social, and economic areas. Given the extreme economic dislocations of the 1930s, many blacks fought for the removal of all legal barriers to their participation in the movement toward economic recovery and prosperity.

The "New Negro" of the twenties was generally not as preoccupied with desegregating American society as he was with probing alternatives to racism, capitalism, and the political powerlessness of blacks in the United States. Garveyism, Socialism, Communism, and many other political and social movements and ideologies competed for the support of the masses of blacks who saw little likelihood of social improvement under the present system.[93] The Great Depression, however, demonstrated to most Afro-Americans that their social conditions were inextricably tied to those of the larger society, and that legal segregation must be challenged if Afro-Americans were going to contribute to their own and the nation's economic advancement.

The New Deal made little attempt to incorporate a policy of non-discrimination into federally sponsored employment or educational programs directed at the general American populace. But the continued practice of segregation and racial discrimination, especially in light of increased black militancy in opposing Jim Crow, meant that there was greater likelihood of interracial conflict and tension. Racial violence erupted in several cities during the 1930s, with the Harlem Race Riot of 1935 attracting the most national attention.[94]

With the outbreak of conflict in Europe in 1939, there was even greater need for "interracial cooperation" in the United States. The national defense mobilization and the subsequent entrance of the United States into the hostilities required that the country utilize to the fullest extent possible its material and manpower resources, especially those resources located in major industrial areas. When blacks began to be employed in industries from which they had been barred, interracial tension increased and violence sometimes erupted. The most serious wartime interracial violence occurred in Detroit, New York City, and Los Angeles in 1943. In Philadelphia the public transportation strike during the summer of 1944 demonstrated the depth of interracial hostility there. The sometimes tense racial climate in Philadelphia in the 1930s and 1940s led many social organizations to sponsor community-wide educational programs and other efforts to improve interracial understanding. Interracial and intercultural programs became a significant part of community education in both black and white Philadelphia beginning in the 1930s and continuing throughout the 1940s.

The national defense mobilization and wartime industrial expansion brought a number of welcome changes for the depression-ridden citizens of Philadelphia. On the eve of the defense build-up, the economy of the city was still sagging under the weight of high rates of unemployment and low levels of industrial productivity. Throughout the depression years, unemployment rates in Philadelphia were generally higher than those for the nation as a whole. For example, in April 1933, it was reported that 44.8 percent of the work force of the city was unemployed, whereas for the entire nation the highest level of unemployment reached throughout the Depression was 30.9 percent in 1933. In August 1938 Philadelphia had 32.4 percent unemployment, and even after the beginning of national defense mobilization in March 1940, 19.4 percent of the city's workers were still without jobs.[1]

These trends in unemployment were reversed by December 1941, however, when it was reported that only 6.0 percent of the city's work force was idle.[2] Industrial productivity greatly expanded during the defense build-up, and many plants and government installations in the city received defense contracts, especially in shipbuilding, heavy armament, and munitions. By 1942 war contracts were also being given to textile, clothing, leather, chemical, and other industries. Labor shortages in several areas developed as early as 1940, but Philadelphia was not considered an official "shortage area" until the summer of 1944.[3] With the end of the war, substantial labor cutbacks were made by the city's industries, but levels of civilian employment were higher in 1947 and 1950 than in 1940. In April 1947, for example, only 6.5 percent of the city's work force was unemployed, and in April 1950, this figure had risen to only 6.6 percent.[4]

Socioeconomic conditions for black Philadelphians during the 1940s did not necessarily reflect the general economic improvement reported for the city as a whole. In 1940 blacks were 13.1 percent of the city's population. Between 1930 and 1940, their numbers increased from 219,599 to 250,880, or 13.6 percent, while the total population of the city decreased from 1,950,961 to 1,931,334, or by 1 percent. During World War II there was another large migration of southern blacks to Philadelphia. By 1950 the city's total population had increased to 2,071,607 (a 7 percent increase), but the black population had reached 376,041 (a 49.9 percent increase). Thus, by 1950, blacks were 18.1 percent of the Philadelphia population—as shown by table 1 in chapter 1.[5]

With the increase in the black population came a significant shift in the pattern of distribution of blacks in the city. Before 1930, the black community was centered in South Philadelphia. By 1940, however, the largest concentration of blacks was found in North Philadelphia. Thus, rather than a "black belt," as in New York and Chicago, Philadelphia had a number of small and large black neighborhoods scattered throughout the city.[6] A statement prepared by the Philadelphia Housing Association in November 1947 reported that between 1930 and 1940 "within the city 28 wards showed a percentage decrease [in population] while only 20 showed an increase. The 'traditional colored districts' in North [Central], South and West Philadelphia have absorbed not only the entire net growth, but also many Negro families from other parts of the city, especially those displaced by demolition in the center of the city and along the waterfront."[7] These conditions resulted in a housing shortage and great overcrowding in the predominantly black areas, which in turn led to higher rents in those sections. The association also pointed out that in 1940 in census tracts inhabited by blacks, 81 percent of the housing units were built before 1900, as against 33 percent in the rest of the city.[8]

The wartime migration of southern blacks to Philadelphia only aggravated the housing shortage. The Armstrong Association reported that almost one-half of the black families in Philadelphia in 1950 lived in areas certified for redevelopment, as opposed to one-eighth of white families. Overcrowding was three times greater among black households.[9] Between 1945 and 1955, there were 140,000 new housing units provided for white residents in the city, while only 1,044 (or 0.7 percent) were set aside for blacks.[10]

According to 1940 census data for the city, 29.4 percent of blacks in the labor force were unemployed, of whom 25.8 percent were experienced workers. Only 15.1 percent of whites in the labor force were unemployed, and 10.2 percent of experienced workers. Moreover, 6.8 percent of black workers were still on public emergency projects, while only 2.1 percent of the white work force was so employed. There were also great differences in the occupational distribution of white and black workers. For example, in 1940, 77.0 percent of the black male workers in Philadelphia were employed in the less desirable and lower-paid jobs, such as factory operatives, domestic and other service work, and unskilled laborers. Only 35.9 percent of the white male workers in the city were listed in these categories. The two largest job categories for white females were clerical, sales, and related workers (35.5 percent) and factory operatives (30 percent). But 60.3 percent of employed black females were in domestic service, and 14.4 percent were in some other form of service occupation (see table 12).[11]

Initially the expansion in wartime production in the city did not affect the occupational distribution of black workers. Studies of the industrial opportunities for blacks in the defense industries found that many employers were still reluctant to hire black workers. Consequently, the unskilled and semiskilled industrial labor needs were generally filled by white workers, especially in the period from 1939 to 1941. In areas of labor shortages—that is, in skilled and highly technical areas—most blacks could not have competed for these positions even if there were no discrimination, because they often did not possess the necessary training. This state of affairs led to a twofold campaign on the part of a number of organizations in the black community: to encourage blacks, especially black youth, to enroll in defense training courses, and to mobilize to break down race barriers in the defense industries of the city. These campaigns, however, met with only limited success.[12]

Surveys of the employment conditions for blacks in the war industries of Philadelphia in 1942 and 1944 further supported the contention that blacks were still the victims of discrimination. In June 1942 the staff of the War Production Board in Philadelphia voiced its belief that "the problem for Negroes . . . was not one of employment but of the types of occupations Negroes would hold and their opportunities for advancement into skilled work."[13] By 1944 some change in the employment status of blacks was noted by the Armstrong Association, probably spurred by the labor shortage and the president's Executive Order 8802 forbidding discrimination in hiring because of race, creed, or national origin by plants and industries holding government contracts. The association surveyed twenty-four Philadelphia companies in June 1944 and found that 16.6 percent of the blacks employed were skilled workers and almost 30 percent were classified as semiskilled. These were considered very high percentages. But it was also noted that no blacks were listed as stenographers, typists, or clerks in the twenty-four firms. The Armstrong Association concluded that despite encourag-

Table 12
Employed persons (except in public emergency work) in Philadelphia in 1940, by occupation, sex, and race

Occupation	Males						Females					
	Total	White		Black		Other	Total	White		Black		Other
		Number	Percentage	Number	Percentage			Number	Percentage	Number	Percentage	
Total	485,086	441,667	100.0%	42,550	100.0%	869	218,612	187,581	100.0%	30,990	100.0%	41
Professional and semiprofessional workers	30,416	29,211	6.6	1,179	2.8	26	23,417	22,540	12.0	864	2.8	13
Farmers and farm managers	228	224		4		—a	15	13		2		—
Proprietors, managers, and officials, except farm	50,963	49,602	11.2	1,190	2.8	171	6,385	6,143	3.3	241	0.8	1
Clerical, sales, and kindred workers	92,971	90,126	20.4	2,801	6.6	44	67,348	66,638	35.5	705	2.3	5
Craftsmen, foremen, and kindred workers	99,002	95,297	21.6	3,676	8.6	29	3,662	3,544	1.9	118	0.4	—
Operatives and kindred workers	117,878	108,906	24.7	8,686	20.4	286	61,633	56,184	30.0	5,440	17.6	9

Domestic service workers	1,931	517	0.1	1,363	3.2	51	28,472	9,767	5.2	18,698	60.3	7
Protective service workers	15,637	15,027	3.4	586	1.4	24	122	115	0.1	7	7	—
Service workers, except domestic and protective	33,125	22,998	5.2	9,939	23.4	188	24,309	19,852	10.6	4,452	14.4	5
Farm laborers and foremen	533	487	0.1	46	0.1	—	20	15		5		—
Laborers, except farm and mine	38,698	25,892	5.9	12,760	30.0	46	1,065	838	0.4	227	0.7	—
Occupation not reported	3,704	3,380	0.8	320	0.8	4	2,164	1,932	1.0	231	0.7	1

Source: G. Gordon Brown, *Law Administration and Negro-White Relations in Philadelphia* (Philadelphia, 1947), p. 45.
Note: a. Less than one-tenth of one percent.

ing trends in some industries, the hiring of black workers at all skilled levels had not taken place at these Philadelphia companies.[14]

These findings suggest that there was a wide area for improvement in the employment conditions for blacks in Philadelphia in the early 1940s. But attempts to provide equal opportunities and facilities for blacks in housing, public services, and employment were often opposed, sometimes violently, by many white citizens and organizations. Indeed, in the period from 1930 to 1950 one finds reference to almost as many instances of interracial conflict in the city as examples of interracial cooperation.

Interracial cooperation and conflict in Philadelphia, 1930–50

Throughout the first half of the twentieth century many attempts were made at interracial cooperation among the black and white citizens of Philadelphia. The Philadelphia branch of the NAACP, which was organized in 1913, and the Armstrong Association, founded in 1908, initially were interracial organizations interested in the problems of blacks in the city.[15] In the 1920s the Interracial Commission of Philadelphia sponsored a few activities aimed at improving race relations and gave its support to the attempts of the black community to end segregation in the Philadelphia public schools.[16]

During the 1930s there was a great increase in the number of interracial activities sponsored by religious denominations in the city. The Federation of Christian Churches in Philadelphia inaugurated "Interracial Sunday" in February 1930.[17] It became "Race Relations Sunday" in the latter part of the decade. On this Sunday in February, in various churches throughout the city, sermons were preached on the need for greater cooperation and tolerance between the black and white communities.[18] Beginning in April 1931, the Philadelphia Quakers sponsored several interracial conferences and were active in promoting the Race Relations Institute held each summer during the decade at Swarthmore College, outside of Philadelphia. Prominent black and white leaders attended the institute and gave speeches and lectures on racial issues, which were then publicized throughout the Philadelphia metropolitan area.[19]

The Philadelphia archdiocese of the Roman Catholic Church also involved itself in the promotion of interracial activities. In May 1936, the archdiocese sponsored a campaign to improve interracial understanding and openly supported the intergroup activities of individual parishes.[20] But the racial prejudices of many white Catholics often caused a great deal of racial tension. In February 1941, for example, several priests in the Gesu Catholic Church in North Philadelphia made statements to the effect that they did not want black families to move into the neighborhood surrounding the church. These priests were joined by other ministers and individuals who were opposed to the residence of blacks in certain sections of North and West Philadelphia. On 16 March 1941 concerned members of the black community held a public protest meeting at the Douglass School in North Philadelphia and chose a committee to meet with Dennis Cardinal Dougherty, archbishop of Philadelphia, in order to make an official protest against the statements of the priests and ask for their removal from the local parishes. Cardinal Dougherty condemned racial prejudice and promised to look into the matter, but the priests were not removed.[21] As a result of this and several other incidents, another series of interracial lectures and programs was sponsored by the Catholic Church in Philadelphia.[22]

In December 1935 an "Interracial Church" made its debut in the city. The congregation was made up of persons of all faiths and races interested in the improvement of race relations locally. The group held nondenominational religious services at various host churches throughout the city.[23] During the 1930s and 1940s the branches of the YMCA and YWCA sponsored interracial meetings and conferences in an attempt to break down the barriers between white and black Christian youth. After the official desegregation of the association in 1946, these activities became much more common.[24]

During the 1940s a number of nonreligious social organizations in Philadelphia were active in trying to improve race relations. The Fellowship House, which opened in April 1941, was operated by black and white teenagers who had worked with the Committee on Race Relations of the Society of Friends during the 1930s. Jews and Christians, Protestants and Catholics, blacks and whites were among the supporters of Fellowship House, and its activities included weekly meetings to discuss racial and religious problems, the distribution of literature on brotherhood and interracial cooperation, and the creation of other "fellowship organizations" throughout the city.[25]

An increase in racial incidents and the resurgence of white-supremacist organizations led in October 1941 to the formation of the Philadelphia Fellowship Commission, a citywide community relations organization made up of eight local social agencies.[26] Only organizations or community agencies could belong to the commission, but by 1947 over five thousand persons belonged to the Fellowship Center and Library. The commission tried to assist and coordinate the programs of the constituent agencies, to act as mediator in interracial problems, and to conduct educational programs. When an incident occurred or a problem arose, the officers of the commission would determine whether the situation should be handled by the organization itself or referred to one of the more specialized member groups. The Fellowship Commission was also instrumental in the formation of the Committee on School and Community Tensions by the public school superintendent in 1944.[27]

The number of interracial incidents in the public schools began to increase in the early 1940s. Superintendent Alexander Stoddard decided to appoint Dr. Tanner G. Duckrey (a black) as his special assistant in July 1943. Duckrey was to give particular attention to the areas of race relations and intergroup tensions in the city schools.[28] In April 1944, Superintendent Stoddard announced the formation of a Committee of Thirty, made up of teachers and public school administrators, to "study race, religious and class tensions in the schools and recommend procedures."[29] Then, in September 1944, the Committee on School and Community Tensions was formed. Its members were school personnel and officials of local community agencies and organizations.[30] At the first meeting, held on 14 September 1944, Edwin W. Adams, associate superintendent of public schools and chairman of the committee, stated that its purpose was "the development of techniques for gathering information on school and community tensions and conflicts in order to

Dr. Tanner G. Duckrey, former principal of Paul Lawrence Dunbar Public School, and appointed in July 1943 special assistant to the superintendent of the Philadelphia public schools. Duckrey was the first black appointed to an administrative position within the Department of Superintendence of the public school system. (Courtesy of the Philadelphia Tribune)

monitor the school-community racial situation in the city."[31] The committee met throughout the remainder of the decade and made several recommendations to the school administration on interracial problems.[32]

The Pennsylvania State Temporary Commission on the Urban Colored Population, which completed its main report on the general social, economic, and educational conditions for blacks throughout the state in January 1943, had begun to work on "post-war planning." However, because of "increasing reports of racial tension throughout the State, the Commission at its July, 1943, meeting instructed its staff to suspend post-war planning and concentrate on the immediate racial situation."[33] The commission sponsored several conferences, developed a comprehensive program to prevent racial clashes, and established several programs to minimize racial friction and promote goodwill.[34]

The bloody Detroit Race Riot of the summer of 1943 led to the suggestion by several civic leaders that the municipal government establish a permanent committee on race relations to avoid a similar situation in Philadelphia. In August 1943 Mayor Bernard Samuel appointed forty-five prominent citizens to the City-Wide Interracial Committee, which would investigate interracial relations in employment, housing, and other areas. In December 1943 attorney Raymond Pace Alexander presented to the committee a comprehensive report on discrimination in hiring practices of the Philadelphia city government. On the basis of this report and other investigations, the committee concluded that there was a need for a permanent bureau or commission to investigate and intervene in incidents of discrimination.[35]

Despite these activities, racial incidents continued to occur. In August 1934 a full-scale race riot occurred in North Philadelphia after a white merchant on Ridge Avenue attacked a black woman and her baby in one of the food markets.[36] In December 1940 the black press reported that a black youth had been attacked by a white mob in South Philadelphia.[37] A black family was driven from their newly purchased home in North Philadelphia by a mob of armed white residents in March 1942, and a similar incident occurred on Grays Ferry Avenue in South Philadelphia in March 1943.[38] And a new low in race relations was reached with the Philadelphia transit strike during the summer of 1944.

The major issue in the Philadelphia Transportation Company (PTC) strike was the upgrading of black workers. From as early as 1941, there had been a shortage of streetcar motormen for the city's transit system. In 1942 and 1943 blacks had been hired and trained as motormen for the transit systems of New York and Washington, D.C.[39] In Philadelphia the local chapters of the National Negro Congress and the

NAACP began to push for the hiring of blacks in these positions in the city's transportation system as early as December 1942, but PTC officials continually refused to upgrade blacks, using as an excuse the possible opposition of the Philadelphia Rapid Transit Employees Union (PRTEU).[40] When the transit company requested one hundred white motormen from the United States Employment Office in 1943, however, the Fair Employment Practices Commission and War Manpower Commission entered the situation, and the FEPC decided to hold hearings in December.[41]

An upcoming election for union representation of the transit workers led to the postponement of further action. In that election in March 1944, three unions were competing for the employees' endorsement, and one group, the Transit Workers Union, supported the upgrading of black workers. The election was won by the Transit Workers Union, which received more votes than the other two unions combined. Meanwhile, the War Manpower Commission ruled that all male employees for the transit company were to be hired through the United States Employment Service, and hiring practices were to be nondiscriminatory. As a result, in July 1944, the PTC accepted three black applicants from the Employment Service and five blacks already employed by the company for training as streetcar motormen.[42]

White employees of the PTC then met and decided that on 1 August 1944, the first day blacks were supposed to drive streetcars in Philadelphia, they would go on strike. During the first few days of the walkout, several attempts were made to get the striking workers to return to their jobs. Then, on 3 August 1944, President Roosevelt asked Henry Stimson, the Secretary of the Army, to take charge of the PTC. Stimson sent Major General Phillip Hayes to Philadelphia. The Transit Workers Union had urged workers to return to their job, but to no avail. On 5 August General Hayes informed the local press and union officials that any workers who did not return to work by Monday, 7 August, would be removed from the company payroll and would lose their army deferments. On Sunday, PTC workers were signing pledges to return to their jobs and the leaders of the strike went to jail for violation of the Smith-Connally Act, which prohibted the instigation of a strike when a facility was in possession of the federal government.[43]

The strike by white employees of the PTC because of the upgrading of black workers suggested to many Philadelphians that future attempts to employ or upgrade black workers in other wartime or post-war industries might also meet with strong opposition. Several black and white leaders in Philadelphia advocated the support of the growing movement to set up a national or local fair employment practices commission to adjudicate disputes over the hiring of minority workers.[44] As was mentioned in chapter 5, the national movement for the passage of fair employment practice laws was begun in 1940 in order to insure that black and other minority workers would not be the victims of discrimination by industries receiving government defense contracts.[45] With the president's creation of the Fair Employment Practices Commission in 1941, and the opening of the Philadelphia office in October 1942, blacks who believed they were being discriminated against in hiring could make a formal complaint to the local FEPC office. As the war drew to a close, however, several groups began to push for the creation of a permanent FEPC. Between 1945 and 1950, Congress debated the passage of a fair hiring law, but opposition to the measure was great and no law was passed.[46]

During the postwar era and into the early fifties, however, attempts to gain the passage of state and local FEPC laws were meeting with some degree of success. Between 1945 and 1951, New York, New Jersey, Massachusetts, Connecticut, Rhode Island, New Mexico, Oregon, Washington, and Colorado passed fair employment practice laws.[47] In Pennsylvania the mobilization for the passage of state FEPC law began in 1944. Bills were introduced into almost every session of the General Assembly from 1945 to 1955, when a measure was finally passed.[48] In November 1945 a bill was introduced into the Philadelphia City Council for the creation of a local FEPC.[49] Though the bill was not acted upon, several community organizations continued to lobby and hold rallies in support of the measure. The Council on Equal Job Opportunity, the local NAACP, the United People's Action Committee, the Jewish Community Relations Council, and other organizations sponsored numerous public meetings and distributed literature on the need for such an ordinance in Philadelphia.[50]

In November 1947 another bill for the creation of a FEPC was introduced into the Philadelphia City Council by Louis Schwartz, and in January 1948 the Law Committee of the Council announced that public hearings on the measure would be held on 19 February 1948. Over seven hundred persons attended the hearings, and those who spoke in opposition to the measure were completely ineffective. The Law Committee voted unanimously to send the bill to the full Council. Despite some last-minute efforts by "business and patriotic groups" to generate opposition to the measure, the FEPC ordinance was enacted unanimously by the City Council on 11 March and signed by Mayor Bernard Samuel the next day.[51]

Under the terms of the ordinance, employers could not refuse to hire, labor unions were forbidden to deny membership, and employment agencies that were open to the general public were not to prohibit the registration, of any individual because of race, color, religion, national origin, or ancestry. The Philadelphia Fair Employment Practices Commission, the executive arm of the ordinance, was empowered to receive, investigate, and adjust charges involving discrimination in employment. Five commissioners were provided for in the ordinance, three appointed by the mayor and two appointed by the president of the City Council. In the first year of operation, 1 June 1948 to 31 May 1949, the commission received 204 cases, of which 155 were closed "to the satisfaction of all parties concerned."[52]

The first annual report of the Philadelphia FEPC discussed at length "the use of education to reduce prejudice and fears." The commission pointed out that "for the employer and worker, discrimination is frequently rooted in prejudice or in fear. It may be fear of loss of business, or fear of 'labor trouble' or fear of change. Both prejudice and these untested fears tend to evaporate when people work together and get to know each other better. Knowledge that fair employment practices work successfully also tends to abate such fears." This belief that education could improve interracial understanding was a general one in the social science and educational literature of the period; indeed, when the new city charter was enacted in Philadelphia in 1951, the FEPC was replaced by the Commission on Human Relations, whose activities would become almost entirely educational, although it was empowered to "adjust" or make recommendations about discriminatory hiring practices.[53] In Philadelphia throughout the period from 1930 to 1950, and afterward, educational activities were sponsored by various organizations and institutions, including the public schools, in hopes of improving race relations and interracial understanding among citizens.

Intercultural education in Philadelphia, 1930–50

During the first half of the twentieth century, the study of race and race relations changed in a number of fundamental ways. During the first twenty years, the social sciences, especially psychology and sociology, were dominated by Social Darwinian ideas (and ideals) developed in the last quarter of the nineteenth century.[54] As we have seen, the mental testing movement in the United States can be viewed as an attempt by some psychologists to measure the intellectual differences between "inferior" and "superior" races.[55] Some sociologists used the Social Darwinian notions of "social evolution" and "race survival" to account for specific developments in societies: for example, racial prejudice was considered a mechanism for group maintenance. Robert Park wrote in 1917

Dr. Sadie T. M. Alexander, a former member of the Philadelphia Commission on Human Relations, with a group of pupils from the Philadelphia area. (Courtesy of the Philadelphia Tribune)

that racial prejudice "may be regarded as a spontaneous more or less instinctive defense-reaction, the practical effect of which is to restrict free competition between the races." According to Park, the existence of racial castes in American society reinforced racial prejudice through the isolation of racial groups. "Isolation is at once a cause and effect of race prejudice," wrote Park, "it is a vicious circle—isolation, prejudices; prejudices, isolation."[56]

In his discussion of the "race relations cycle," Park theorized about the nature of interracial contacts. The cycle proceeded in four stages: contact, conflict, accommodation, and assimilation. After the initial contact of different racial groups, Park argued, a period of conflict arose that ended only when "one group has put the other in its place." This ushered in the period of accommodation, which was characterized by a caste system in which a very clearly outlined form of "racial etiquette" defined the nature of interracial relationships. The final stage, assimilation, saw the development of "primary relations" or interpersonal intimacy among individuals of the two races. Without some degree of "personal intimacy," myths and legends about racial groups would persist, and the formal system of racial etiquette would continue.[57]

Gunnar Myrdal, in his famous study of the American racial situation, An American Dilemma (1944), criticized Park and other American sociologists for having too fatalistic a view of social forces in general and race relations in particular. Myrdal attacked the acceptance of Social Darwinian "naturalistic laws" that defined the nature of race relations. He proposed a dynamic view of social relations: the "Negro Problem" should be approached scientifically, with a specific goal in mind. That goal should be, according to Myrdal, the realization of the "American Creed." This creed, or national ethos, consisted of the basic beliefs of all Americans "in liberty, equality, justice and fair opportunity for everybody." The American dilemma was thus the conflict between the "higher valuations" of the American Creed, and the "other valuations— which refer to various smaller groups of mankind or to a particular occasion; are commonly referred to as 'irrational' or 'prejudiced,' sometimes even by people who express and stress them. They are defended in terms of tradition, expediency or utility."[58]

Although there were important differences between their positions, both Park and Myrdal supported the belief that education should be used to improve interracial understanding. Through interracial activities and programs, contacts between the races could bring about some degree of "personal intimacy"; fears and myths could be dispelled through educational programs in schools and other formal and informal social gatherings. The social engineering Myrdal advocated to solve the so-called Negro Problem would entail a great deal of education to make clear the "irrationality" of certain other valuations of black and white Americans. During the 1930s and 1940s, there was a substantial increase in the number of books, articles, and statements on improving race relations through education. We also find the introduction of "intercultural education" into the curricula of schools and school systems throughout the country. These programs tried to improve intergroup understanding and to inform schoolchildren about the cultures of the various groups which made up American society.[59]

In Philadelphia, as in many other places, racial tensions and violence led to a variety of activities to improve black-white relations, most of which could be considered educational. The interracial committees and organizations that were formed during the period from 1930 to 1950 developed elaborate educational programs. The Philadelphia Fellowship Commission saw as one of its major functions the production of educational materials—press releases, pamphlets, and films—"to keep the public informed about the conditions as they actually are and what is being done about them."[60] It also sponsored a number of activities in the Philadelphia public schools: film-discussion programs for students, "Intercultural Leadership Seminars" for school administrators and provided literature for intercultural and interracial discussion groups.[61] The Early Childhood Project, begun on the initiative of the Fellowship Commission, was conducted by the Bureau of Intercultural Education, a private organization, in a public elementary school in the late 1940s. It involved children in kindergarten and in the first and second grades, and sought to determine the racial "attitude-formation process" of youngsters of that age. The results of the study were used in orientation programs for teachers and administrators in newly desegregated public schools in the city.[62]

The Pennsylvania State Temporary Commission on the Conditions of the Urban Colored Population and the City-Wide Interracial Committee not only made recommendations to other organizations about interracial cooperation, but also sponsored conferences, lectures, and public meetings in Philadelphia and throughout the state on race relations.[63] The YMCA and the YWCA, especially after 1945, educated young people in the city about some of the racial problems they would have to confront as adults.[64] As was mentioned earlier the school superintendent, Alexander J. Stoddard, formed a Committee of Thirty in April 1944 to look into the interracial conditions in the schools. In the fall of 1944, the superintendent sponsored a conference at which over five hundred educators discussed "Patterns of Prejudices and Tensions" and "Constructive Approaches to Intercultural Problems," as well as changes needed in the public school curricula to portray more accurately the history and cultures of minority groups in the United States.[65]

Individual public and parochial schools established intercultural programs and clubs. The Fellowship House developed the High School Fellowship Movement, which in 1947 was operating in over fifty schools, with over twenty-five hundred members. "Fellowship Clubs," formed in the public schools, worked to affect "the whole life of the school community: clubs, sports, assemblies, lunchroom practices, student government, student publications and other activities." Some students served on "conciliation teams," which attempted to settle interracial conflicts that arose in the schools.[66]

With all of this interracial activity in Philadelphia, one might ask, what did members of the black community have to say about the new emphasis on race relations, minority problems, and intercultural education? A perusal of the black press in the city during the period reveals enthusiasm: it appears that for the most part blacks in Philadelphia agreed with the contemporary belief that racial prejudice was the result of "ignorance and fear." Many blacks supported and joined the campaigns to improve race relations through greater interracial contacts and intercultural education. Considering the pattern of white violence and discrimination against blacks during the first quarter of the century, these calls for greater interracial cooperation and understanding were a welcome change.[67]

At the same time, however, blacks in Philadelphia were continually reminded that only some whites subscribed to the ideal of interracial cooperation and tolerance. Throughout the period of "interracial understanding," blacks were immersed in a struggle for adequate housing, equal access to employment and public accommodations, and better schools. Postwar Philadelphia witnessed a resurgence of the Ku Klux Klan in the city, as well as the formation of numerous interracial committees.[68] There was the enactment of a fair employment practices ordinance, as well as the laying off of thousands of black workers in Philadelphia industries, because blacks were still "the last hired and first fired."[69] In 1937 the dual eligibility lists for teacher appointments in the Philadelphia public schools were abolished, but by 1950 the vast majority of black students and teachers were in predominantly black or all-black public schools.[70] There is little doubt that there was a need to improve race relations in Philadelphia in the 1930s and 1940s and that this need was recognized, but there is little evidence that the campaigns to increase interracial understanding and tolerance had any significant impact upon the overall social conditions of the majority of black citizens. Thus, while some blacks involved themselves in interracial activities and programs, others continued to work to improve social and educational conditions within the black community.

Secondary Education, Vocational Training, and the Problems of Black Youth

In examining the major social and economic issues facing the Philadelphia black community between 1930 and 1950, the problems of black youth stand second only to the more general problem of unemployment. Black teenagers were the victims of the racism and prejudices of teachers and administrators in the public schools, the discriminatory hiring practices of employers, and social and racial conditions in the city at large. Black parents and citizens were well aware of the problems facing black youth, and the community mobilized on more than one occasion to ameliorate them and to attack juvenile delinquency and gang violence. But the effectiveness of these community education programs was limited by the inability of blacks to provide employment and wholesome recreational activities for their youth. The Philadelphia black community tried desperately to assist its young people in their movement into adulthood, but in many instances the community was simply in no position to solve the problems of black youth in the schools, on the job, and in the streets of the city.

Black youth and the public secondary schools

In the first three decades of the twentieth century, the enrollment of blacks in the public secondary schools of Philadelphia was extremely low. One of the major reasons was that after age sixteen school attendance was not compulsory; and even before that age many blacks had dropped out of the public schools and usually were not pursued by attendance officers.[1] In 1920, for example, it was estimated that of the 1,625 students enrolled in the public junior high schools, 52 (or 3.2 percent) were black. Out of a senior high school population of 20,390, there were 545 black pupils, or 2.7 percent. In 1930, of the 37,809 pupils enrolled in the junior high schools, 2,422, or 6.4 percent, were black;

167

and of the 34,929 students in the public senior high schools, 2,006, or 5.7 percent, were black. By 1940, the total enrollment in the junior high schools had reached 41,377, and black pupils numbered 8,625, or 20.8 percent; in the senior high schools there were 51,272 pupils, of whom 5,455, or 10.6 percent, were black. It should also be noted that blacks were 20.5 percent of the total public school population in 1940 but only 13.1 percent of the city population. Throughout the period from 1920 to 1940, the percentage of blacks enrolled in the public elementary schools exceeded the percentage of blacks in the total population, while the percentage of blacks in the secondary schools was always lower.[2] But by 1950 blacks were 18.3 percent of the total city population and approximately 27.8 percent of the public secondary school enrollment.[3]

In studies of blacks in the Philadelphia public schools, it was often pointed out that as the black enrollment increased, especially in the period after 1930, black students became more and more segregated. This situation obtained in both the elementary and secondary public schools.[4] The Pennsylvania State Temporary Commission on the Conditions of the Urban Colored Population, created by the state legislature to assess the problems of urban blacks reported that "in 1941, there were forty-five elementary schools in Philadelphia in which 40% or more of the pupils were Negroes. Included in these forty-five elementary schools were twelve all-Negro schools with Negro principals, teachers and students."[5]

The United States Commission on Civil Rights reported that by 1950 in Philadelphia 84.8 percent of the black public elementary school pupils were enrolled in majority-black schools, and 63.2 percent attended elementary schools that were 90 to 100 percent black.[6] In the public secondary schools, the Pennsylvania State Temporary Commission reported that in 1935 over 50 percent of the black senior high school students were enrolled in three schools, and in 1941 there were seven public junior high schools and two senior high schools having 40 percent or more black pupils.[7] A 1945 report on black secondary school enrollments revealed that this trend was producing a large number of majority-black public secondary schools in Philadelphia.[8]

Black students enrolled in the public senior high schools, especially before 1945, usually took the "academic" or college preparatory course of study. There were several reasons for this choice. Many of the black pupils in the public high schools were interested in going to college and eventually entering one of the professions.[9] The college preparatory course would guarantee the graduate sufficient credits for college admission. Moreover, studies of the employment opportunities for black high school graduates in Philadelphia revealed that there were few advantages to going on to high school other than preparation for college. A study of high school graduates and dropouts in Philadelphia conducted by the Board of Public Education reported that in the period from January 1937 to June 1938, black high school graduates were slightly better able to secure employment than black high school dropouts. However, whereas 23 out of every 100 white high school graduates were unemployed during that period, 42 out of every 100 black high school graduates were without jobs.[10] In a 1939 study of the industrial opportunities for black youth, the board reported that of the many reasons given for the nonemployment of blacks in Philadelphia industries, "the two foremost . . . were prejudice on the part of employers and the non-acceptance of Negroes as co-workers by white employees."[11]

In another, more extensive examination of the trends in black employment conducted by researchers from the Board of Public Education in 1942, questionnaires were received from 224 black high school graduates of 1940.

> Of 127 girls 114 had worked since graduation and 71 had jobs at the time of the inquiry. Of 97 boys 88 had worked since graduation and 53 were working when they answered the questionnaire. Most of those who [were employed] had odd jobs—domestic work or child care for girls and work as porters, errand boys and unskilled labor for the boys. A few were in college and as many as 25 had civil service jobs. . . .
>
> The Negro graduate felt a need of help in securing better occupational opportunities. They were often too timid to stand the risk of being insulted or turned away.[12]

According to the report, the major reasons given by employers for not hiring blacks were "never thought of it; traditional not to; fear of employee or customer reaction; personal prejudice plus a belief in racial superiority (they believed in special kinds of work for whites and for Negroes); union attitudes; [and] attitudes of employment agencies."[13] Therefore, it is not surprising that black high school graduates in Philadelphia before World War II fared less well than white graduates in the job market, and only slightly better than black high school dropouts.

To account for the low enrollments of blacks in public secondary schools in Philadelphia during the first four decades of this century, we have to examine not only the employment opportunities for black high school graduates, but also the "social psychological" conditions for black students in the public schools. Incidents of racial discrimination and violence in the public secondary schools were often reported in the black press of the city. For example, in February 1924, when black parents protested against the segregation of all of the black students into one class at Philadelphia High School for Girls, the principal responded that the grouping was based on the I.Q. test scores of the students. It was later revealed that black students with low, average, and high I.Q. scores had been placed in the same disputed class.[14]

Black students were often the victims of discrimination at school athletic programs as well as at social functions and on class trips. Occasionally, the discriminatory actions of individual secondary school teachers against black students were reported in the newspapers.[15] The Pennsylvania State Temporary Commission presented the results of interviews with over five hundred black secondary and college students on the topic of discrimination in the public high schools. The students stated that they could recall "numerous instances of prejudice," especially when public school events, such as swimming meets and basketball games, were held in places which excluded or restricted blacks.[16]

The commission also presented an analysis of the textbooks then in use in the public elementary and secondary schools throughout the state, and concluded that "it is unmistakable that taken as a whole, they [the textbooks] omit, or deride, or treat very unsatisfactorily the accomplishments of other racial and cultural groups. Whatever may be the difficulties of textbook writing, there is no justification for the injustices done Negroes by most of the textbooks now used in our schools."[17] The commission went on to point out that there were books and materials that could be used "that would provide teachers and students with a wide knowledge of the constructive side of the American Negro."[18]

Before 1940 black pupils left the public secondary schools of Philadelphia for a wide variety of reasons. Many were interested in securing full-time employment to support themselves or their families. Others found it difficult to adjust to high school for one reason or another, and decided to drop out. Limitations in the employment opportunities for black youth in Philadelphia, no matter how much schooling they might have had, also had the effect of discouraging blacks from remaining in high school. But beginning with several of the youth programs of the New Deal, and subsequently in the defense and vocational training programs of the pre–World War II era, an attempt was made by black and white educators and leaders to encourage black youth to enroll in the defense training courses offered throughout the city. Many black teenagers in Philadelphia, almost for the first time, began to see some concrete value in remaining in or returning to school.

Vocation and defense training for black youth in Philadelphia

Few black students in the public secondary schools were enrolled in industrial or vocational courses of study before the early 1940s. The

Armstrong Association of Philadelphia conducted a survey of the four vocational-technical public schools in the city in April 1940 and found that of the 7,490 students enrolled, only 667, or 9 percent, were black. At the same time, well over half of the black students attending the vocational schools were enrolled in dressmaking (272), home economics (98), and beauty culture (48).[19] Blacks interested in vocational courses in those fields, or in tailoring, auto mechanics, and commercial subjects, could also take them at one of two private black vocational institutes in the Philadelphia area, the Berean School and the Downingtown Industrial School.

The Berean School, founded by Rev. Matthew Anderson in 1899 and located in North Philadelphia, provided a number of business and vocational courses for blacks at relatively low cost.[20] After 1933, however, Berean began to specialize in business and commercial courses and required high school graduation for admission to day classes. By 1945 the Berean School had become Berean Business College, a two-year business school, and offered stenographic-secretarial training and business administration.[21] The Downingtown Industrial School, founded in 1904 by Rev. William Creditt, was located in Downingtown, Pennsylvania, twenty-five miles outside of Philadelphia.[22] The school offered secondary vocational courses but was primarily a boarding school, and did not offer evening classes, although many blacks from Philadelphia were enrolled at the school throughout its history.[23]

The need for black students in general to enroll in vocational training courses was highlighted in 1930 by the National Urban League's "Vocational Opportunity Campaign," which was aimed at young blacks in large cities and tried to persuade them "to prepare for future industrial employment" by taking vocational training courses. Urban League officials were particularly active in this area, since they believed that the main reason blacks could not secure jobs in manufacturing and skilled trades was that they did not possess advanced technical skills and training.[24] In Philadelphia "Vocational Opportunity Week," sponsored by the Armstrong Association, was observed at various times in the late 1930s and 1940s. The programs consisted of a wide variety of educational activities, aimed especially at black youth, to inform them of the need "To Prepare Today for Tomorrow's Jobs."[25] However, the Armstrong Association itself acknowledged the limited success of these campaigns in its reports on black enrollment in vocational courses, especially in the 1930s.[26]

With the New Deal came several new programs for the training of black youth. The Works Projects Administration (WPA) in Philadelphia sponsored adult education and vocational training programs that were administered by the Board of Public Education. Classes were offered in commercial and business areas, trades education and industrial subjects, as well as traditional academic courses.[27] The National Youth Administration (NYA) provided jobs and funds for black youth in the city, opened four "Negro Youth Centers," and sponsored the Negro Chorus, under the direction of W. Franklin Hoxter.[28]

In 1939 and 1940, with the national defense mobilization, many of the NYA and WPA agencies shifted from general vocational courses to defense training in their educational programs. In Philadelphia the Board of Public Education began to offer two types of defense training instruction: "(1) Supplementary instruction for workers employed in industries essential to national defense, or in closely allied industries. (2) Pre-employment training for persons selected from the registers of the public employment service who would look forward to employment in industries essential to national defense."[29] Defense courses were provided for teenagers employed by the NYA and adults from the WPA rolls. According to Charles Bauder, the director of the defense training program in the city, between July 1940 and September 1941 there were 42,716 students enrolled in the board's defense training courses.[30]

In October 1939 officials of New Deal and defense agencies in the city began to address the problems of black workers in the new defense industries. At the first meeting of the State Advisory Council on Negro Affairs for the state Department of Labor and Industry on 28 October 1939, black and white leaders, businessmen, and school officials agreed that "Negro boys and girls should be trained to fit into some scheme of things rather than just fields in which Negroes are known to settle."[31] Campaigns were launched in the Philadelphia black community in 1940 and 1941 to encourage high school dropouts to enroll in the defense training courses.[32] The Armstrong Association contacted firms and defense plants in the city "to make such firms conscious of Negro labor. As of April, 1941, roughly 65 firms have been contacted. Indirectly we have been in touch with many more."[33] Charles Shorter, then director of industrial research at the association, declared that "in the main our job in connection with the local defense program up to the present time has been in the form of an educational one."

> We have steered Negroes to places of training, we have educated employers on the facts concerning Negro employment conditions. We have been laying the groundwork in preparation for the future, stressing training for the unprepared and education for the uninformed, in order to make them conscious of our problems of unemployment. When these two objectives have been fully developed our entire program will then be devoted to the matter of job placement.[34]

By April 1941 the director of the Defense Training Program in Philadelphia was able to report that 9 percent of the enrollment in the
courses was black. This was close to the percentage of blacks in the total
city population.[35]

In order to gauge the occupational success of blacks who were enrolled in and graduated from the various defense training programs in
Philadelphia, several follow-up studies were conducted by the Pennsylvania State Temporary Commission on the Conditions of the Urban
Colored Population. In one survey, conducted in October 1941, ninety-
nine black enrollees in the Vocational Education for National Defense
(VEND) programs were questioned. The state commission found that
"48% of the persons surveyed had completed their respective courses,
42% did not; and 10% answered in such a manner as to make their
tabulation unsatisfactory. Of the 48% who had completed their respective courses not one of them was employed in a job for which the given
course had prepared them."[36] Many of the trainees who had dropped
out of the courses did so because they had secured employment; but
it was again pointed out that not one of the employed dropouts had a
job in an area for which he had been trained.[37]

The conclusions from a second, more comprehensive, survey of
black trainees in VEND programs were also significant. Of the 562 black
former enrollees in VEND programs contacted by the State Temporary
Commission in November 1941, 403, or 72 percent, were employed.
But 78 percent of the employed black ex-trainees were found to be
engaged in occupations other than those for which they were trained;
only 3 percent were working in defense industries. This seemed to indicate that "despite the national emergency Negroes are rarely employed
even after they have been trained for employment by agencies financed
by the Federal Government." And since 250, or 62 percent, of the 403
who were employed had not finished the defense training course, the
commission concluded that in Philadelphia "completion of [defense]
training is not any advantage to the Negro in securing employment."[38]

In June 1942 interviews were conducted with the staff of the United
States Employment Service, the Industrial Division of the Regional
Office of the War Production Board, the Armstrong Association, the
Industrial Department of the Chamber of Commerce, and several other
agencies in Philadelphia on the gains made by blacks in local defense
industries. The conclusions were generally the same: "that Negroes were
not becoming integrated into the local industries in proportion to their
available manpower."[39] Among the reasons given for this situation were
the reluctance of employers to change existing employment practices
for fear of "disrupting or retarding" production, the need for blacks to

gain membership in trade unions in several vital industries, and discrimination against blacks in civil service appointments.[40]

The peak of employment for black workers in general and black youth in particular in wartime Philadelphia came between July and October 1943. Between 1945 and 1950 unemployment again became a problem for large numbers of blacks in Philadelphia and throughout the country.[41] The increase in unemployment during the post–World War II era aggravated the already serious social problems facing black youth in Philadelphia.

Juvenile delinquency and the gang problem, 1930–50

The Great Depression drastically changed the employment situation for American youth. Before the 1930s, adolescents who had left school or needed part-time employment to support themselves or their families could generally find some kind of job. But the economic crisis of the thirties forced heads of households to take jobs that previously had gone to young people, and employers laid off many youngsters who already had jobs. It was estimated that in 1930, 27.5 percent of the potential workers in the fifteen to twenty-four-year-old age group were unemployed. By November 1937 unemployment in this group had risen to 35.9 percent. And as late as April 1940, after the beginning of the national defense mobilization, 22 percent of the potential workers in this age group were unemployed.[42]

The idleness caused by the Depression forced some American teenagers to remain in school in hopes of improving their chances of employment, while others were left to their own devices to try to fill their spare time and their pockets. Soon many Americans came to realize that in the midst of their economic crisis was the beginning of a "youth crisis." Thus, when President Franklin Roosevelt began to set into motion his agencies for dealing with the depressed economic conditions throughout the country, he also decided to launch "A New Deal for Youth."[43] On 31 March 1933 Roosevelt signed the bill for the creation of the Civilian Conservation Corps (CCC), a program designed to help relieve poverty and provide training for young men by employing them in conservation work on the nation's forests, parks, and public lands.[44] On 26 June 1935 the president issued an executive order setting up the National Youth Administration to give unemployed youth "their chance in school, their terms as apprentices, and their opportunity for jobs—a chance to work and earn for themselves."[45] These youth agencies, as well as several other New Deal programs, provided aid and employment and helped to solve some of the problems of unemployed youth during the depression decade.

Nationally, employment conditions during the 1930s were generally worse for black youth than for white youth. Whereas before the Depression many black teenagers could at least hope to gain the traditional "Negro jobs," the hard times of the thirties meant that blacks were pushed out of even these menial positions. In November 1937, for example, the federal government revealed that of the black youths aged fifteen to twenty-four officially in the labor force in 1937, approximately 35 percent were unemployed, compared to 29 percent of white youth.[46]

In the nine-year life of the CCC, the agency enrolled over two and one-half million persons, of whom almost two hundred thousand were black. Although it provided jobs and skills for many black youths who otherwise would have been unemployed, some researchers believe the corps did not live up to its potential for assisting young black victims of the Depression.[47] The National Youth Administration (NYA) in November 1938 employed about sixty-three thousand black youths on the Student Aid and Work Program. This represented approximately 11 percent of the youth then being aided.[48] In the 1939–40 school year, the NYA School Work Program employed 58,181 blacks (12.9 percent of the total number), and in 1943–44, 10,829 (18.2 percent).[49]

We can gain some indication of the magnitude of teenage unemployment in Philadelphia from the statistics compiled on the number of employment certificates issued to teenaged workers by the Junior Employment Service, a division of the Bureau of Compulsory Education of the Board of Public Education. In 1930, at the outset of the Depression, 18,736 employment certificates were issued to teenagers (fourteen to sixteen years old) who had found employment (an 11 percent drop since 1929), 181 of them to black teenagers.[50] In the 1930–31 school year, 10,783 certificates were issued, 137 to black students. However, 7,545 (70 percent) of the 1930–31 certificates were returned by the employers during the year because the students had been laid off.[51] In the 1932–33 school year, only 3,240 were issued. During the 1920s the largest number of the employment certificates was distributed in the 1926–27 school year, when 23,317 were given out to underaged students who had found employment.[52] These figures provide some indication of the shift in the employment conditions for teenagers in Philadelphia during the early years of the Depression.[53]

In the Philadelphia black community in the early 1930s, the severe unemployment among teenagers led to an increase in juvenile delinquency. The concern expressed in the black press over the rise in juvenile crime was reinforced by other studies conducted throughout the decade.[54] The report of the Pennsylvania State Temporary Commission presented and analyzed several studies and some important statistics on juvenile delinquency in the Philadelphia black community. Although these statistics must be used with extreme caution, the following statement by the judges of the Municipal Court of Philadelphia sheds a good deal of light on the extent of the problem.

> The total number of delinquent children in Philadelphia in 1920 was 4270; in 1930, 6280; in 1935, 4704; and in 1940, 3513. In the same years these figures included Negro delinquent children as follows: 1920, 676; 1930, 1446; 1935, 1742; 1940, 1513. In other words, Negroes constituted in 1920—16% of all juvenile delinquency cases; in 1930, 23%; in 1935, 37%; and in 1940, 43%. It will also be observed that, for instance, in 1940 when Negro children were 15.5% of the total school population, Negro juvenile delinquency was 43% of all juvenile delinquency cases, or in other words, the Negro delinquency rate was almost three times the average delinquency rate, and was four times the delinquency rate among white children alone. What is more, Negro children were involved in 51% of the more serious offenses.
>
> The ratio of delinquency has varied widely; for instance, in 1920, 43 Negro children of ages 7 to 15 were arrested out of every 1000 Negro children of these ages. This number increased to 48 in 1930, declined to 43 in 1932, reached the all time high of 50 in 1934, and has since declined again to 37 in 1940.[55]

The State Temporary Commission discussed several of the reasons for the high rate of juvenile delinquency among blacks in Philadelphia and throughout the state. The first reason given was that "racial discrimination in the administration of justice tends to promote law violation among Negroes." It was pointed out that "since officers of the law will arrest a Negro or a member of a minority group, for the same violations for which a native white person would not be arrested, the number of arrests is faulty as a measure of the volume of crime and delinquency."[56] The unfavorable socioeconomic conditions for blacks in Philadelphia— segregation, discrimination, and the depressed social environment— helped to account for the high rate of juvenile delinquency.[57] The commission concluded that "crime and delinquency rates, as they relate excessively to any social group, are but symptoms of general social maladjustment. In order to remedy the situation, emphasis must be placed upon those constructive factors already within each of the several municipalities. Full social justice in citizenship, suitable employment, proper recreational facilities, better housing and related improvements will result in the eradication of excessive rates of Negro crime and delinquency. . . . Otherwise, there can be no significant improvement in the high incidence of crime and delinquency among Negroes."[58] As we shall see, in the 1930s and 1940s campaigns sponsored by black social and community agencies would help to stem somewhat the growth of juvenile delinquency in the black community.

Another important problem for black youth in Philadelphia during this period was the existence of juvenile gangs. The earliest of these groups seem to have been formed to carry out criminal activities, such as burglaries.[59] Later, groups of young people living in a section or area of the city would band together to protect themselves and their neighborhood from other groups or individuals interested in "invading their territory." In West Philadelphia during the 1930s and 1940s the most notorious gangs were the Tops and the Bottoms, the names suggesting the parts of West Philadelphia that they inhabited and "protected."[60] The lack of adequate employment and recreational facilities tended to aggravate the gang problem among black teenagers, and in the 1940s juvenile gang activity increased in many black neighborhoods.[61]

Various federal, state, and community agencies and organizations began to sponsor educational and recreational activities for black teenagers in the 1930s. The National Youth Administration, which came to Pennsylvania in December 1935, opened a Regional Office for Negro Affairs in Philadelphia. Rufus Watson, a former juvenile court lawyer, was appointed the director of the office. Watson saw as one of the major goals of the NYA programs "the provision of wholesome activities to keep Negro youth away from the pernicious influence of their environment."[62]

The NYA program for black youth centered on the activities provided at four black community centers and several recreational playfields opened in the city beginning in March 1936. The St. Simon's Youth Center, located in the parish house of St. Simon's Episcopal Church in South Philadelphia, employed over forty black youths and provided a large number of activities, including plays, carnivals, musicals, athletic teams, and various clubs. The Northwest Center, on Twenty-second Street in North Philadelphia, was developed with the cooperation of John Brodhead, principal of the Arnold Public School, and several parents in the neighborhood; black social clubs donated recreational equipment. Attendance at the center averaged over 1,600 persons per week in 1936. The Mt. Pisgah Youth Center in West Philadelphia was opened in February 1936. In addition to its recreational and athletic facilities, the Mt. Pisgah Center had a small printing press and supplied programs, membership cards, tickets, and other printed materials to all of the centers. St. Ignatius Youth Center, also located in West Philadelphia, provided educational and recreational activities for an average of 175 persons daily in 1936. The (NYA) Negro Chorus was organized at the St. Ignatius Center but later moved to the Dunbar

School in North Philadelphia for its regular meetings. Through the "Colored Playfield Project," the NYA provided recreational areas throughout the city for black youth and employed many teenagers in the renovation of vacant lots and other properties for use as playfields. The Philadelphia Board of Public Education provided equipment for many of the playgrounds opened by the NYA.[63]

In 1936 the Pennsylvania State Negro Council sponsored a series of reports, lectures, and panels on juvenile delinquency "to develop the spirit and power of understanding and solidarity among Negroes in Pennsylvania by encouraging intelligent discussion of the problems confronting Negroes."[64] These public meetings and conferences on juvenile delinquency were an important part of the council's community education program during the 1930s. At the council meeting held at Cheyney State Teachers College on 6 June 1936, officials of the National Urban League and the Armstrong Association discussed the rise in juvenile delinquency among blacks in Philadelphia.[65] Subsequently, members of the council prepared a report on the topic and sponsored programs for parents, teachers, and students in several predominantly black public schools in Philadelphia on the ways of improving the social conditions for black youth.[66]

The predominantly black public schools initiated a number of drives to end juvenile delinquency among blacks. The Reynolds Public School, Vaux and Sulzberger junior high schools, and later the Simon Gratz High School sponsored forums and debates to inform their black student bodies of the possible harm that delinquent activities would bring to themselves and to others.[67] The Board of Education supported the individual schools and parent-teacher associations in these activities and allowed many schools to open their playing yards after school hours and during the summer for use by children in the neighborhoods.[68]

The community centers in predominantly black neighborhoods of Philadelphia continued to serve an important educational and recreational function for black youth, even after the demise of NYA and WPA programs. The Wharton Settlement House and the McDowell Community Center in North Philadelphia, St. John's Settlement in South Philadelphia, the Mantua Community Center in West Philadelphia, and the branches of the YMCA and YWCA throughout the city provided a wide variety of afterschool activities for black youth to fill spare time that could have been occupied with delinquent activities.[69]

Campaigns for the prevention and control of juvenile delinquency often became community-wide efforts involving not only persons and groups that worked directly with youth, but also some individuals who felt they could contribute to the solution of this intractable social problem. Philadelphia chapters of the Elks, the local branches of the NAACP and National Negro Congress, and several other black social organizations sponsored programs for black teenagers, and established youth sections within their own groups to campaign against juvenile delinquency.[70] The Youth Council of the Philadelphia NAACP, organized in May 1935, was involved in many other activities as well, including the sponsoring of community lectures on the problem of lynching and the need to abolish poll taxes for voting.[71] The council also launched several protest campaigns against employment discrimination in defense industries and organized programs to improve interracial tolerance among youth in the city.[72]

The various civic leagues in North, West, and South Philadelphia also had active youth sections. As was mentioned earlier, the North Philadelphia Civic League served as the parent organization for the very successful North Philadelphia Youth Movement, formed in January 1937 under the leadership of Sam Evans. The jobs campaign, however, was only one of the more important activities of the Youth Movement.[73] In the late 1930s and early 1940s, juvenile crime and gang warfare were rampant in the predominantly black section of North Philadelphia east of Broad Street. Sam Evans suggested that the teenagers in the neighborhood should be given greater responsibility for policing the area, and

Samuel Evans, president of the North Philadelphia Youth Movement and originator of Youth City, 1939–40. (Courtesy of the Philadelphia Tribune)

came up with idea for "Youth City."[74] Patterned after Father Flanagan's Boys Town, Youth City was to be run by the black teenagers elected to the offices of mayor, district attorney, and city councilman. Following the election in May 1940, the young officials of Youth City not only declared war on juvenile delinquency within their municipality, but also worked to improve the health, safety, and recreational facilities available to the residents.[75] Many local, state, and national leaders, both black and white, lent their spiritual and financial support to the project.[76] Among the individuals receiving awards from Youth City officials for their work on behalf of black youth were Mary McLeod Bethune, Col. Benjamin O. Davis, and Mrs. Eleanor Roosevelt.[77]

In March 1942 Youth City began to experience financial difficulties, but through "Youth City Sunday" and other fund-raising campaigns it was able to continue operating through 1944.[78] During its years of greatest activity, Youth City served as a model for other sections of the city and demonstrated that there were ways of dealing positively and creatively with the problem of juvenile delinquency.[79]

Throughout the 1930s and 1940s there were numerous conferences, meetings, lectures, and other activities dealing with the problems of black youth and juvenile delinquency.[80] There is reason to believe that the decline in black juvenile delinquency during the late 1940s was at least partly the result of these campaigns and activities. The annual report of the Municipal Court of Philadelphia for 1950 reported a definite decrease in the total number of cases disposed of, from a peak of 9,238 in 1945 to 6,193 in 1950.[81] According to the records of the court, the total number of children under sixteen who appeared before the judges decreased 29 percent between 1930 and 1950. During the same period, the number of white children in the city seven to fifteen years old decreased 29 percent, while the number of black children in this age group increased 78 percent. Philadelphia was, in effect, losing an average of approximately 3,800 white children each year of the twenty-one year period, and was annually gaining approximately 1,100 black children. In 1930, 10 percent of the children of juvenile court age in Philadelphia were black; in 1940, 16 percent; and in 1950, 21 percent.[82]

The "Negro delinquency ratio" in 1950 was 41 delinquents per 1,000 black children in the city, four times the ratio for white children. However, the ratio in 1930 was 48 per 1,000 black children, and in 1934 it had reached 50. For black males aged seven to fifteen years, the delinquency ratio fluctuated between 1940 and 1950: in 1940 it was 57 per 1,000; in 1944 it was up to 76; but in 1950 it was down to 52. The ratio of black female delinquents per 1,000 black girls aged seven to fifteen rose from 7 in 1940 to 12 in 1950.[83] Although these figures provide only an indication of the amount of juvenile delinquency in Philadelphia during the period from 1940 to 1950, there seems to be little doubt that there was a decrease in the number of juvenile court cases involving blacks during a decade of great increase in the number of black children in the city.

In viewing the social, economic, and educational situation for black youth in Philadelphia from 1930 to 1950, especially in comparison with white youth, it is apparent that blacks were operating under many disadvantages. Until 1940 blacks were underrepresented in the secondary school population. Though the college enrollment figures for black high school graduates were low, blacks who did attend high school overwhelmingly were enrolled in the college preparatory course of study. Even during the national defense mobilization, there was no substantial increase in the percentage of blacks enrolled in vocational courses. Studies of the employment status of Philadelphia public high school graduates revealed that black high school graduates were much more likely to be unemployed in the late 1930s than their white classmates. Blacks who completed defense training courses were no more likely to be employed in the defense industries than blacks who had dropped out of these courses. These conditions may help to account for the low enrollment of blacks in public vocational schools and courses. Studies of employment opportunities for black workers in Philadelphia pointed out that the major reasons given for the nonemployment of blacks in local industries were not that the employers felt blacks were lazy or unqualified, but the personal prejudices of the employers and the official discrimination of the labor unions.

The general social conditions for blacks in Philadelphia in the 1930s and 1940s spawned many of the problems facing black youth. Lack of recreational facilities and employment helped to create a situation where teenage gangs and juvenile delinquency could flourish. To prevent and control juvenile delinquency, many social agencies and organizations working in the black community sponsored educational and recreational programs for black youth and encouraged them to stay in school. Gang violence continued, however, and the rate of juvenile delinquency among blacks remained relatively high. Social conditions for black youth in Philadelphia during the thirties and forties were dismal. To a very great extent, the general social and economic conditions in Philadelphia determined the educational and industrial opportunities that were to be made available to black youth. And in the period from 1930 to 1950, these opportunities were generally very limited.

Change
and Continuity
in
Black Philadelphia

On the basis of the experience of Africans in the United States to the end of the nineteenth century, W. E. B. Du Bois in his now-classic discourse on *The Souls of Black Folk* concluded that black Americans were afflicted with a kind of "double-consciousness." "It is a peculiar sensation, the double-consciousness, this sense of always looking at one's self through the eyes of others, of measuring one's soul by the tape of a world that looks on in amused contempt and pity. One ever feels his two-ness—an American, a Negro; two souls, two thoughts, two unreconciled strivings; two warring ideals in one dark body, whose dogged strength alone keeps it from being torn asunder." Double-consciousness was seen as one of the burdens borne by blacks in a country controlled and dominated by hostile whites. Tension and conflict were inherent in this condition because of the clash of values at a fundamental level of self-awareness and identity. At the same time, most black Americans were well aware that there were deficiencies on both sides: that there were disadvantages associated with any attempt to become "truly American," and that it was unlikely that blacks in the United States could ever be "truly African." Du Bois was aware of the dilemma and posited a third objective for the African-American, suggesting that the two sides of his nature be merged "into a better and truer self."

> In this merging he wishes neither of the older selves to be lost. He would not Africanize America, for America has too much to teach the world and Africa. He would not bleach his Negro soul in a flood of white Americanism, for he knows that Negro blood has a message for the world. He simply wishes to make it possible for a man to be both a Negro and an American, without being cursed and spit upon by his fellows, without having the doors of opportunity closed roughly in his face.[1]

The continued attempts of the African in the United States to become "a co-worker in the kingdom of culture" would not only require a vast improvement in the social, political, and economic conditions for blacks in this country, but also a fundamental change in American society. Unless the Afro-American was provided the opportunity to "use his best powers and latent genius," both cultures would be deprived of potential strengths and resources. Afro-Americans were profoundly aware of their need to advance themselves in American society, and Afro-American history and literature of the late nineteenth and early twentieth centuries are replete with statements and activities aimed at "Negro improvement."[2] Du Bois, for example, in his recommendations to the Philadelphia Negro in 1898, pointed out that "simply because the ancestors of the present white inhabitants of America went out of the way barbarously to mistreat and enslave the ancestors of the present black inhabitants gives those blacks no right to ask that the civilization and morality of the land be seriously menaced for their benefit."

> Men have a right to demand that the members of a civilized community be civilized; that the fabric of human culture, so laboriously woven, be not wantonly or ignorantly destroyed. Consequently a nation may rightly demand of a people it has consciously and intentionally wronged, not indeed complete civilization in thirty or one hundred years, but at least every effort and sacrifice possible on their part toward making themselves fit members of the community within a reasonable length of time; that thus they may become a source of strength and help instead of a national burden.

Du Bois recommended that the Philadelphia Negro "bend his energy to the solving of his own social problems. . . . For the accomplishment of this the Negro has the right to demand freedom for self development, and no more aid from without than is really helpful for furthering that development."

> Such aid must of necessity be considerable: it must furnish schools and reformatories, and relief and preventive agencies; but the bulk of the work of raising the Negro must be done by the Negro himself, and the greatest help for him will be not to hinder and curtail and discourage his efforts. Against prejudice, injustice and wrong the Negro ought to protest energetically and continuously, but he must never forget that he protests because those things hinder his own efforts, and those efforts are the key to his future.[3]

Thus, according to Du Bois, though mutual obligations had to be met, Afro-Americans in Philadelphia had primary responsibility for their social advancement.

In surveying the overall social conditions for black Philadelphians during the first half of the twentieth century, we find that while some conditions improved as a result of black and white efforts, other conditions remained the same or even worsened due to the failure of the dominant white majority to meet its obligations and afford most black citizens the opportunity to earn a decent living. At the same time, since black public and community education reflected the social and political conditions for the black minority, there were some changes and many continuities in the education of black Philadelphia between 1900 and 1950.

The black population increased sixfold during the first half of the twentieth century: from 62,613 in 1900 to 378,968 in 1950. From the densely settled back alleys and narrow streets of South Philadelphia's seventh ward, blacks moved into almost every section of the city, establishing small and large enclaves, usually surrounded by larger white communities. But by 1950 there was an extremely high concentration of blacks in North Central, South, and West Philadelphia, and we find the beginnings of a number of "black belts" in these sections. The 50 percent increase in the black population following the wartime expansion of employment opportunities was almost completely absorbed by these three areas (see Map 3).[4]

In the early 1900s blacks generally lived in the most dilapidated, unsanitary, overcrowded housing in the city. As the number of blacks increased, those who could afford to moved out of the tenements and slums into middle-income, predominantly white neighborhoods in North and West Philadelphia. This movement was highly visible, and therefore an object of scrutiny for housing officials and an object of alarm for many white residents. For officials of the Philadelphia Housing Association, the Armstrong Association, and other organizations interested in black housing, this trend signaled a break in the exclusionary practices of realtors in several sections of the city. At the same time, the masses of lower-income blacks remained in inadequate, and sometimes dangerous, quarters well into the 1940s. The opening of the James Weldon Johnson, Glenwood, and Richard Allen housing projects in the early 1940s brought some relief, and the proportion of the black population living in substandard housing dropped from 45 percent in 1940 to 35 percent in 1950. Unfortunately, because of the 50 percent increase in the size of the black population during that decade, the number of blacks in substandard housing was greater in 1950 than in 1940. There was little basic change in the housing conditions for the masses of black Philadelphians during the first fifty years of this century.[5]

There were, however, significant changes in the occupational dis-

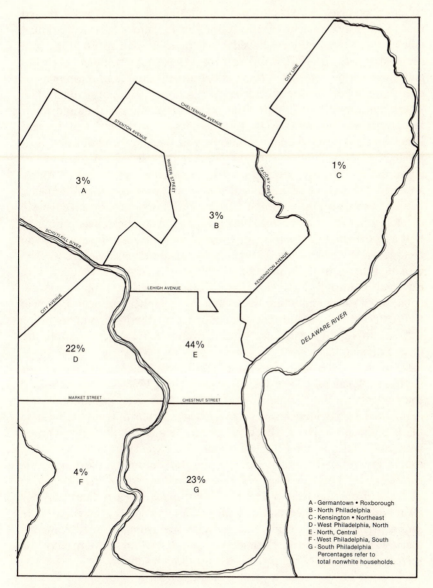

CHELTENHAM AVENUE

CITY LINE

STENTON AVENUE

WISTER STREET

TACONY CREEK

SCHUYLKILL RIVER

KENSINGTON AVENUE

CITY AVENUE

LEHIGH AVENUE

DELAWARE RIVER

MARKET STREET

CHESTNUT STREET

3%
A

1%
C

3%
B

22%
D

44%
E

4%
F

23%
G

A - Germantown • Roxborough
B - North Philadelphia
C - Kensington • Northeast
D - West Philadelphia, North
E - North, Central
F - West Philadelphia, South
G - South Philadelphia
  Percentages refer to
  total nonwhite households.

Map 3. Distribution of nonwhite households in Philadelphia by major sections, 1950.

tribution of black workers from 1900 to 1950. Du Bois had reported that in 1898 most black males employed in Philadelphia were unskilled laborers, and that most employed black females were in domestic and personal service. In 1953 the Armstrong Association compiled statistics and information on the occupational distribution and employment conditions for blacks in Philadelphia, based on 1950 census data. The association found that despite "the expansion of industrial employment for Negro workers in the last two decades, Negroes are still by and large to be found in the largest numbers in the most onerous and least productive jobs." The researchers pointed out that 75 percent of all white male workers were employed in skilled or semiskilled positions, and only 36 percent of black males were so employed. Black females, however, were no longer confined to domestic service; 43.9 percent were employed in skilled and semiskilled positions. The researchers estimated that approximately 28 percent of these black females were employed in factories. But whereas only 11.9 percent of white female workers were in unskilled areas, over 56 percent of the employed black females were classified as unskilled workers.[6] The disparity in the occupational distribution of black and white workers in Philadelphia had decreased over the half century, but the persistence of racial discrimination in hiring was an important continuity in the overall employment picture for black Philadelphians.

Politically, we again find some significant changes and continuities for black Philadelphia over the fifty years. Until 1936 blacks maintained their allegiance to the party of Lincoln. The city government was dominated by Republicans, but party bosses often did not respond to black political demands. Black politicians tended to be rather conservative and did not press black interests; most were satisfied with a few minor appointments and patronage jobs for delivering the black vote each election. The New Deal era, however, witnessed the mass defection of blacks from the Republican to the Democratic Party, and between 1936 and 1951 the two parties had to compete for the black vote. In presidential elections during this period, votes from the predominantly black wards went to the Democratic candidates, but in state and municipal elections Republicans still received much support.[7]

The 1930s witnessed a great increase in the number of blacks from Philadelphia elected to political office. In 1928 there were only two blacks, both Republicans, in the state house of representatives; by 1939 there were five black representatives, four of them Democrats. The split in the black vote during the 1930s again manifested itself in the 1940s in the elections for the state house of representatives. For example, in 1946 five black Republicans were elected to the General Assembly from

Philadelphia in the wake of the Republican landslide throughout the state and nation, but in 1950 two black Republicans and four black Democrats were elected.[8] The late 1940s were a period of decline for the Republican Party in Philadelphia, and black Democrats won in 1950 in the predominantly black areas as the Democratic reform movement began its sweep of the city. This signaled the end of the split in the black vote, which remained almost completely Democratic for the next two decades.

Despite the change in party affiliation in the 1930s, political powerlessness was a continuous and persistent condition for black Philadelphia throughout the first half of the twentieth century. The Republican Party dominated political activity in Philadelphia before 1930, and blacks, who usually voted Republican, were considered one of the cornerstones of machine power. Black political demands, such as an equal rights law or public school desegregation, did not have to be met if a more powerful constituency objected. Black and immigrant voters had nowhere else to turn for redress of political grievances. Black politicians were chosen by the party, and offered to black voters as the only acceptable candidates. Those black politicians who exercised some degree of independence and moved to implement black demands soon fell out of favor with party leaders and often were no longer supported by the machine, as was the case with John C. Asbury and Andrew Stevens in 1924. Black politicians, as well as the black vote, were in the hip pocket of the Republican bosses.

The re-emergence of the Democratic Party during the 1930s and the activities of John Kelly, Francis Biddle, and other Democratic leaders to gain black support meant that the two major political parties would not merely refrain from alienating black voters, but would begin to move on black political demands. Appointment of blacks by *both* parties to high positions within the state and local government, the passage of an equal rights law, and the creation of the black National Guard units were the more significant political victories of black Philadelphia during the 1930s. Gradually, as more and more accusations of political corruption and bossism were hurled at the Republican city government, and Democratic candidates became more viable alternatives, blacks, like many other Philadelphians, began to shift their votes to the Democratic columns. Blacks supported Democratic candidates to a greater extent than whites in the presidential elections of 1940, 1944, 1948, and 1952 but in local elections for mayor, governor, and the Pennsylvania General Assembly during that same period, blacks continued to vote for Republican candidates. In the 1943 mayoral election, for example, Republican Bernard Samuel received 55.4 percent of the votes in the largely black wards, and in 1947 Samuel was re-elected, receiving 63.0 percent of the votes from these areas.[9] In the Republican sweep of 1946, five black Republicans defeated the black and white Democrats who ran for the Pennsylvania General Assembly from the black wards. In 1949, however, following revelations of "well-organized systems of extortion . . . in the Fire Marshal's Office, the Department of Public Works, the Water Bureau, and the Department of Supplies and Purchases," 50.1 percent of the votes from predominantly black wards went to the Main Line reformer Joseph Clark in his successful campaign for the office of city controller. In the 1951 special election to approve a new city charter, blacks, as well as most other Philadelphians, cast their votes in favor of the reform measure.[10] With the mayoral election later that year, the black vote was fastened securely to the emerging Democratic organization. Following the expansion and consolidation of the Democratic political organization in the 1950s and 1960s, the black vote was considered to be in the hip pocket of the new Democratic machine politicians. Most importantly, black Philadelphians again lacked sufficient political power to get public officials to support black political demands such as the further desegregation of the public school system.[11]

In examining the politics of black public schooling in Philadelphia between 1900 and 1950, we find again that the most significant changes took place during the thirties. The appointment of a representative of the black minority to the school board, the merging of the dual eligibility lists for appointments to the public elementary schools, and the decision to allow blacks to compete for positions in the public secondary schools were the most important political changes during the first half of this century. However, with regard to the most significant political issue involving the public schools—the official and unofficial segregation of black teachers and students—the overall political powerlessness of the black community allowed public school officials to respond to increasing black enrollments with further segregation.

With the help of the wartime migration of thousands of southern blacks to Philadelphia and the exit of thousands of white families to the suburbs, blacks went from 20.4 percent of the total enrollment in the public school system in 1940 to 30.2 percent in 1950 (see table 6 above). Throughout the 1940s the Educational Equality League, under the leadership of Floyd L. Logan, continued its role as the major supporter of minority rights in the public schools of the Philadelphia area.[12] Following the official desegregation of the faculties of public secondary schools in 1937, black educators began to take examinations for positions in the junior and senior high schools. A suitable score on the National Teachers

Examination (NTE) and successful performance at an oral interview with four or five principals and department heads in the areas of specialization often resulted in appointment, although during some years, as was the case in the late 1930s, there were long lists of qualified candidates for very few positions. No blacks received appointments as regular teachers in the public secondary schools between 1937 and 1942.[13] Some blacks did not receive high scores on the written examinations, but more often than not it appeared that the black applicant had done poorly at the oral interview: for some reason black candidates for secondary school positions were unable to convince the orals committee that they were sufficiently qualified and articulate to teach in public secondary schools.

Black teachers began registering complaints with Floyd Logan and the Educational Equality League, and in the case of Ruth Wright Hayre, the league decided to intervene. Mrs. Hayre was allowed to appear before a second orals committee after both the league and Superintendent Alexander Stoddard agreed that the first group of examiners had treated her unfairly. A black principal was added to the second committee, and Mrs. Hayre passed the exam with a very high rating. In September 1942 she received an appointment at Sulzberger Junior High School as an instructor of English. Once minority administrators began to participate on the orals committees and the Educational Equality League began to act as a watchdog for the educational interests of the black community, other blacks managed to get appointments as principals and teachers in the junior high schools of the city.[14] But it was not until February 1946 that the first black educator was appointed to a senior high school. Mrs. Hayre had reached the top of the eligibility list in the field of English and was appointed first a teacher, and later principal, at William Penn High School. The ice was broken, and several other blacks gained positions in the senior high schools.[15]

These appointments were very well received in the black community of Philadelphia. There was a general belief that the public school system was beginning to provide opportunities for blacks to teach in the senior high schools because the school administrators were trying to meet the needs and interests of the black community. This may have been the case. However, from the perspective of the Educational Equality League and other informed black citizens and educators, the school officials had merely succumbed to reality—many of these junior and senior high schools were predominantly black, and many of the white teachers wanted transfers to other schools. Dr. Daniel Brooks, former principal of Reynolds Public School, regularly during the decade published school statistics and noted the increasing segregation in the public junior and senior high schools; and in 1948 and 1949–50 the Educational Equality League conducted surveys of the conditions for blacks in the public schools in general.[16]

The league found that between 1932 and 1948 the number of black "teachers, counselors, and secretaries" had increased from 285 in 1932 to 497 in the 1947–48 school year. It also reported that approximately 159 black teachers were in schools that had previously had all-white faculties, and that there were 53 black teachers and counselors in public secondary schools. In the 1949–50 school year, the league found that of the 186 public elementary schools in the city, 10 were all-black, and 30 were at least 75 percent black but had predominantly white faculties. There were also 140 public elementary schools without a single black faculty member. Only 6 of the more than 75 black secondary school teachers

William Penn High School for Girls in North Philadelphia. (Source: PBPE)

were in schools where the enrollment was still predominantly white. The league suggested some reasons for the increasing "racial isolation" in the public schools:

> Some elementary schools have become predominantly Negro because white children in the area are allowed to have bus transportation to schools outside the area in which they live.
>
> Other schools, notably Sulzberger Junior High, have become 99% colored because of the skillful zoning maneuvers. The zoning line is so arranged that the white section of the area sends its children to Beeber [School].

The league cited several instances where school officials had divided or zoned the administrative districts so that some schools would remain predominantly white while others remained predominantly black.

As the number of black pupils enrolled in the public schools increased during the 1940s, school officials' support for lessening the degree of racial segregation decreased. Some form of designation by race was used to insure that black teachers did not end up teaching where they were not wanted. The Educational Equality League reported that during the 1948–49 school year, "one Negro teacher was refused a transfer to a school with an approximate 50% Negro enrollment, in a section of the city previously predominantly white on the basis of 'The time is not yet ripe.' . . . Another Negro teacher was advised not to accept a transfer to a predominantly white senior high on the grounds that he might meet prejudiced treatment and 'low rating' by the administration."[17] After several complaints that black students had been prevented from attending public schools where the enrollment was predominantly white, the Educational Equality League and black parents and citizens held several meetings with school officials, but there was no evidence of a change in policy or practice. Then, in May 1950, Walter Biddle Saul, president of the school board, told a committee of black and white citizens that the public school system was not discriminating against black teachers, but that school officials often took into account "community feelings" in making appointments of black teachers to white schools. President Saul also made it clear that any further efforts to desegregate the school system would go forward "carefully and slowly."[18]

The politics of black public education in Philadelphia over the first half of the century were dominated by the issue of official and unofficial racial segregation in the public school system. Segregation was a persistent problem, not merely because blacks were often deprived of access to public resources to which they were entitled as citizens, but also because it limited black Philadelphians' ability to help themselves. The absence of black teachers in the junior and senior high schools very likely contributed to the high dropout rates among blacks before 1940. The exclusion of black teachers from appointments to the public secondary schools was opposed by virtually every segment of the black community, but not all segments agreed with some black teachers that separate black public schools should be promoted by the school board. Thus, another reason for the intractability of the segregation issue was that some elements within the black community benefited from the practice. And the political powerlessness of the black community inhibited its leaders' ability to lessen the negative impact of segregation on the quality of public education received by black children. Segregation was problematic, but desegregation, far from resolving the issues, actually brought with it a new set of problems.

The experience of black teachers in the public secondary schools illustrates this point. Under official segregation, black teachers were barred from employment in the public junior high schools, which consisted of grades seven, eight, and nine, but they taught grades seven and eight in the separate black grammar schools. Following the official desegregation of the public secondary schools, black educators were teaching black students in grades seven, eight, and nine, but in an environment where their white colleagues openly questioned the mental capabilities of black pupils. Black teachers witnessed the interactions between some white teachers and administrators and black students, and most were not in a position to intercede. In the separate public school, the incompetent teacher or insensitive educator was dealt with by the black principal and staff. It was only the rare educator who openly protested against the bigotry, insensitivity, and incompetence to which black children were subjected in many newly desegregated classrooms. Segregation had its drawbacks, but desegregation was "no crystal stair."[19]

When we turn to the community education of black Philadelphia, we also find that segregation was an important continuity throughout the first half of the century, but that an increase in interracial educational activities took place after 1930. More importantly, however, throughout the fifty-year period under examination, black social advancement remained the overriding concern and underlying theme of the vast majority of community education programs, whether segregated or desegregated. Before 1930 the major thrusts of organized community-wide educational activities were the Afro-American heritage and racial pride, individual and community development, and black political and social advancement. During the 1930s and 1940s, black Philadelphia continued to observe Negro History Week; the Christian Street YMCA, the Southwest and Belmont YWCAs, and the black churches continued to bring speakers to the city to lecture on Afro-American history; and the black newspapers continued to publish weekly columns, features, and editorials that dealt with the history of the black experience.[20]

Whereas the impact of the migration of southern blacks was a major issue at community education forums and conferences during World War I and the twenties, the Great Depression slowed the southern influx, and unemployment and juvenile delinquency came to dominate these gatherings. Throughout the first half of the century, however, the problems facing black students and teachers in the Philadelphia public school system were regular topics of discussion at community meetings. The problematic relationship between the school administration and the black community was another important continuity in the public education of black Philadelphia. Public school officials wrote about "the problem of the colored child." Increasing black enrollments led to the policy of creating more separate black public schools. The problem of large numbers of overaged blacks students who achieved low scores on the newly introduced "intelligence tests" led to the policy of providing special industrial curricula in black and predominantly black elementary and junior high schools. The problem of the black teacher instructing the white child led to the practice of segregating black teachers. The problem of black pupils in mixed neighborhoods attending predominantly white schools led to the practice of gerrymandering school district lines to minimize racial integration.

Most black Philadelphians believed that one or more of these practices was detrimental to the education of black children and was contrary to the community's basic objective of social advancement. These discriminatory policies and practices were thus viewed as problems for the black community and were vigorously protested. The ability of black leaders to bring about a favorable change in the conditions in the public schools rested on the amount of political power wielded by the black community: the problems in the public schools did not exist in a vacuum, but were part of the larger political environment for the black minority. Therefore, the greatest change in the public school situation came about during the 1930s, when both the Democratic and Republican parties were actively courting the black vote. The existence of an organization such as the Educational Equality League to press for changes and serve as the guardian of the interests of blacks in the public school system also promoted educational advancements.

After 1940 there was a great increase in interracial educational activities throughout the Philadelphia area. Black Philadelphians were pleased with the moves toward greater interracial tolerance and understanding and the attempts to call attention to the particular problems facing the black minority, and participation in these intercultural programs definitely helped to advance the social, political, and economic interests of the black community. The increase in these programs coincided with a decline in programs for raising race consciousness and increasing race pride. Indeed, many black organizations went through identity crises during the late 1940s and early 1950s, believing that the demand for the abolition of social proscriptions on the basis of race, creed, color, or ancestry also required the abandonment of these distinctions in mobilizing for black social advancement. They agreed that no group or individual should be barred from participation in the campaign for public school desegregation, the enfranchisement of the black South, or the end of lynch law because of race, creed, or color, but did this mean that there should be no all-black advancement organizations? In Philadelphia, after black teachers had begun to teach white students in the public schools, the ostensible objectives of the Pennsylvania Association of Teachers of Colored Children appeared somehow limited, too narrow. The organization went out of existence in the late 1940s, and many black educators became involved in the emerging Philadelphia Federation of Teachers, which was actively seeking their support.[21] Many black educators shared the concerns of the teachers' organization for improvements in educational conditions for black and white children and in the working conditions for all teachers. These black educators had come to believe that black social advancement could be achieved through participation in larger, interracial organizations.

Community education in black Philadelphia changed somewhat as a result of the new interest in interracial cooperation and understanding, but the change was in keeping with the overall objective of black social advancement. This "ethos of advancement," which manifested itself in most of the social and educational strivings of the black community, goes a long way toward explaining community activities and educational configurations. It helps to explain why some members of the community supported "voluntary segregation" for self-development, assistance, and protection, while others advocated an end to official Jim Crow and discrimination as a prelude to greater racial integration in American institutions and society at large. Voluntary segregation and racial integration were considered by their advocates strategies for the advancement of the social, political, and economic conditions of Afro-Americans. This makes it fairly clear why one position, as opposed to other possible alternatives, appeared to have more support in the black community at a given time. For example, in the 1920s, neither the black nor the white community of Philadelphia was overly responsive to pleas for greater "interracial understanding and cooperation," and blacks received little white support in their campaigns to desegregate the public school system. In the 1940s, however, greater interracial cooperation was needed for the war effort, and black and white Philadelphians worked together to expose racially discriminatory practices in employment, housing, schooling, and other important areas.

The vision of life or *paideia* of Afro-Americans, which probably had at its core this "ethos of advancement," was shared by only a few members of the dominant white society in Philadelphia. Although the Irish Jewish, Polish, and Italian communities may also have possessed their own "ethos of advancement," which served as the underlying belief or value for community educational activities, black social advancement, or even racial justice, was not a value cherished by the white majority or the cultural and religious minorities. As Du Bois had noted at the turn of the century, the black American did not wish to "bleach his Negro soul in a flood of white Americanism, for he knows that Negro blood has a message to the world. He simply wishes to make it possible for a man to be both a Negro and an American . . . without having the doors of opportunity closed roughly in his face." Throughout the first half of the twentieth century, Afro-American social advancement remained a primary objective for the public and community education of black Philadelphia.

In studies of blacks in urban America, race relations and the increase in the degree of segregation in the city, in the schools, and on the job tend to dominate the discussion of black social conditions. These writers seem to suggest that the increase in the number of blacks and their concentration in a few sections of the city lessened the likelihood of improvements in the overall social conditions of the black population. The Great Migration, which brought thousands of blacks to northern cities, increased the possibility of racial conflicts and hostilities in these urban areas. Thus, the migration is characterized as having a negative impact upon the resident black community.[22] But in Philadelphia, although the increase in the number of blacks may have made racial conflicts more frequent, it surely made them less violent and destructive to the black community. During the antebellum period, the forays of white mobs into black neighborhoods were an almost annual occurrence, and blacks often fled their homes, jobs, and the city itself when threatened by white racist mobs. But in 1918, when white immigrants attacked law-abiding black citizens who had purchased homes in sections of South Philadelphia, the black community moved on the defensive. Blacks knew they were not in Dixie now, and did not have to suffer the abuse of white mobs. After 1918 there was no major race rioting in Philadelphia.[23]

The increase in the black population also greatly improved the bargaining position of the community in the political arena as local politicians in pursuit of black votes supported the social, political, and educational demands of black leaders. As we have seen, when the two political parties in Philadelphia were competing for black votes, many black educational demands were met. The increasing proportion of black children in the public school system encouraged black leaders and organizations to continue to protest against the lack of black input into the decision-making process in the city schools. Eventually, the black community was able to get one of its most prominent members appointed to the school board, and changes were made in employment practices with regard to black teachers.

In the last few years some educational historians have become disturbed by research findings that suggest that American public education has historically been "racist, sexist, bureaucratic, and dominated by middle-class white Anglo-Saxon culture."[24] Several social scientists and historians have investigated the impact of schooling on the social mobility of various groups in American society and found that social class, rural or urban background, time of entrance into the United States, race, and religion were as important in accounting for the upward social mobility of ethnic groups in the United States as amount of schooling. Christopher Jencks, Milton Gordon, Colin Greer, Michael Katz, and others found that many white ethnic groups moved from lower-class to middle-class status as a result of a combination of favorable social, economic, and political factors. Throughout most of the twentieth century, schooling was only one of the contributors to this upward social movement, and generally one of the less important ones.[25] This investigation of blacks in Philadelphia between 1900 and 1950 found not only that more public schooling did not greatly improve the overall social status of blacks, but also that at times the public schools were considered more an obstacle to the achievement of the larger goal of black social advancement.

But it should be kept in mind that most black Philadelphians, and Afro-Americans in general, were well aware that the public schools were not designed to bring about their freedom and social advancement. If the inadequacy of the public educational facilities available to blacks in the southern states was unconvincing, then those blacks who went to school, became qualified for certain positions, but were refused employment because of their race could testify on the "role of schooling in upward social mobility." The way blacks were treated in the public schools was more than an indication that white school officials believed that they knew (better than blacks themselves) what was educationally best for black children. Black parents and citizens told school officials that they did not want their children "Jim Crowed" in public schools. Blacks in Philadelphia asked that black teachers be allowed to teach in public schools with white pupils. Black organizations requested that a black be appointed to the Board of Public Education. The response of school officials to these requests was favorable only after they were included in the overall political demands of the black electorate in the city. Therefore, it is not surprising that few black Philadelphians looked to the public school system for their social, economic, or political liberation.

Nonetheless, most Afro-Americans in Philadelphia considered ignorance a form of slavery, and believed that education could serve as an important path toward freedom. Therefore, in spite of conditions in the public schools, blacks could still value schooling and education, and continue to work to drive ignorance from their community. Black social organizations during the first half of this century became involved in numerous community education programs to insure that black citizens would not be ignorant of the important social, political, and economic issues facing the community. The success of these efforts is difficult to assess: the impact of a historical lecture or cultural exposition upon an individual or community does not easily lend itself to empirical investigation, other than personal interviews of individuals immediately following the event. But programs to inform blacks about political issues and candidates, or strategies for achieving a specific educational or economic goal can be considered effective if the objective sought by the program's sponsors was ultimately achieved. As we have seen, some of the community education programs in black Philadelphia were effective; others were not. However, blacks continued to educate themselves about those things that were important to their advancement in the city. This was another important continuity in the education of the Philadelphia black community between 1900 and 1950.

Community and public education in black Philadelphia has been a primary concern of this study. Since most social problems, such as segregation in public education or other accommodations, affected both upper- and lower-status blacks, there has been little discussion of class consciousness among blacks in Philadelphia. At the same time, greater emphasis on the social class background of the supporters and opponents of issues in the community would not necessarily add to our understanding of the differences of opinion. For example, the fact that the black teachers who supported separate public schools were "middle-class" does not explain why they supported segregated schooling. Many middle-class teachers and lower-class black workers were among the supporters of "voluntary segregation" for black social advancement. During the 1920s, when it was in the interests of black teachers to support segregated schooling, many openly advocated separate public schools in the face of widespread opposition to the practice in the black community. During the 1930s, however, when public school desegregation was in their best interest, most black teachers supported the campaigns of the Educational Equality League and the other middle- and lower-class blacks who lobbied for a change in public school policies and practices. Self-interest on the part of the teachers seems to be a reasonable explanation for their actions. Some writers have overemphasized class consciousness and underemphasized pure self-interest in trying to account for the accommodating behavior of some black leaders and organizations when dealing with the white majority.[26]

In black Philadelphia between 1900 and 1950, almost all of the community leaders would be considered middle-class, but not all of them were considered "race men" and "race women." Some so-called race leaders in the city were known to put their own personal interests or the interests of some small clique ahead of those of the whole group.[27] Fortunately, black Philadelphia had many leaders who were also race men and women, who worked through the various race institutions and organizations to improve social conditions in the black community. The race leaders, black and white social organizations and institutions, black parents, average citizens, as well as the public schools, were all extremely important in the overall education of black Philadelphia throughout the first half of the twentieth century.

Epilogue

The Supreme Court decision in *Brown v. Board of Education* (1954) that declared segregation in American public education unconstitutional initiated an entirely new era in the history and development of black education in the United States. The effects of the decision were not confined to the "solid South," where dual systems of public education flourished; eventually the Brown decision moved north into cities and states where *de jure* school segregation had been outlawed for almost a century. Although the ruling was viewed as a major victory in the long struggle of Afro-Americans for basic civil rights and simple justice, the hope that public school desegregation would soon bring improvements in the educational opportunities of black and other minority students was not fully realized. Southern whites brought suits to stall the implementation of desegregation orders, and several southern legislatures enacted laws that attempted to nullify the Court's decision or called for the withholding of state funds to any local school district that moved to desegregate its public schools. When these measures proved unsuccessful, some state officials tried to block desegregation orders by threatening state military intervention, thus forcing the federal government to send troops to southern cities to protect citizens involved in the desegregation process. The most effective strategy for avoiding racial integration, however, was the decision on the part of white parents to remove their children from the public schools and to enroll them in the newly created "white academies." As a result, in many areas the public school systems became predominantly black, and the new private schools enrolled the majority of white students. Following the exodus of white pupils, many state legislators became more reluctant to support increased, or even adequate, appropriations for the predominantly black public school systems.[1]

In the North the Brown decision initially had little impact because it primarily addressed *de jure* segregation, and much of the racial isolation in northern public school systems was the result of housing and demographic patterns. But a closer examination of the policies and practices of many northern school boards revealed that through various

199

quasilegal maneuvers, such as the shifting of school boundaries within the districts, school officials were able to create separate black and other minority public schools. Moreover, many parents of children attending these schools complained of the inferior quality of the schooling provided minority students in the system. With regard to textbooks and materials available, experience of teachers, physical plant, curricular innovations, and several other measures, public schools in minority neighborhoods were noticeably inferior to those in other sections of the school district.[2]

In Philadelphia, the political reform movement of the late 1940s and 1950s hit the public school administration in the 1960s. One of the major reforms sought was a lessening of racial isolation in the public schools. In the late 1950s and early 1960s reports and studies by school board members, civic organizations, and outside consultants chronicled a long list of woes affecting the school system. Insufficient funding of the public schools led to low teacher salaries and inability to recruit and retain competent educators, outdated educational materials and textbooks, and, most importantly, low academic achievement levels compared to other large cities. Moreover, by the early 1960s a majority of the pupils enrolled in the public schools were black; and just as traditionally black students had inherited antiquated, rundown, inadequate school buildings abandoned by white students, blacks had now been bequeathed a tired, rundown public school system. Even though blacks were a majority in the public schools, they retained their minority status in the city, state, and nation at large and continued to be the victims of the social deprivation imposed by the dominant white majority.[3]

There were some attempts in the early 1960s to reduce the degree of segregation following the filing of a suit by the Educational Equality League and the local NAACP on behalf of a black parent, Terry Chisholm, who wanted his child to attend the underused neighborhood "white" public school, rather than the more distant, overcrowded school for the "colored." The school administration was granted a continuance by the court after it submitted an "Implementation Plan for Its Announced Policy of Fostering Integration." There was some movement of black students from overcrowded buildings to underused, predominantly white schools, and a few black teachers desegregated the faculties of schools in predominantly white areas, but the school system could not significantly alter the patterns of school segregation without massive busing of black and white pupils. Such a move, however, would very likely have resulted in a more rapid exit of white children from the public school system.[4]

Rather than emphasize school desegregation, the school board, under the leadership of former mayor Richardson Dilworth, decided to try to improve the quality of public schooling. It hired in 1967 Mark Shedd, a Harvard-trained administrator and former superintendent of the Englewood, New Jersey, public schools, to bring about some improvements and innovations in the Philadelphia schools. A number of experimental programs were launched, and Shedd began to move to decentralize the school administration and increase community input into the running of the schools. The attempt to decentralize the school system failed, however, because of the unwillingness of those with power —the school board, school administrators, and teachers' organizations— to relinquish some degree of control over the schools, and Shedd's inability to muster sufficient support from the black community to pressure the school board to implement greater community control.[5]

Conflict between the new superintendent and the political and educational establishment began only two months after Mark Shedd assumed his position. On 17 November 1967 a mass school walkout of about thirty-five hundred black high school students took place to protest against the general quality of public schooling and present a list of demands for changes, including the teaching of Afro-American history, the right to wear traditional African garb in school, the organizing of black clubs and social groups within the schools, and the changing of the names of several predominantly black high schools to honor black leaders. The students rallied at the Board of Education building, and several of their leaders were invited into a meeting with Shedd and other school officials. While the conference was in progress, some of the students outside allegedly climbed atop parked cars, and Police Commissioner Frank Rizzo ordered two busloads of uniformed police to disperse the crowd. Using what were considered by many observers excessively brutal tactics, the police attacked the students. Fifty-seven persons were arrested, most of them juveniles, and twenty-two were seriously injured.[6]

In the aftermath of what the police termed a riot, Superintendent Shedd and board President Dilworth condemned the actions of the police, but Commissioner Rizzo was supported by Mayor James Tate. The lines of battle had been drawn, and in subsequent confrontations between the school administration and the city government, the mayor, police commissioner, and the City Council were usually on one side of the issue, and the superintendent, school president, and the black community on the other. There were several incidents of violence in the public schools, including the killing in February 1971 of Samson Freedman, a teacher at Leeds Junior High School, by a black student. In this case and others, Mayor Tate and Commissioner Rizzo accused the school leadership of "excessive permissiveness" in dealing with trouble-makers in the schools. The continuing fiscal crisis of the public school system was also laid at the feet of the school administration, and little political support was given to a $90 million school bond issue, which was rejected by voters in May 1969. Although Mayor Tate supported a $60 million bond issue that passed in November, he vetoed a city tax on liquor that was passed by the City Council in May 1971. This veto, plus the failure of the school board to get emergency funds from the city or state, signaled the beginning of massive cutbacks in personnel, extracurricular activities, and building construction in the Philadelphia public school system. And in the November 1971 mayoral election, Police Commissioner Rizzo made Superintendent Shedd and the public schools an issue, promising to fire Shedd "within seconds" of his election. In December 1971, following the Rizzo victory, Mark Shedd was forced to resign. The second era of reform had ended for the Philadelphia public schools.[7]

Although many of the larger political and economic problems involving the public schools in the 1950s and 1960s directly or indirectly affected black public education, the continuing political impotence of the black community meant that black leaders and organizations had only minimal influence on decisions affecting the public schooling of black children. There were several reasons for this state of affairs. In the many essays and books that have examined black politics in Philadelphia during this period, writers and researchers have generally concluded that because of the attachment of the black vote to the Democratic Party, and the inability (or unwillingness) of Republicans to seek the support of black voters, blacks "do not benefit from the political system to any special extent, and have achieved no major changes in their political, economic, and social status as a result of the operations of the political system in Philadelphia."[8] Thus, the pattern of black participation in local politics in the 1950s, 1960s, and early 1970s resembled that of the pre-1932 era, when the black vote was firmly attached to the Republican machine. The one-party orientation of black voters limited the need for the political establishment to make concessions on black political demands, since the black vote was generally taken for granted by the Democratic politicians in power.

Black protest activities, such as mass demonstrations and boycotts, appear to have been only slightly more successful than political participation in gaining black social and political demands during the 1950s and 1960s. For example, John H. Strange estimated that between April 1963 and June 1965 there were at least seventy-eight protest demonstrations conducted by black organizations against local and federal government officials and agencies and local business firms, and at least forty-two threats of demonstrations and boycotts by black leaders and organizations. However, after examining the actual improvements in black social or economic conditions resulting from these protests, Strange concluded that "protest activities in Philadelphia have resulted in few changes."

> Those protests reviewed . . . resulted in the hiring of five journeymen, the installation of traffic lights, the opening of several hundred jobs to Blacks, and the investigation of discriminatory educational practices. But life is still much the same for Blacks in Philadelphia. The public schools are still segregated, Blacks are still employed in lower level occupations by industry, as well as by the city government. More than twice as many Blacks as whites are still unemployed. Blacks still receive harsher treatment by police than whites.[9]

Even in the most successful black protest demonstration during the 1960s, the one that eventually led to the desegregation of Girard College, nine months of demonstrations and years of litigation produced an important symbolic victory for the black community but very little change in the educational opportunities available to most black children in the city.

In 1954 the Educational Equality League began working with attorney Raymond Pace Alexander, later judge in the Court of Common Pleas, Philadelphia, on a legal suit to bring about the desegregation of Girard College. Stephen Girard, a prominent Philadelphia merchant, banker, and financier of the early nineteenth century, provided in his will over $6 million in trust for the education of "poor white orphan boys." Girard College was opened in 1848 in North Philadelphia. Each time the suggestion was made that poor *black* orphan boys be admitted to the school, the private board of trustees cited the Stephen Girard will. The league took the case to the U.S. Supreme Court, which upheld the position of the trustees in June 1958. Even with this setback, the Educational Equality League and the local branch of the NAACP under the leadership of attorney Cecil B. Moore continued to pursue the issue in the courts, and throughout the 1960s sporadic nonviolent direct action protests were organized around the school. Finally, in 1968, the U.S. Supreme Court agreed to set aside the stipulations of the Girard will, and in September of that year the College admitted the first black orphan boys.[10]

The desegregation of Girard College was considered a major victory for the league and the NAACP; however, it had only a limited effect on the availability of quality schooling for most black Philadelphians. Some of the problems facing blacks in the Philadelphia public school system during the 1950s and 1960s were addressed by Floyd Logan and the league, which during this period was a virtual one-man show, with Logan gathering the appropriate support according to the issue being addressed. When legal problems were tackled, Logan went to the NAACP for support and assistance, as in the Girard College suit. When black teachers called on the league to investigate discrimination in appointments or promotions in the public school system, Logan sought the advice and support of the Philadelphia Teachers Association, the Black Teachers Forum, the Educators Roundtable, and other teachers' organizations in the city. Although Logan served as an effective lobbyist for the black community on specific issues and problems as they arose, he could do little to stem the general deterioration in the public schooling made available to black citizens.

As was mentioned, there were numerous surveys of the Philadelphia public school system by interested insiders and outsiders during the late fifties and early sixties. All of these studies noted the differences in the quality of public schooling available in black and white areas. The Spe-

Cecil B. Moore, former president of the North Philadelphia branch of the NAACP, and demonstrators in front of the Girard College in 1965. (Photo by Jack T. Franklin)

Demonstrations at Girard College. (Photos by Jack T. Franklin)

cial Committee on Nondiscrimination, consisting of three school board members and one hundred representatives from various civic groups, was created by the Board of Public Education in February 1963 to review school policies and practices. The committee's report was released in July 1964. It noted, among other things, that predominantly black public schools in Philadelphia were "usually also the oldest, had more part-time classes, more overcrowding, the least experienced teachers, the lowest student achievement levels, the highest drop-out rates, the highest proportion of black faculty, and the least adequate textbooks, supplies, and equipment."[11] The Odell Report issued in February 1965 echoed the findings and recommendations of the Committee on Nondiscrimination. Dr. William Odell, hired by the school board to make a comprehensive study of the system, found that there was need for improvement in administrative, curricular, and instructional areas. Average achievement levels in the basic skills were low throughout the system, but in predominantly black schools pupils were averaging two and three years below grade level. Odell recommended that expenditures per pupil be raised from $391 a year in 1959–60 to $650 by 1966–67, and that the school system improve its curricular, testing, and personnel practices.[12]

Many black parents and community leaders were disturbed by the continual reports of the deficiencies in the public schooling of black children, but there was little that black leaders could do because most of the changes needed would require an increase in revenues or a reallocation of limited funds. The antagonism between the reform Dilworth board and superintendent and the Democratic city government lessened the likelihood of strong support from the Democratic organization for increases in real estate taxes for the public schools, and any reallocation of school funds away from predominantly white areas would have led to a deterioration in the local public schools and increased enrollment in private or parochial schools by white students, thus exacerbating racial isolation in the schools. Sporadically throughout the 1960s, black parents and citizens crowded into school board meetings to testify about specific problems such as overcrowding and lack of adequate supplies at various schools, and by the end of the decade Philadelphia was one of the centers of the "Quality Integrated Education" movement.[13] But the lack of black political power within the city government and Democratic organization meant that many important political decisions affecting public education would not necessarily reflect the needs and interests of the black community.

As was the case during the first half of the century, the problems of blacks in the public school system were the major topics of discussion at community education programs in black Philadelphia in the 1950s, 1960s, and 1970s. The need to lower juvenile delinquency and dropout rates was a particular concern during the 1950s, while the growing number of "functional illiterates" being graduated from the public school system became an issue at parent-teacher conferences, Home and School Association forums and school board meetings in the 1960s. Black teachers and administrators were particularly active in developing and implementing new programs and strategies to improve the educational achievement of lower-income, inner-city youths. In July 1958, for example, Project WINGS was launched at William Penn High School for Girls by Dr. Ruth Wright Hayre, the principal, to "encourage our girls to achieve excellence—or at least their best—through guidance, parental cooperation, and an enriched cultural program." Among the results of the program were decreases in the percentage of dropouts, increases in the number of graduates entering college, and improvements in attendance rates and motivation among the predominantly black student body at the school.[14] When Marcus Foster was appointed principal of Simon Gratz High School in North Philadelphia, according to one observer, Gratz was "the epitome of inner-city education in Philadelphia—a model of everything it should not be. It was the kind of school that most people who had never been there were afraid even to visit."

> The very name could evoke images of dark halls teeming with knife-wielding gangs. Gratz was a dumping ground, and students who had a choice did their best to go somewhere else. More important than any specific faults—the antiquated, inadequate facilities; the high ratio of permanent substitutes; the low morale of the faculty; the students' sub-normal reading levels—was the fact that Gratz was a poor black school, the ultimate symbol of failure.[15]

Foster came to the school in 1966 and began by meeting with the parents as well as the students in an effort to get "academic achievers" to return to the school. He increased the number of academic and vocational courses offered, and developed a special humanities program and classes on African art and culture. Federal grants were awarded the school to develop new curricular materials focusing on the problems of the inner city. The Honor Society was reinstated; a band, and drama club were organized; and Foster managed to gain college scholarships for many of the graduating seniors. New contacts were made with business and professional groups to train students not going on to college for jobs in industry. At several schools, black and white educators and administrators began to change the climate of failure that pervaded public schooling for blacks in Philadelphia. Federal funds for "compensatory education" brought projects Get Set, Head Start, Upward

Bound, and various other educational enrichment programs to the public schools and provided some hope that the school system was finally attempting to meet the needs of the black community.

With the end of the second reform era, however, following the election of Police Commissioner Frank Rizzo as mayor, the Philadelphia public school system entered another period of retrenchment and fiscal instability. The antagonism between the school administration and the city government meant that requests for increased funding by the city or the state would not receive the full support of city officials. The militancy of the teachers' union during the late 1960s had led to increases of up to 24 percent in teacher and other staff salaries over four

Dr. Ruth Wright Hayre, principal of William Penn High School for Girls and later a district superintendent of the Philadelphia public school system, shown in the photograph on the left presenting commendations for academic achievement to outstanding students. (Courtesy of the Philadelphia Tribune)

or five years, and the city government was attempting to force the school board to make significant cuts in programs and personnel. Summer school was eliminated in 1971; school building construction and expansion were halted; and by the middle of the decade, school officials were laying off teachers' aides and, finally, regular public school teachers. At the same time, the average achievement level of pupils in the system, as well as the morale of the staff, continued to drop, and each school year there were threats that the schools would have to close early because of lack of operating funds. The predominantly black public school system had become a victim of the renewed political struggle between the black community and the new city government.[16]

The deterioration in the relations between the black community and the Democratic city government had begun long before the Rizzo era made racial issues paramount in partisan and nonpartisan politics. Black leaders saw that fewer and fewer of the goods and services pro-

vided in predominantly white neighborhoods were reaching black neighborhoods in North and West Philadelphia. Urban renewal almost immediately turned into "Negro removal" in several sections of North and South Philadelphia east of Broad Street. City wage taxes were paid by all employed persons in Philadelphia, but the municipal services purchased with those taxes were distributed disproportionately. Black neighborhoods were allowed to deteriorate while funds were made avail-

Judge Raymond Pace Alexander and a group of children celebrating "World Peace Through Law" and the Geneva Peace Conference c. 1955. (Courtesy of the Philadelphia Tribune)

able to other areas of machine strength for numerous redevelopment projects.[17] These and related issues, such as the persistently high rates of unemployment among blacks, further estranged black citizens from the Democratic city organization.

The only major election won by a black candidate in the late 1950s was for the congressional seat in the Second District, which included the predominantly black sections of North and West Philadelphia. Unfortunately, Robert N. C. Nix rarely addressed the major problems facing his predominantly black constituency and kept a low profile with regard to the larger issues facing Afro-Americans in general. Unlike many of his contemporaries—William Dawson and Ralph Metcalf in

Chicago, and Adam Clayton Powell, Jr., in New York City—who had their base of support primarily within the black community, Nix completely embraced the Democratic machine.[18] Nix's opponents within the community were in no position to challenge him as long as he had the support of the Democratic organization. Nix was finally unseated in the Democratic primary of 1978, despite the support of the Democratic organization. His black constituency had decided that they would rather have a black freshman, William Gray, representing their interests in Congress, than Nix with his twenty years of seniority.

Although there were some changes in the actual conditions for blacks in Philadelphia between 1950 and 1979, there were no significant changes in power balances. For example, the major change with regard to the public schools was the attainment of a black majority in the city school system. However, the dominant white majority in the city and state still controls the public school system, so that the major difference between the situation in 1925 or 1935 and that in 1979 is that more black students are now in segregated public schools with inadequate

Students of Simon Gratz High School in front of a memorial of Marcus Foster, former principal of the school and superintendent of Oakland (California) public schools. He was killed in 1975. (Courtesy of the Philadelphia Tribune)

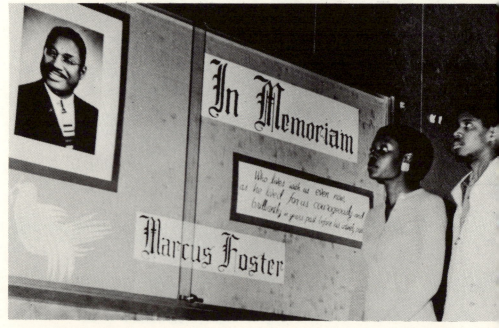

E. *Washington Rhodes, publisher of the* Philadelphia Tribune, *and Congressman Robert N. C. Nix of the Second District of Pennsylvania (Philadelphia). (Courtesy of the Philadelphia Tribune)*

supplies and frustrated and disillusioned teachers. The desegregation of Girard College was accomplished in 1968, but only a few blacks each year are admitted. The election of the first black congressman from the city brought no sharper focus on the problems facing black folk in North and West Philadelphia. The leadership provided by newspaper editors, ministers, and lawyers during the earlier era appeared to be lacking in the 1960s and 1970s, while black politicians vied for the support of the Democratic machine. Unfortunately, talented and capable leadership was in short supply in black Philadelphia after 1960.

The persistent failure of the public school system to provide black pupils with basic literacy skills and specialized knowledge in certain areas remains a problem for black Philadelphia. Whereas in earlier decades campaigns were launched to encourage black youth to remain in school, a campaign against "functional illiteracy"—the inability to read and write well enough to function as a young adult in contemporary American society—has yet to materialize. Against the opposition of unsympathetic city and school officials, however, black and white Philadelphians must continue to work to improve the public schooling made available to black and other minority children, for, as W. E. B. Du Bois declared in 1923: "first and foremost and more important than anything else, Negro children must not be allowed to grow up in ignorance. This is worse than segregation, worse than anything we could contemplate."[19]

Appendixes
Notes
A Note on Sources
Selected Bibliography

Appendix 1
Committees Working
with Black Migrants
to Philadelphia

The Round Table Conference for Work Among Colored People in Philadelphia

Organizations, 1917

Anthony Benezet School
Armstrong Association of
  Philadelphia
Cheyney Training School
Children's Bureau
Children's Aid Society
Downingtown Industrial School
Eighth Ward Settlement House
Happy Day Nursery
Home for Destitute Colored
  Children
Home for the Homeless
House of St. Michael's and All
  Angels
House of the Holy Child
Joseph Sturge Mission
Lincoln Day Nursery
Lincoln University
Mercy Hospital

Philadelphia Association for the
  Protection of Colored Women
Seybert Institution
Shelter for Colored Orphans
Society for Organizing Charity
Society for the Protection of
  Children
Spring Street Settlement
Starr Center
St. Mary's Mission
Travelers' Aid Society
Western Soup Society
Western District Colored School
Whittier Centre
Wissahickon Boys Club
South West Branch, Young Men's
  Christian Association
Young Women's Christian
  Association

Note: The Round Table Conference was in existence until January 1921, when the Executive Committee voted to merge it with the Conference of Institutions for the Care and Training of Children in Philadelphia; see letter from J. Prentice Murphy, president of the Round Table Conference, to John Ihlder, 29 December 1920, Box 21, f. 120, PHA Papers, TUUA.

Negro Migration Committee, 1917

Subcommittees and Members

Committee on Receiving Immigrants:

Travelers' Aid Society
Philadelphia Association for the Protection of Colored Women

Committee on Housing and Sanitation:

Philadelphia Housing Association
Octavia Hill Association

Committee on Employment:

Armstrong Association of Philadelphia

Committee on Relief:

Society for Organizing Charity
Children's Bureau

Committee on the Courts:

The Legal Aid Society
House of Detention—H. P. Richardson

Committee on Education:

Louis Nusbaum, Philadelphia Public Schools
J. R. Paul Brock, Principal, Durham School

Committee on Recreation:

Bureau of Recreation
Armstrong Association of Philadelphia

Committee on Churches:

Rev. W. F. Graham, Archdeacon Henry L. Phillips

Source: Letter John Ihlder to J. Pancoast, November 5, 1917, Box 21, f.121, PHA Papers, TUUA.

Table 13

Enrollment of black children in Philadelphia public schools, 1919-40

Year	Grades 1 to 8			Kindergarten			Special Classes		
	Enroll-ment[a]	Black	Percent-age	Enroll-ment	Black	Percent-age	Enroll-ment	Black	Percent-age
1919	186,830	14,133	7.6%	8,525	549	6.4%	2,868	749	26.1%
1920	187,290	14,369	7.7	8,174	520	6.4	3,035	787	25.9
1921	191,502	16,305	8.5	8,147	560	6.9	3,823	1,043	27.3
1922	194,636	17,016	8.7	8,983	645	7.2	4,127	1,031	25.0
1923	192,487	18,754	9.7	8,861	781	8.8	5,176	1,456	28.1
1924	189,069	20,076	10.6	8,937	1,019	11.4	5,749	1,957	34.0
1925	184,020	21,270	11.6	9,445	995	10.5	6,531	2,071	31.7
1926	182,241	21,770	11.9	9,350	1,056	12.4	7,666	2,263	29.5
1927	177,649	23,161	13.0	9,579	1,068	11.1	8,376	2,740	32.7
1928	170,344	23,226	13.6	9,568	947	9.9	9,549	3,067	32.1
1929	166,486	23,892	14.4	9,857	1,094	11.1	9,817	3,266	33.3
1930	166,313	25,568	15.4	10,018	1,156	11.5	10,371	3,454	33.3
1931	162,032	25,983	16.0	9,795	1,179	12.0	10,514	3,328	31.7
1932	158,648	26,375	16.6	9,956	1,370	13.8	10,665	3,666	34.4
1933	154,499	27,116	17.6	10,148	1,669	16.4	10,614	3,763	35.5
1934	154,278	27,766	18.0	9,748	1,471	15.1	10,961	4,071	37.1
1935	150,048	28,912	19.3	9,975	1,485	14.9	10,984	4,270	38.9
1936	145,422	29,371	20.2	9,899	1,498	15.1	10,678	4,027	37.7
1937	139,676	30,258	21.7	9,653	1,532	15.9	10,225	4,077	39.9
1938	138,059	29,646	21.5	9,954	1,578	15.9	10,356	4,265	41.2
1939	134,738	29,046	21.6	9,906	1,583	16.0	10,461	4,508	43.1
1940	131,993	30,126	22.8	9,904	1,518	15.3	9,800	4,388	44.8

Source: Final Report of the Pennsylvania State Temporary Commission on the Conditions of the Urban Colored Population (Harrisburg, Pa., 1943), p. 412.
Note: a. For year ending 30 June.

Table 14
Enrollment of black children in Philadelphia junior and
senior high schools, 1919–40

Year	Junior High School			Senior High School		
	Enroll-ment	Black	Percent-age	Enroll-ment	Black	Percent-age
1919	1,606	39	2.4%	20,390	545	2.7%
1920	1,625	52	3.2	22,171	657	3.0
1921	4,960	85	1.7	26,233	650	2.5
1922	7,200	215	3.0	29,918	952	3.2
1923	7,839	281	3.6	30,807	1,040	3.4
1924	16,059	374	2.3	30,465	1,276	4.2
1925	21,215	837	3.9	30,131	1,297	4.3
1926	21,418	1,021	4.8	30,458	1,383	4.5
1927	27,171	1,161	4.3	30,960	1,547	5.0
1928	35,542	1,925	5.4	31,622	1,692	5.4
1929	37,608	2,300	6.1	32,223	1,718	5.3
1930	37,809	2,422	6.4	34,929	2,006	5.7
1931	41,357	2,576	6.2	38,432	2,449	6.4
1932	42,492	3,860	9.1	42,330	2,634	6.2
1933	44,054	4,286	9.7	46,456	3,187	6.9
1934	42,831	4,782	11.2	48,352	3,411	7.1
1935	42,979	4,887	11.4	50,491	4,009	7.9
1936	43,173	5,052	11.7	51,758	4,436	8.6
1937	45,128	5,310	11.8	51,872	4,798	9.2
1938	45,534	7,126	15.6	49,711	4,851	9.8
1939	45,149	8,623	19.1	42,025	4,874	9.4
1940	41,377	8,625	20.8	51,272	5,455	10.6

Source: Final Report of the Pennsylvania State Temporary Commission on the
Conditions of the Urban Colored Population (Harrisburg, 1943), p. 414.

Notes

Abbreviations

The Annals	The Annals of the American Academy of Social and Political Science
HSP	Historical Society of Pennsylvania
JNE	Journal of Negro Education
JNH	Journal of Negro History
KC	Philadelphia Board of Public Education, Kennedy Center
PAS	Pennsylvania Abolition Society
PHA	Philadelphia Housing Association
PBPE	Philadelphia Board of Public Education
PMHB	Pennsylvania Magazine of History and Biography
TUUA	Temple University, Urban Archives

Introduction

1. Lawrence A. Cremin, *American Education: The Colonial Experience, 1607–1783* (New York, 1970), p. xi.

2. Ibid., p. xiii.

3. Lawrence A. Cremin, *Traditions of American Education* (New York, 1977), pp. 19–38. For another excellent examination of the educational configurations in several American towns and cities during the late nineteenth and early twentieth centuries, see Patricia A. Graham, *Community and Class in American Education, 1865–1918* (New York, 1974).

4. Cremin, *Traditions of American Education*, pp. viii, 48–87; see also Lawrence A. Cremin, *Public Education* (New York, 1976).

5. The different values and social goals to be served by the newly established public schools for blacks and whites are discussed in detail in Vincent P. Franklin, "American Values, Social Goals, and the Desegregated School: A Historical Perspective," in *New Perspectives on Black Educational History*, ed. V. P. Franklin and James D. Anderson (Boston, 1978), pp. 193–201.

6. Although this is the first book-length study of the education of a minority group in the United States, there are several essays that suggest that some minorities used education to improve their socioeconomic status in urban America. See, for example, Timothy L. Smith, "Immigrant Social Aspirations and American Education, 1880–1930," *American Quarterly* 21

(1969): 523–43; Richard A. Varbero, "Philadelphia's South Italians in the 1920s," in *The Peoples of Philadelphia: A History of Ethnic Groups and Lower Class Life, 1790–1940*, ed. Allen F. Davis and Mark H. Haller (Philadelphia, 1973), pp. 255–76; and M. Mark Stolarik, "Immigration, Education, and Social Mobility of Slovaks, 1870–1930," in *Immigrants and Religion in Urban America*, eds. Randall M. Miller and Thomas D. Marzik (Philadelphia, 1977), pp. 103–16; see also Gerd Korman, *Industrialization, Immigrants, and Americanizers: The View from Milwaukee, 1866–1921* (Madison, 1967).

Chapter 1. The Black Community and Race Relations before 1920

1. For a discussion of blacks in seventeenth-century Philadelphia, see Edward Turner, *The Negro in Pennsylvania, Slavery-Servitude-Freedom, 1639–1861* (1911; reprint ed., New York, 1969), pp. 1–25; and W. E. B. Du Bois, *The Philadelphia Negro—A Social Study* (1899; reprint ed., New York, 1967), pp. 10–14. (All page references are to reprint editions.)

2. Turner, *The Negro in Pennsylvania*, pp. 1–17. The areas that will be discussed throughout the book are within the boundaries of the city of Philadelphia. Before 1854 this area was designated the "County" of Philadelphia; in 1854, the City and County became coterminous. In the colonial era the black community was within the boundaries of the City. For a discussion of the changing boundaries of Philadelphia, see Allen F. Davis's Introduction to Davis and Haller, *The Peoples of Philadelphia*, pp. 6–9.

3. Turner, *The Negro in Pennsylvania*, pp. 109–12; Du Bois, *The Philadelphia Negro*, pp. 11–17.

4. Turner, *The Negro in Pennsylvania*, p. 113.

5. Ibid., "Legal Status of the Slave," pp. 17–28.

6. The Act of 1726 is quoted in Du Bois, *The Philadelphia Negro*, p. 15.

7. Turner, *The Negro in Pennsylvania*, pp. 64–74; see also Ira V. Brown, *The Negro in Pennsylvania History* (Gettysburg, Pa., 1970), pp. 3–6; Thomas Drake, *Quakers and Slavery in America* (New Haven, 1950), pp. 90–93; Sidney V. James, *A People among Peoples: Quaker Benevolence in Eighteenth Century America* (Cambridge, Mass., 1963), pp. 134–36.

8. The original full title of the reorganized society was "the Pennsylvania Society for Promoting the Abolition of Slavery, for the Relief of Free Negroes Unlawfully Held in Bondage, and for Improving the Condition of the African Race"; see Brown, *The Negro in Pennsylvania History*, p. 6.

9. The activities of the Pennsylvania Abolition Society (PAS) to provide schooling for free blacks are discussed in chapter 2.

10. For a discussion of the attempts to pass the Act of Manumission in the Pennsylvania Assembly, see Arthur I. Zilversmit, *The First Emancipation: The Abolition of Slavery in the North* (Chicago, 1967), pp. 124–37. See also Turner, *The Negro in Pennsylvania*, pp. 77–82, and Brown, *The Negro in Pennsylvania History*, pp. 6–9.

11. The Act of 1780 is reprinted in Richard R. Wright, Jr., *The*

Negro in Pennsylvania: A Study in Economic History (1911; reprint ed., New York, 1969), pp. 203–7.

12. Census data on the black population in Philadelphia from 1790 to 1860 may be found in Turner, *The Negro in Pennsylvania*, p. 253; and Du Bois, *The Philadelphia Negro*, p. 47.

13. Richard Allen, *The Life Experience and Gospel Labors of Rev. Richard Allen*, quoted in Carol George, *Segregated Sabbaths: Richard Allen and the Rise of Independent Black Churches, 1760–1840* (New York, 1973), p. 26.

14. Ibid., p. 51.

15. Charles Wesley, *Richard Allen: Apostle of Freedom* (Washington, 1935), p. 60. See also George, *Segregated Sabbaths*, pp. 26–48. These works contain important information on the origins of the black community of Philadelphia.

16. Sam Bass Warner, Jr., *The Private City: Philadelphia in Three Periods of Growth* (Philadelphia, 1968), pp. 4–7.

17. These censuses were used extensively by Du Bois in his study of the Philadelphia Negro; for a discussion, see pp. 43–45.

18. Theodore J. Hershberg, "Free Blacks in Antebellum Philadelphia," in Davis and Haller, *The Peoples of Philadelphia*, p. 124.

19. Ibid., pp. 112–18.

20. Charles Godfred Leland, quoted in John Runcie, "Hunting the Nigs in Philadelphia: The Race Riot of August 1834," *Pennsylvania History* 39 (1972): 189.

21. Ibid., p. 188.

22. Elizabeth M. Geffen, "Violence in Philadelphia in the 1840's and 1850's," *Pennsylvania History* 36 (1969): 386–87.

23. George Lippard, *The Quaker City; or the Monks of Monk Hall* (1844; reprint ed., Philadelphia, 1876), p. 409; Geffen, "Violence in Philadelphia," p. 388.

24. Du Bois, *The Philadelphia Negro*, pp. 36–37; Warner, *The Private City*, pp. 140–42.

25. William Dusinberre, *Civil War Issues in Philadelphia, 1856–1865* (Philadelphia, 1965), p. 13.

26. Frederick Binder, "Pennsylvania Negro Regiments in the Civil War," *JNH* 27 (1952): 388–89.

27. Ibid., p. 380; Winnifred K. Mackay, "Philadelphia During the Civil War, 1861–1865," *PMHB* 70 (1946): 35–38.

28. Binder, "Pennsylvania Negro Regiments," pp. 415–17; Horace Montgomery, "A Union Officer's Recollections of the Negro as a Soldier," *Pennsylvania History* 28 (1961): 156–86 passim.

29. Philip S. Foner, "The Battle to End Discrimination against Negroes on Philadelphia Street Cars: (Part I) Background and Beginning of Battle," *Pennsylvania History* 40 (1973): 278–85; Ira Brown, "Pennsylvania and the Rights of the Negro, 1865–1887," *Pennsylvania History* 28 (1961): 45–57.

30. Philip S. Foner, "The Battle to End Discrimination against

Negroes on Pennsylvania Street Cars: (Part II) The Victory," *Pennsylvania History* 40 (1973): 371.

31. Ibid., pp. 373–79; Brown, *The Negro in Pennsylvania History*, pp. 45–49.

32. For a thorough account of the movement to disenfranchise the black population of Pennsylvania, see Turner, *The Negro in Pennsylvania*, pp. 169–93; Brown, *The Negro in Pennsylvania History*, pp. 21–23.

33. Before the election of 1870, a rumor circulated that Negroes would be prevented from voting. As a result, General E. M. Gregory, United States Marshal for the eastern district of Pennsylvania, intervened to insure that blacks would be allowed to vote. The presence of troops at the polls was later protested by the mayor of Philadelphia and the governor of the state; see Brown, "Pennsylvania and the Rights of the Negro," pp. 49–52.

34. Ibid.; Foner, "The Victory," pp. 378–79. For a general discussion of Negro voting in the North in the post-Civil War era, see Leslie Fishel, "The Negro in Northern Politics 1870–1900," *Mississippi Valley Historical Review* 42 (1955): 466–89; Leslie Fishel, "Northern Prejudice and Negro Suffrage, 1865–1870," *JNH* 34 (1954): 8–26.

35. Warner, *The Private City*, pp. 125–26.

36. Ibid.

37. Philadelphia is north of the Mason-Dixon line; however, it is very close to this border. Philip S. Foner concluded that during the antebellum period, Philadelphia was "the most anti-Negro city in the North and the most segregated metropolis above the Mason-Dixon line." See "Background and Beginning of the Battle," p. 261.

38. U.S. Department of Commerce, Bureau of the Census, *Immigrants and Their Children*, by Niles Carpenter (Washington, D.C., 1927), pp. 11–43; Adna F. Weber, *The Growth of Cities in the Nineteenth Century: A Study in Statistics*, 2d ed. (Ithaca, N.Y., 1965), pp. 20–40.

39. Ibid.; see also Lyle W. Dorsell, ed., *The Challenge of the City, 1860–1910* (Lexington, Conn., 1968), pp. v–vii.

40. Caroline Golab, "The Immigrant and the City: Poles, Italians, and Jews in Philadelphia, 1870–1920," in Davis and Haller, *The Peoples of Philadelphia*, p. 204.

41. Ibid., p. 205; and Caroline Golab, *Immigrant Destinations* (Philadelphia, 1977), pp. 11–27.

42. U.S. Department of Commerce, Bureau of the Census, *Negro Population, 1790–1915* (Washington, D.C., 1918), Table 10, p. 93; Du Bois, *The Philadelphia Negro*, p. 47.

43. Dorsell, *The Challenge of the City*, pp. v–viii; George Mowry, "The Urban Reform Tradition," reprinted in Dorsell, *The Challenge of the City*, pp. 94–99.

44. Ibid.; Roy Lubove, *The Progressives and the Slums: Tenement House Reform in New York City, 1890–1917* (Pittsburgh, Pa. 1962), pp. 244–45.

45. William Issel, "Modernization in Philadelphia School Reform,

1882–1905," *PMHB* 94 (1970): 360; see also Bonnie Fox, "Philadelphia Progressives: A Test of the Hofstadter- Hays Thesis," *Pennsylvania History* 34 (1967): 372–94; Robert Bloom, "Edwin A. Van Valkenburg and the *North American*, 1899–1924," *Pennsylvania History* 31 (1954): 109–27; Donald Disbrow, "Herbert Welsh, Editor of *City and State*, 1895–1904," *PMHB* 94 (1970): 62–74; Lloyd M. Abernathy, "Insurgency in Philadelphia, 1905," *PMHB* 87 (1963): 3–20.

46. For a more complete discussion of the school reorganization in 1905, see chapter 2.

47. E. Digby Baltzell, Introduction to the 1967 edition of *The Philadelphia Negro*, p. xviii; see also Samuel P. Hays, "The Politics of Reform in Municipal Government in the Progressive Era," *Pacific Northwest Quarterly* 55 (1964): 157–69.

48. Du Bois, quoted by Baltzell, Introduction to *The Philadelphia Negro*, p. xix.

49. Ibid., p. ix. Unfortunately, Du Bois is rarely cited as a pioneering sociologist.

50. Du Bois, ibid., p. 1.

51. Ibid., p. 389.

52. Ibid., p. 394.

53. If one considers Washington and Baltimore "southern or border cities," Philadelphia had the largest black population of any city in the "North"; see U.S. Bureau of Census, *Negro Population, 1790–1915*, Table 10, p. 93.

54. Ibid.; see also table 2 above.

55. Du Bois, *The Philadelphia Negro*, p. 74.

56. Ibid., p. 92.

57. U.S. Bureau of the Census, *Negro Population, 1790–1915*, "Illiteracy in Cities," Table 30, pp. 432–33. The figures on the percentages of black illiteracy were—1910: Boston, 3.5; New York City, 6.4; Pittsburgh, 6.6; St. Louis, 12.4; Chicago, 4.0; Cleveland, 4.1; Detroit, 3.5; Philadelphia, 7.8.

58. Du Bois, *The Philadelphia Negro*, p. 145; see also I. Eaton, "Special Report on Domestic Service in the Seventh Ward of Philadelphia," also in *The Philadelphia Negro*, pp. 427–529 passim.

59. U.S. Department of Commerce, Bureau of the Census, *Thirteenth Census of the United States*, Vol. 4, Population: *Occupation Statistics* (Washington, D.C., 1914), pp. 590–92.

60. Emmett J. Scott, *The Negro Migration during the War* (New York, 1920), p. 55.

61. Ibid., p. 14; see also Chicago Commission on Race Relations, *The Negro in Chicago* (Chicago, 1922), pp. 122–33; John Hope Franklin, *From Slavery to Freedom: A History of Negro Americans*, 3d ed. (New York, 1967), pp. 471–76; Robert B. Grant, ed., *The Black Man Comes to the City: A Documentary Account from the Great Migration to the Great Depression* (Chicago, 1972), pp. 31–40; Robert C. Weaver, *The Negro*

Ghetto (New York, 1948), pp. 25–32; St. Clair Drake and Horace Clayton, *Black Metropolis: A Study of Negro Life in a Northern City* (New York, 1945), pp. 58–64.

62. Scott, *The Negro Migration*, p. 17; Vincent P. Franklin, "The Persistence of School Segregation in the Urban North—A Historical Perspective," *Journal of Ethnic Studies* 1 (1974): 54–58.

63. Sadie T. Mossell, "The Standard of Living Among 100 Negro Migrant Families in Philadelphia," *The Annals* 98 (November 1921): 174.

64. Wright, *The Negro in Pennsylvania*, pp. 64–65.

65. Mossell, "The Standard of Living," p. 177.

66. Commonwealth of Pennsylvania, Department of Welfare, *Negro Survey of Pennsylvania* (Harrisburg, Pa., 1928), pp. 36–37.

67. Charity Organization Society of New York City, "The Negro in the Cities of the North," *Charities* 15 (7 October 1905).

68. "Industrial Conditions of the Negro in the North," *The Annals* 27 (May 1906); "The Negro's Progress in Fifty Years," *The Annals* 49 (September 1913).

69. For a comprehensive bibliography of articles and books on the migration, see Frank V. Ross and Louise V. Kennedy, *A Bibliography of Negro Migration* (New York, 1934).

70. Guichard Parris and Lester Brooks, *Blacks in the City: A History of the National Urban League* (Boston, 1971), p. 4.

71. Armstrong Association of Philadelphia, *Annual Reports, 1910–20* (Philadelphia, 1911–21); Philadelphia Association for the Protection of Colored Women, *Annual Reports, 1908–15* (Philadelphia, 1909–16). The reports may be found at the Historical Society of Pennsylvania (HSP).

72. John T. Emlen, "The Movement for the Betterment of the Negro in Philadelphia," *The Annals* 49 (September 1913): 90.

73. Armstrong Association, *Seventh Annual Report, 1915* (Philadelphia 1916), pp. 3–5 (HSP).

74. Parris and Brooks, *Blacks in the City*, p. 89.

75. Ibid., pp. 89–93; *Philadelphia Tribune*, 3 February 1917, p. 1; Nancy Weiss, *The National Urban League, 1910–1940* (New York, 1974), p. 109.

76. Minutes of the Round Table Conference for Work among the Colored Peoples of Philadelphia, 13 February 1917, box 21, f. 23, PHA Papers, TUUA; *Philadelphia Tribune*, 17 March 1917, p. 1. For a listing of groups belonging to the Round Table Conference in 1917, see Appendix 1.

77. Minutes of the Round Table Conference, 13 February 1917.

78. For a list of groups and individuals on subcommittees of the Negro Migration Committee, see Appendix 1.

79. PHA, *Annual Report, 1917* (Philadelphia, 1918), p. 8, PHA (Urb 29), box 1, f. 2, TUUA; "Negro Migration Study," 1917, conducted by Anna Gibson, box 21, f. 123, PHA Papers, TUUA.

80. PHA, *Annual Report, 1917*, pp. 8–9.

81. John T. Emlen to John Ihlder, 14 August 1919; John Ihlder to

John T. Emlen, 28 August 1919, box 21, f. 126, Letters, PHA Papers, TUUA.

82. PHA, "Know Your City—Housing the Negro Migrants" (August 1923), PHA Pamphlet Collection, TUUA. A thesis was completed under the sponsorship of the Philadelphia Housing Association by William Fuller, entitled, "The Negro Migration to Philadelphia, 1924"; see PHA Pamphlet Collection, TUUA.

83. For a discussion of the "intolerable" housing conditions that led to municipal action, see chapter 5.

84. The black newspapers in Philadelphia in 1896 are discussed by Du Bois in *The Philadelphia Negro*, pp. 228–30. In 1917 there were at least three black newspapers in Philadelphia, the *Tribune*, the *Courant*, and the *Public Journal*. The *Christian Recorder*, a publication of the A.M.E. Church, also came out of Philadelphia. However, back issues survive only for the *Tribune* and the *Recorder*.

85. George Simpson, *The Negro in the Philadelphia Press* (Philadelphia, 1936). This doctoral dissertation analyzed the four major white dailies in the city in the period from 1908 to 1932, and found that most news items on blacks dealt with "Negro crime."

86. Incidents of racial violence were reported in the *Philadelphia Tribune* on the following dates: 25 July 1914, p. 1; 7 November 1914, p. 1; 2 January 1915, p. 1; 24 April 1915, p. 1; 8 January 1916, p. 1; 8 July 1916, p. 1; 26 March 1917, p. 1; 2 June 1917, p. 1.

87. *Philadelphia Tribune*, 28 July 1917, pp. 1 and 4; 4 August 1917, p. 4.

88. PHA, *Annual Report*, 1917, p. 7.

89. *Philadelphia Tribune*, 6 July 1918, p. 4.

90. *Philadelphia Inquirer*, 28 July 1918, p. 15; *Philadelphia Tribune*, 3 August 1918, p. 1.

91. Variants of the story appeared in the following Philadelphia newspapers on 29 July 1918: *Public Ledger, Record, Press, North American, Evening Bulletin, Inquirer*. See also Vincent P. Franklin, "The Philadelphia Race Riot of 1918," *PMHB* 99 (1975): 336–50.

92. Franklin, "The Philadelphia Race Riot," pp. 336–50.

93. *Philadelphia Tribune*, 12 October 1918, p. 1; 2 November 1918, p. 1; 25 January 1919, p. 1; 3 May 1919, p. 1; 2 August 1919, p. 1.

94. Ibid., 17 August 1918, p. 1; 28 September 1918, p. 1; 4 January 1919, p. 1; 29 March 1919, p. 1.

95. A sample of the ideas of the "Old Philadelphians" about the migrants may be found in the study of Sadie T. Mossell (Alexander). "The incident [the race riot of 1918] explains the attitude of the Negro public of Philadelphia toward the coming of the migrant. As in the case of the probation officer so in numerous other occurrences, the colored people of every class received harsh treatment at the hands of the white public. This was virtually unknown to the Philadelphia Negro, for the city had long possessed a relatively small population of Negroes of culture, education and

some financial means. They had always enjoyed the same social and educational facilities as the whites and courteous treatment from them. But, with the increase in population by a group of generally uneducated and untrained persons these privileges were withdrawn as has already been discussed. The old colored citizens of Philadelphia resented this, placed the blame at the migrant's door and stood aloof from him." See "The Standard of Living," p. 177. Miss Mossell was a sociologist, not a historian.

96. The *Philadelphia Tribune* began publishing in 1884, but back issues survive only from 6 January 1912 to the present. The first article extant on the migration is dated 24 February 1912, p. 4.

97. Two excellent summaries of the activities of the Armstrong Association may be found in the *Philadelphia Tribune*, 6 June 1914, p. 1; and 13 March 1920, p. 1.

98. *Philadelphia Tribune*, 6 January 1912, n.p.; 10 February 1912, p. 1; 8 May 1915, p. 2. The activities of the Philadelphia Association for the Protection of Colored Women were similar to those of the Southwest Young Women's Christian Association; see chapter 4.

99. *Philadelphia Tribune*, 19 August 1916, p. 1; 9 September 1916, p. 1; Charles Brooks, *The Official History of the First African Baptist Church of Philadelphia* (Philadelphia, 1922), pp. 41–43.

100. Mossell, "The Standard of Living," p. 177; *Philadelphia Tribune*, 5 April 1919, p. 5.

101. *Philadelphia Tribune*, 19 May 1917, n.p.

102. In the various surveys of the migrants who came to Philadelphia, many reported that improved educational opportunity was one of their major reasons for leaving the South. See Wright, *The Negro in Pennsylvania*, pp. 55–57; and "Negro Migration Study, 1924" in PHA Papers, TUUA.

Chapter 2. The Schooling of the Philadelphia Negro

1. Winthrop Jordan, *White Over Black: American Attitudes toward the Negro, 1550–1812* (New York, 1969), p. 133. Jordan's source of information was the *South Carolina Gazette* (Charleston), 18 July 1740.

2. Richard I. Shelling, "Benjamin Franklin and the Dr. Bray Associates," *PMHB* 63 (1939): 285–86; Nancy S. Hornick, "Anthony Benezet and the Africans' School: Toward a Theory of Full Equality," *PMHB* 99 (1975): 403–4.

3. Hornick, "Anthony Benezet and the Africans' School," pp. 404–16; Turner, *The Negro in Pennsylvania*, pp. 128–29.

4. Wesley, *Richard Allen: Apostle of Freedom*, pp. 96–97; George, *Segregated Sabbaths*, pp. 3–4; see also Margaret H. Bacon, *History of the Pennsylvania Society for Promoting the Abolition of Slavery; the Relief of Negroes Unlawfully Held in Bondage; and for Improving the Condition of the African Race* (Philadelphia, 1959), pp. 12–14.

5. The various record books of the committees of the PAS may be found in the PAS Papers at the Historical Society of Pennsylvania (Philadelphia).

6. Committee for Improving the Condition of the Free Blacks, Minutes, 1790–1802, PAS Papers, HSP.

7. Discussions and monthly reports on the schools available to blacks in Philadelphia may be found in the reports of the Committee on Education, 1790–1802, PAS Papers, HSP. These reports discuss the activities of the schools financed by the committee or Board of Education, and other schools for blacks in the city during this period.

8. Board of Education, 1819, quoted in Bacon, *History of the PAS,* pp. 16–17.

9. Many of these schools were discussed in the reports of the PAS Board of Education, 1797–1819. See also John K. Alexander, "Philadelphia's Other Half: Attitudes Toward Poverty and the Meaning of Poverty in Philadelphia, 1760–1800" (Ph.D. diss., University of Chicago, 1973), pp. 223–25; George, *Segregated Sabbaths,* pp. 76–77; Carter G. Woodson, *The Education of the Negro Prior to 1861* (1919; reprint ed., New York, 1968), pp. 144–45.

10. "Preamble of the Pennsylvania Augustine Society for the Education of People of Colour, 1818," reprinted in *A Documentary History of the Negro People in the United States from the Colonial Period to the Establishment of the NAACP,* ed. Herbert Aptheker (Secaucus, N.J., 1951), pp. 72–73; Henry Silcox, "A Comparative Study of School Desegregation, 1800–1881: The Boston and Philadelphia Experience" (Ed.D. diss., Temple University, 1972), pp. 51–52.

11. Silcox, "A Comparative Study of School Desegregation," pp. 52–86, describes the various private venture schools started by blacks. The 1850 survey by Benjamin C. Bacon (see n. 18) discussed both the public and private schools for blacks in the city. In this study, the public schooling of blacks is primarily discussed. Though some blacks did attend private and parochial schools, for the black community as a whole, public schooling was definitely the most important throughout the nineteenth and twentieth centuries.

12. James Wickersham, *A History of Education in Pennsylvania* (Lancaster, Pa., 1886), pp. 263–68.

13. Ibid.; see also Joseph J. McCadden, *Education in Pennsylvania, 1801–1835, and Its Debt to Roberts Vaux* (Philadelphia, 1937), pp. 19–21.

14. Quoted in Harry C. Silcox, "Delay and Neglect: Negro Public Education in Antebellum Philadelphia, 1800–1860," *PMHB* 97 (1973): 448.

15. Ibid., pp. 448–49.

16. Ibid., p. 449.

17. Ibid., pp. 450–56. Turner mistakenly gives the date of the opening of the Mary Street School as 1820; see *The Negro in Pennsylvania,* pp. 130–31.

18. Benjamin C. Bacon, *Statistics of the Colored People of Philadelphia* (Philadelphia, 1856), pp. 4–6.

19. Silcox, "Delay and Neglect," pp. 452–53.

20. Ibid., pp. 456–57.

21. Ibid., p. 458.

22. See chapter 1 and table 1.

23. Silcox, "Delay and Neglect," p. 462.

24. According to the Common School Laws of Pennsylvania of 1854, "the directors or controllers of the several districts of the State are hereby authorized and required to establish within their respective districts, separate schools for the tuition of negro and mullatto [sic] children whenever such schools can be so located as to accommodate twenty or more pupils; and whenever such separate schools shall be established, and kept open four months in any year, the directors or controllers shall not be compelled to admit such pupils into other schools in the district." See *The Common School Laws of Pennsylvania and Decisions of the Superintendent with Explanatory Instructions and Forms*, prepared by Henry C. Hickok (Harrisburg, Pa., 1857), p. 15.

25. Silcox, "Delay and Neglect," pp. 463–64.

26. Silcox, "A Comparative Study of School Desegregation," p. 55; Silcox, "Philadelphia Negro Educator: Jacob C. White, Jr.," *PMHB* 97 (1973): 75–98.

27. Franklin, *From Slavery to Freedom*, p. 342; Brown, *The Negro in Pennsylvania History*, p. 52.

28. Brown, *The Negro in Pennsylvania History*, pp. 52–53.

29. *Journal of the Senate of the Commonwealth of Pennsylvania for the Session at Harrisburg on the 4th day of January 1881* (Harrisburg, Pa., 1881), pp. 696, 927, 969, 1091, 1335, and 1382; Franklin, "The Persistence of School Segregation in the Urban North," pp. 52–53.

30. Brown, *The Negro in Pennsylvania History*, pp. 52–55.

31. William Issel, "Modernization in Philadelphia School Reform," p. 358; Charles Nash, *The History of Legislative and Administrative Changes Affecting the Philadelphia Public Schools, 1869–1921* (Philadelphia, 1943), pp. 15–19, 53–59.

32. For an examination of the administration of Edward Brooks in the Philadelphia public schools, see Nash, *The History of Legislative Changes*, pp. 39–40.

33. Ibid., p. 63; V. A. Ciampa, "Martin Grove Brumbaugh, Pioneering Superintendent of the Philadelphia Public Schools," *Pennsylvania History* 7 (1940): 31–41; "Dinner in Honor of Governor Brumbaugh," *School and Society* 1 (9 January 1915): 55–56.

34. Issel, "Modernization in Philadelphia School Reform," p. 380.

35. "Dinner in Honor of Governor Brumbaugh," p. 56; *Smulls Legislative Handbook and Manual of the State of Pennsylvania, 1915* (Harrisburg, Pa., 1915), p. 224.

36. For a discussion of the movement for "scientific management" of the public schools, see Raymond Callahan, *Education and the Cult of Efficiency: A Study of the Social Forces That Have Shaped the Administration of the Public Schools* (Chicago, 1962), pp. 19–41.

37. For a discussion of the "backwardness" of the Philadelphia public school system during this period, see Nash, *The History of Legislative Changes*, pp. 79–97.

38. Brumbaugh came to the superintendency in September 1906; thus most of the "Report of the Superintendent" for 1906 dealt with the final months of the tenure of his predecessor, Edward Brooks. The report for 1907, then, can be considered Brumbaugh's first full year's report as superintendent.

39. PBPE, *Annual Report, 1907* (Philadelphia, 1908), pp. 27–28. (Hereafter cited as: PBPE, *Annual Report, 1907*, "Report of the Superintendent.")

40. Ibid., pp. 39–42.

41. Ibid., p. 38.

42. Ibid., p. 32.

43. Ibid., p. 44.

44. Ibid., p. 42. This statement was probably not true for 1907, and was definitely incorrect for 1910. According to the Bureau of the Census, in 1910 in Negro population six to fourteen years of age, "New Orleans leads and Washington, D.C. comes next, while Philadelphia, New York, and St. Louis stand high in the list. In numbers in school, Washington stands first, New Orleans comes next, then Baltimore, Philadelphia, and New York." See U.S. Department of Commerce, Bureau of the Census, *Negro Population, 1790–1915*, p. 389.

45. Brumbaugh seems to have been well aware of the so-called "tipping-point phenomenon," which was rediscovered by educational researchers in the early 1960s; see, for example, U.S. Commission on Civil Rights, *Racial Isolation in the Public Schools*, vol. 1 (Washington, D.C., 1967), pp. 20–25. Quotation from PBPE, *Annual Report, 1907*, "Report of the Superintendent," pp. 42–43.

46. Ibid., p. 44.

47. PBPE, *Report of the Bureau of Compulsory Education, 1908* (Philadelphia, 1909), p. 13.

48. Oliver Cornman, "The Retardation of the Pupils of Five City School Systems," *Psychological Clinic* 1 (1907–8): 245–57. The five cities examined by Cornman were Philadelphia, Boston, New York, Camden (New Jersey), and Kansas City (Missouri).

49. Percentage of "retarded children in Philadelphia" given ibid., p. 251. The rates in the other four cities for June 1906 were: Boston, 51.0 percent; New York, 59.9 percent; Camden, 72.7 percent (September 1905); Kansas City, 77.6 percent. Cornman pointed out that the high rates of retardation in several of the cities were due to the fact that "pupils are

already over age on entering school," and "in some cities large numbers of foreign-born children are retarded on account of difficulty with the language." Ibid., p. 254.

50. See chapters 3 and 6.

51. PBPE, *Annual Report, 1908*, "Report of the Superintendent," p. 52.

52. Ibid., pp. 43–44.

53. The controversy over the separate eligibility list dominated the issue of separate schools in Philadelphia in the 1930s; see chapter 6. A description of the use of the separate lists and the process of appointing black teachers may be found in the *Philadelphia Tribune*, 24 February 1912, p. 1.

54. This account is based on an interview with a black teacher, Mary S. Beckett, who "founded" a black public school in Philadelphia in 1900. Ms. Beckett's account of the founding of the Meehan School is in Etta Williamson, "The History of the Separate Public Schools for Negroes in Pennsylvania" (M.A. thesis, Howard University, 1935), pp. 83–84.

55. The "creation" of separate black schools by the Board of Public Education was often reported in the *Philadelphia Tribune*; see, for example, 23 October 1920, p. 7; 11 December 1920, p. 1; 26 February 1921, p. 1.

56. In the annual reports of the Board of Public Education, the separate black schools were designated until 1926 by the word "colored" or by an asterisk next to the name of the school. Martha Washington School was designated a "colored" school beginning with the annual report for 1920; see p. 369. Marie S. Chase was listed as the principal.

57. Byron Phillips, "Retardation in the Elementary Schools of Philadelphia," *Psychological Clinic* 6 (1912–13): 82–83. There were no data presented to explain why he felt that supervision was an important factor in the reduction of "retardation."

58. Ibid., p. 109.

59. Ibid., p. 121.

60. For a detailed description of the conditions of southern black elementary education during this period, see W. E. B. Du Bois and A. G. Dill, *The Common School and the Negro American* (1911; reprint ed., New York, 1968).

61. Not many researchers were interested in discussing the practice of "demoting" children one or two grades when they came to northern public schools from the South, but Louise V. Kennedy, in her study *The Negro Peasant Turns Cityward* (1930; reprint ed., New York, 1971), pp. 192–200, examines this and several other educational changes wrought by the migration of southern blacks to the North.

62. Henry H. Goddard, "Four Hundred Feeble-Minded Children Classified by the Binet Method," *Pedagogical Seminary* 17 (1910): 396. Goddard mentioned that for the previous four years, he and his colleagues at the Vineland Institute had been using methods for classification of

children that "we picked up here and there. These are, perhaps we may say, mechanical methods or better, methods of motor control, or methods of testing the intelligence in other ways than by appealing directly to the intelligence and having the child answer questions." See p. 390.

63. Henry H. Goddard, "Two Thousand Normal Children Measured by the Binet Measuring Scale of Intelligence," *Pedagogical Seminary* 18 (1911): 232–39.

64. Ibid., p. 233.

65. Goddard made comparisons between "city and country students" in his testing of "two thousand normal children"; ibid., pp. 251–55.

66. The application of the new tests to immigrant children has been discussed in numerous books and articles; see, for example, Clarence Karier, "Testing in the Corporate Liberal State," in *Roots of Crisis: American Education in the Twentieth Century,* with Paul Violas and Joel Spring (Chicago, 1973), pp. 108–37; Robert A. Divine, *American Immigration Policy, 1925–1952* (New Haven, 1957), pp. 6–25.

67. Howard W. Odum, "Negro Children in the Public Schools of Philadelphia," *The Annals* 49 (September 1913): 186–208.

68. Rupert Vance, "Howard W. Odum," in *The International Encyclopedia of the Social Sciences,* 2d ed. (New York, 1968), 11: 270–73; Howard W. Odum, *The Social and Mental Traits of the Negro: Research into the Conditions of the Negro Race in Southern Towns* (New York, 1910).

69. Odum, "Negro Children in the Public Schools of Philadelphia," p. 186.

70. Ibid., p. 187.

71. Ibid., p. 190.

72. Ibid., pp. 193–94.

73. Ibid., p. 199. The study suggested by Odum came close to being carried out in the 1960s with the famous (or infamous) Coleman Report. See U.S. National Center for Educational Statistics, *Equality of Educational Opportunity,* by James Coleman et al. (Washington, D.C., 1966).

74. Odum, "Negro Children in the Public Schools of Philadelphia," p. 220. It would be easier to accept or refute many of these judgments had Odum included notes in this summary of his study.

75. The tests used were the Binet-Simon, the Thorndike A-T Association Test, the Ebbinghaus Sentence Completion Test, and Thorndike's Opposites Test. The application of the tests is discussed ibid., pp. 201–4. It should also be noted that Odum was testing Negro children in Philadelphia at the same time as, or a few months after, Henry Goddard had tested the two thousand "normal" white students. Both stated that the testings were carried out in the fall of 1910; see Odum, "Negro Children in the Public Schools of Philadelphia," p. 187, and Goddard, "Testing of Two Thousand," p. 233.

76. Odum, "Negro Children in the Public Schools of Philadelphia," p. 205.

77. Odum, *Social and Mental Traits of the Negro*, pp. 42–54.

78. Odum, "Negro Children in the Public Schools of Philadelphia," pp. 207–8.

79. There have been several studies of these so-called scientific experiments; see, for example, William Stanton, *The Leopard's Spots: Scientific Attitudes toward Race in America, 1815–1859* (Chicago, 1960); John Haller, *Outcasts of Evolution: Scientific Attitudes of Racial Inferiority, 1859–1900* (Urbana, Ill., 1971).

80. Ibid. See also George Frederickson, *The Black Image in the White Mind: The Debate on Afro-American Character and Destiny, 1817–1914* (New York, 1971); I. A. Newby, *Jim Crow's Defense: Anti-Negro Thought in America, 1900–1930* (Baton Rouge, La., 1965).

81. Byron Phillips, "The Binet Tests Applied to Colored Children," *Psychological Clinic* 8 (1914–15): 190–91.

82. Ibid., p. 196.

83. Odum, *Social and Mental Traits of the Negro*, pp. 38–39.

84. For a discussion of the attitudes and opinions behind mental testing, see Karier, "Testing in the Corporate Liberal State," pp. 108–35; Edgar B. Gumbert and Joel H. Spring, *The Superschool and Superstate: American Education in the Twentieth Century, 1918–1970* (New York, 1974), pp. 87–114.

85. Kennedy, *Negro Peasant Turns Cityward*, p. 198.

86. *Philadelphia Tribune*, 11 December 1943, p. 20. Brooks was writing a series of articles on his observations of education for blacks in Philadelphia for the previous twenty-five years.

87. See chapter 6.

88. It is very difficult to keep track of the number of separate black schools because there was no source that consistently presented their names and locations throughout the period under investigation. For example, in the annual reports of the Philadelphia Board of Public Education, the black schools were not designated after 1925. Thus, each time the number is referred to, the source of the information will be cited.

89. See chapters 3 and 6.

90. PBPE, *Annual Report, 1915*, "Report of the Bureau of Compulsory Education," Table 11, p. 46.

91. PBPE, *Annual Report, 1920*, "Report of the Bureau of Compulsory Education," p. 213.

92. See table 7.

93. See *Philadelphia Tribune*, 18 September 1926, p. 1; 16 October 1926, p. 14; 4 December 1926, p. 1; 10 May 1928, p. 1.

94. The Reynolds School did receive a central heating system in 1916; see PBPE, *Annual Report, 1916*, "Report of the Superintendent of Buildings," p. 250. However, major repairs on the school building did not take place until 1925; see PBPE, *Annual Report, 1925*, "Report of the Superintendent of Buildings," pp. 177–81.

95. For an excellent discussion of the conditions of Philadelphia public school buildings in the early twentieth century, see Nash, *The History of Legislative Changes*, pp. 79–103.

96. *Philadelphia Tribune*, 24 February 1912, p. 1. The delegation of black citizens included Rev. John L. Watkins, Dr. John Sinclair, I. H. Ringgold, Hudson Walters, Walter Sanford, and Dr. Nathan F. Mossell.

97. Ibid., 17 February 1912, p. 4.

98. Ibid., 24 February 1912, p. 1.

99. Ibid., 23 March 1912, p. 4.

100. Ibid., 4 May 1912, p. 4.

101. Ibid., 6 March 1915, Statements critical of the segregated school system are found in the *Philadelphia Tribune* on 8 June 1912, p. 4; 15 March 1913, n. p.; 19 April 1913, p. 4; and 19 July 1913, p. 4.

102. PBPE, *Annual Report, 1914*, "Report of the Superintendent," p. 34. Discussions of the introduction of vocational or industrial or manual education into the public schools are found in the reports of the superintendent for 1910–16.

103. PBPE, *Annual Report, 1916*, pp. 361–71.

104. Ibid., p. 362.

105. Armstrong Association of Philadelphia, *A Comparative Study of the Occupations and Wages of the Children of Working Age in Potter and Durham Schools in Philadelphia* (Philadelphia, 1913), HSP; idem, *Fifth Annual Report* (1914), p. 14, HSP; John T. Emlen, "Negro Children of Working Age in the Durham School," *Southern Workman* 47 (1913): 417–19.

106. Emlen, "Negro Children of Working Age," p. 418.

107. Ibid., pp. 418–19.

108. For a positive statement by the *Philadelphia Tribune* about the introduction of manual training into the schools, see 12 September 1914, p. 1.

109. W. E. B. Du Bois, "Education," *The Crisis* 3 (July 1915): 132–34.

110. *Philadelphia Tribune*, 24 July 1915, p. 1.

111. Ibid. The organizations that agreed to monitor the conditions for blacks in the public schools were the Armstrong Association of Philadelphia, the Philadelphia branch of the NAACP, the Professional Club, and the Emancipation Association.

112. For a discussion of the change in the industrial opportunities for blacks in Philadelphia during World War I, see chapter 1.

113. The reasons for the introduction of industrial education into American public schools are examined in Sol Cohen, "The Industrial Education Movement, 1906–1917," *American Quarterly* 20 (1968): 95–110. The immigrant child in the Philadelphia public schools is discussed in chapter 3.

Chapter 3. Politics and the Public Schools in the 1920s

1. For examinations of the general effects of the migration on the North, see Joseph A. Hill, "Recent Northward Migration of the Negro," *Monthly Labor Review* 18 (1924): 1–14; Reynolds Farley, "The Urbanization of Negroes in the United States," *Journal of Social History* 1 (1968): 241–58. For information on the migration to Philadelphia, see Mossell, "The Standard of Living of 100 Negro Migrant Families in Philadelphia"; William D. Fuller, "The Negro Migrant in Philadelphia" (unpublished report for the Philadelphia Housing Association, 1 June 1924), pp. 1–35; PHA Pamphlet Collection, TUUA; Clara A. Hardin, *The Negroes of Philadelphia: The Cultural Adjustment of a Minority Group* (Bryn Mawr, Pa., 1945), pp. 48–49.

2. Du Bois, *The Philadelphia Negro*, pp. 136–46; see also chapter 1.

3. The shifting occupational categories used by the federal census between 1890 and 1930 reflected the changing occupational characteristics of American workers. However, these aggregate data do provide a general indication of occupational trends for blacks in Philadelphia during the period.

4. Du Bois, *The Philadelphia Negro*, p. 109–10.

5. Dean Dutcher, *The Negro in Modern Industrial Society: An Analysis of Changes in the Occupations of Negro Workers, 1910–1920* (Lancaster, Pa., 1930), Tables 20 and 23, pp. 96, 97, 106; Hardin, *The Negroes of Philadelphia*, Table 2, p. 47; see also, Ernest E. Lewis, *The Mobility of the Negro* (New York, 1931) pp. 87–114.

6. Armstrong Association of Philadelphia, "Report of Negro Population and Industries of Philadelphia" (August 1927), MS Box 12, folder (f) 209, Philadelphia Urban League Papers (Urb I), TUUA.

7. Ibid., p. 3. See also Fuller, "The Negro Migrant in Philadelphia," pp. 77–82.

8. Bernard J. Newman, *Housing of the City Negro* (Philadelphia, n.d.), pp. 1–8. Most researchers agree that the pamphlet was published in 1915.

9. The Philadelphia Housing Association conducted surveys of various sections of the city each year. The annual reports for 1920, 1922, 1923, and 1924, entitled "Housing in Philadelphia," may be found at TUUA. Information on the survey of 1921 may be found in A. L. Manly, "Where Negroes Live in Philadelphia," *Opportunity* 1 (1923): 12.

10. Manly, "Where Negroes Live in Philadelphia," p. 13.

11. Ibid., pp. 14–15.

12. T. J. Woofter and Madge H. Priest, *Negro Housing in Philadelphia* (Philadelphia, 1927) (PHA). Some of the activities of the Interracial Commission are discussed in chapter 7.

13. Ibid., pp. 9–21.

14. For information on the activities of the Octavia Hill Association, see John F. Sutherland, "The Origins of Philadelphia's Octavia Hill Asso-

ciation: Social Reform in the 'Contented' City," *PMHB* 99 (1975): 20–44.

15. Woofter and Priest, *Negro Housing in Philadelphia*, pp. 5, 29–30. See also W. Wallace Weaver, *West Philadelphia: A Study of Natural Areas* (Philadelphia, 1930), pp. 138–43; *Philadelphia Tribune*, 26 January 1924, p. 1; 30 January 1926, p. 2.

16. Anna J. Thompson, "Survey of Crime Among Negroes in Philadelphia," *Opportunity* 4 (1926): 217–19, 251–54, 285–86. The survey was conducted under the sponsorship of the Armstrong Association of Philadelphia, and a typescript copy of the study may be found in the Philadelphia Urban League Papers, Box 8, f. 131, TUUA.

17. Many of the general studies of the Great Migration discuss the increase in crime that accompanied the movement; see, for example, Kennedy, *Negro Peasant Turns Cityward*, pp. 182–88.

18. *Final Report of the Pennsylvania State Temporary Commission of the Conditions of the Urban Colored Population* (Harrisburg, Pa., 1943), pp. 412–13, Lawrence Foster, director (mimeographed).

19. In the annual school censuses conducted by the Bureau of Compulsory Education of the Philadelphia Public Schools (1915–30), the number of immigrant children in the city was presented. The above percentages were derived from PBPE, "Reports of the Bureau of Compulsory Education, 1915–1930," in the *Annual Reports of the Philadelphia Board of Public Education, 1915–1930* (Philadelphia, n.d.). A complete set of these annual reports may be found at the Pedagogical Library of the Philadelphia Board of Public Education.

20. PBPE, *Annual Report, 1926*, "Report of the Department of Special Education," pp. 911–12.

21. For a discussion of immigrant children in the parochial schools during the 1920s, see Varbero, "Philadelphia's South Italians in the 1920s," pp. 255–75.

22. PBPE, *Annual Report, 1928*, "Report of the Bureau of Compulsory Education," pp. 480–81.

23. PBPE, *Annual Report, 1930*, "Report of the Bureau of Compulsory Education," Table 5, p. 315.

24. For a discussion of the number of black children in mixed and separate public schools during the 1920s, see W. A. Daniels, "Schools," in *Negro Problems in Cities*, ed. T. J. Woofter, Jr. (New York, 1928), pp. 177–79.

25. For biographical information on black civic leaders in Philadelphia between 1890 and 1930, see Charles White, *Who's Who in Philadelphia: Biographical Sketches of Thirty Prominent Colored Persons of Philadelphia* (Philadelphia, 1912); *Who's Who in Colored America: A Biographical Dictionary of Notable Living Persons of African Descent in America* (New York, 1927–1950); Clement Richardson, ed., *The National Cyclopedia of the Colored Race*, vol. 1 (Montgomery, Ala., 1919).

26. For information on Edward Henry, see *Philadelphia Tribune*, 7 April 1938, p. 1.

27. For information on the activities of Isadore Martin and the Philadelphia branch of the NAACP during the twenties, see NAACP Branch Correspondence, Philadelphia Branch, 1919–1930, Boxes G-186 and G-187, NAACP Collection, Library of Congress (hereafter cited as NAACP Correspondence: Philadelphia, 1919–1930).

28. Hardin, *The Negroes of Philadelphia*, p. 12. This may also be the belief of Miriam Ershkowitz and Joseph Zikmund, editors of *Black Politics in Philadelphia* (New York, 1973). This compilation of articles deals with the twentieth century, but there is no information provided on black politics in the city from 1913 to 1932.

29. Many of these young black lawyers were among the founders of the John Mercer Langston Bar Association, which later came to be an important black legal association; *Philadelphia Tribune*, 9 May 1925, p. 1; 19 April 1928, p. 1.

30. *North American* (Philadelphia), 29 January 1921, pp. 1 and 5. The *Philadelphia Record*, *Public Ledger* and other dailies reported on the event on the same date, but in none of the accounts was the incident involving Representative Asbury mentioned.

31. *Philadelphia Tribune*, 19 February 1921, p. 1; and 26 February, p. 1.

32. There was really no "technicality," but a difference of opinion on what areas of public life were to be subject to the equal rights law. The question was whether hotels and restaurants in the state should be included or not. Governor Brumbaugh wanted the bill to read "excluding hotels and restaurants." For a discussion of the "technicality," see *Journal of the Senate of the Commonwealth of Pennsylvania for the Session Begun at Harrisburgh on the Fifth Day of January, 1915* (Harrisburg, Pa., 1916), pp. 3218–20. For a report on the governer's veto of the measure, see *Philadelphia Tribune*, 3 July 1915, p. 4.

33. For reports on the Republican primary and the elections of 1920, see the *Tribune*, 21 February 1920, p. 1; 27 March 1920, p. 1; 3, 17 April 1920, p. 1; 1 January 1921, p. 1. For the introduction of the Asbury equal rights bill, see *Journal of the House of Representatives of the Commonwealth of Pennsylvania for the Session Begun at Harrisburg on the Fourth Day of January, 1921* (Harrisburg, Pa., 1921), H. B. No. 269, pp. 369, 1022. See also *Philadelphia Tribune*, 2 February 1921, p. 4.

34. *Philadelphia Tribune*, 26 March 1921, p. 1.

35. *Journal of the Senate of the Commonwealth of Pennsylvania for the Session Begun at Harrisburg on the Fourth Day of January, 1921*, Parts I and II (Harrisburg, Pa., 1921), pp. 901, 909, 918–19, 979–80. The bill was introduced into the senate on 30 March 1921, and Senator Barr launched his attack on 4 April 1921.

36. Ibid., pp. 1035–36, 1729; *Philadelphia Tribune*, 23 April 1921, p. 1; 7 May 1921, p. 1.

37. *Journal of the House of Representatives of the Commonwealth of Pennsylvania for the Session Begun at Harrisburg on the Second Day of January, 1923, Part I* (Harrisburg, Pa., 1923), House Bill No. 569, p. 831.

38. There was also an important difference between this bill and the earlier version (1921). The 1923 bill proposed to prohibit discrimination not only in hotels, restaurants and places of public entertainment, but also in education. This measure, however, died in committee.

39. *Philadelphia Tribune,* 15 March 1924, p. 1.

40. This was reported by Edgar W. Roster, a political columnist for the *Tribune,* on 15 May 1926, p. 1.

41. Ibid., 26 April 1924, p. 1; 3 May 1924, p. 1; 8 November 1924, p. 1.

42. A perusal of the *Journal of the House of Representatives of the Commonwealth of Pennsylvania* for the period 1925–1929 reveals that no equal rights bill was introduced.

43. For incidents of discrimination against blacks, see *Philadelphia Tribune,* 24 May 1924, p. 1; 27 December 1924, p. 4; 22 March 1924, p. 9; 5 April 1924, p. 1; 4 August 1927.

44. See Charlene H. Conyers, "A History of the Cheyney State Teachers College, 1837–1951" (Ed. D. diss., New York University, 1960), especially pp. 229–70.

45. Ibid. See also Cheyney Training School for Teachers, *Annual Report, 1917* (Cheyney, Pa., 1917), pp. 15–17 (HSP).

46. Conyers, "A History of Cheyney," pp. 268–74.

47. *Philadelphia Tribune,* 30 October 1920, p. 1.

48. Leslie P. Hill, "The Cheyney Training School for Teachers," *The Crisis* 26 (April 1923): 252–54.

49. Ibid. It is surprising that this entire controversy was not discussed by Conyers in her dissertation on Cheyney State College.

50. G. Edward Dickerson and William Lloyd Imes, "The Cheyney Training School," *The Crisis* 26 (May 1923): 18–21. This statement was endorsed by the Philadelphia branch of the NAACP; see p. 21.

51. W. E. B. Du Bois, "The Tragedy of 'Jim Crow,'" *The Crisis* 26 (August 1923): 169–72.

52. *Journal of the Senate of the Commonwealth of Pennsylvania for the Session Begun in Harrisburg on the Sixth Day of January, 1925* (Harrisburg, Pa., 1926), pp. 312, 383, 418, 456–57, 1272. This bill probably passed the senate on 18 March 1925. The legislative journal does not give the correct date of passage.

53. *Journal of the House of Representatives of the Commonwealth of Pennsylvania for the Session Begun in Harrisburg on the Sixth Day of January, 1925* (Harrisburg, Pa., n.d.), pp. 2428, 2935, 2953, 3017, and 3164. The measure was tabled on 13 April 1925, see p. 3413. For opposition to the Cheyney bill, see *Philadelphia Tribune,* 28 February 1925, p. 1; 7 March 1925, p. 1; 28 March 1925, p. 4; 4 April 1925, p. 1; 18 April 1925, p. 1.

54. William L. Imes, Chairman of NAACP Committee on Schools, to William Dick, secretary of the PBPE, 12 June 1922; copies of letter and protest in Minutes of the PBPE Meeting, 13 June 1922, Kennedy Center, PBPE (hereafter cited as) KC.

55. For information on the conference of 5 July 1922, see Philadelphia NAACP Committee on Public Schools to the Members of the PBPE, 5 June 1924, in Minutes of the PBPE Meeting, 10 June 1924, KC.

56. The creation of the E. M. Stanton School as a separate school is mentioned in the *Philadelphia Tribune*, 23 October 1920, p. 7.

57. William L. Imes to the PBPE, 13 December 1922, in the Minutes of the PBPE Meeting, 18 December 1922, KC.

58. PBPE, *Annual Report, 1926*, "Report of the Superintendent of Buildings," p. 177.

59. Notice of the meeting of 12 May 1923 may be found in NAACP Correspondence: Philadelphia, 1923, Box G-186.

60. For general information on the NAACP convention of 1924, see W. E. B. Du Bois, "In Philadelphia," *The Crisis* 28 (August 1924): 151.

61. For a review of the various sessions of the convention, see *Philadelphia Tribune*, 14 June 1924, p. 1; 21 June 1924, p. 1; 28 June 1924, pp. 1, 4; 5 July 1924, p. 1.

62. Ibid., 13 September 1924, p. 5.

63. Ibid., 31 January 1925, p. 1.

64. Ibid., 14 February 1925, p. 1; 21 February 1925, pp. 4, 9.

65. William L. Imes to the members of the PBPE, 14 February 1925, in the Minutes of the PBPE Meeting, 10 March 1925, KC.

66. PBPE, *Annual Report, 1921*, "Report of the Superintendent of Schools," p. 36.

67. Notice of the change of policy appeared in the *Tribune* on 15 November 1924, p. 15.

68. The "teacher surplus" in the city during the second half of the decade is noted in PBPE, *Annual Report, 1926*, pp. 257–76; *Annual Report, 1927*, pp. 285–86; *Annual Report, 1928*, pp. 11, 288–90; *Annual Report, 1929*, pp. 8–13.

69. *Philadelphia Tribune*, 6 June 1925, p. 1. The PATCC was formed in Philadelphia in 1915. The president in 1925 was George Lyle, a black principal in Philadelphia.

70. Ibid., 4 July 1925, p. 4.

71. Ibid., 12 September 1925, p. 1.

72. Ibid.

73. Ibid., 19 September 1925, p. 1.

74. Ibid.

75. NAACP Correspondence: Philadelphia, Julian St. George White to Robert Bagnall, 30 September 1925, Box G-186.

76. *Philadelphia Tribune*, 19 September 1925, p. 1; 10 October 1925, p. 1.

77. Ibid., 19 September 1925, p. 1.

78. Ibid., 9 January 1926, p. 1.

79. Ibid., 12 April 1924, p. 4; 19 April 1924, p. 1. The editors of the *Tribune* had been calling for the appointment of some black person to the school board from a much earlier date; see, for example, 21 August 1915, p. 4.

80. Ibid., 30 January 1926, p. 2.

81. Julian St. George White, executive secretary of the Philadelphia NAACP, to the members of the PBPE, 6 February 1926, in Minutes of the PBPE Meeting, 9 February 1926, KC.

82. *Philadelphia Tribune*, 27 February 1926, p. 1; 3 April 1926, p. 1.

83. Quoted in *Philadelphia Tribune*, 22 May 1926, p. 1.

84. Ibid., 17 April 1926, p. 1.

85. The funds were to be kept on deposit in the Citizens and Southern Bank in South Philadelphia, founded by Major R. R. Wright, Sr.

86. Ibid., 12 June 1926, p. 1.

87. Ibid., 9 October 1926, p. 4.

88. Ibid., 16 October 1926, p. 1.

89. Ibid., 23 October 1926, pp. 1, 4.

90. Ibid., 11 December 1926, p. 1; 18 December 1926, p. 1.

91. Ibid., 1 January 1927, p. 1; 15 January 1927, p. 1; 29 January 1927, p. 16.

92. The number of separate schools in the city between 1925 and 1927 evidently fluctuated between twelve and fourteen. See, for example, *Philadelphia Tribune*, 4 December 1926, p. 1, which lists fourteen; and Pennsylvania Department of Public Welfare, *Negro Survey of Pennsylvania*, p. 58, which noted that there were twelve separate schools in the city.

93. It is difficult to state the number of rallies that were held because all of them were not necessarily reported in the *Tribune*, and some were sponsored by other groups or individuals, who then turned the contributions over to the Defense Fund Committee. A partial list of places and dates of these rallies may be found in the *Tribune* of 19 February 1927, p. 1.

94. Ibid., 20 October 1927, p. 16.

95. Ibid., 10 November 1927, p. 1. A copy of the letter sent to the local NAACP is reprinted in the newspaper.

96. Ibid., 11 July 1929, p. 16.

97. NAACP Correspondence: Philadelphia, Isadore Martin to Walter White, 25 July 1929, Box G-187.

98. The membership of the Philadelphia NAACP was greatest during the years of its involvement in the school issue, and plummeted after it was no longer as active; see NAACP Correspondence: Philadelphia, 1930, William Pickens to Herbert Millen, President of the Philadelphia branch, 14 October 1930, Box G-187. It has been suggested that the reason the local NAACP did not support issues that concerned the "black masses" was that the organization was dominated by middle-class blacks who were not

overly concerned about "race" issues; see H. Viscount Nelson, "The Philadelphia NAACP: Race Versus Class Consciousness During the Thirties," *Journal of Black Studies* 5 (1975): 255–76.

99. The number attending the rallies varied throughout the year and a half, but reports estimated attendance at from 200 to 2,000 per rally.

100. The precarious economic condition of blacks in Philadelphia during the 1920s also helps to account for the length of time it took the Defense Fund Committee to raise the money.

101. There were several articles in the *Tribune* during the twenties on the political and economic advances that were being made by blacks in Chicago; see, for example, 29 November 1924, p. 4; 3 January 1925, p. 1; 5 March 1927, p. 1.

Chapter 4. Community Education in Black Philadelphia

1. Most sources on the origin of the Free African Society have noted the fact that the organization consciously transcended religious and other differences among blacks in order to work for the improvement of the entire free black community. See, for example, Wesley, *Richard Allen: Apostle of Freedom*, pp. 60–61; George, *Segregated Sabbaths*, pp. 51–53.

2. For a discussion of the activities of the PAS Committee to Visit the Coloured People, see chapter 1. There were whites involved in many of the efforts to inform black Philadelphians about important social and moral issues throughout the period from 1900 to 1930. However, the focus of this chapter is on how the black community educated itself; thus, the predominantly black social organizations are the ones primarily under examination.

3. Dorothy Porter, "The Organized Educational Activities of Negro Literary Societies, 1828–1846," *JNE* 5 (1936): 555–74.

4. Ibid., pp. 557–64. The papers of these and several other nineteenth-century social organizations in Philadelphia may be found in the Leon Gardiner Collection at the HSP.

5. Du Bois, *The Philadelphia Negro*, pp. 221–34. Du Bois was not overly impressed with the community service activities of the black social organizations and did not describe them in detail.

6. The rise of the Negro press is discussed in I. Garland Penn, *The Afro-American Press and Its Editors* (1891; reprint ed., New York, 1969), pp. 25–31.

7. Porter, "The Organized Educational Activities," pp. 557–64; James Spady, "The Afro-American Historical Society: The Nucleus of Black Bibliophiles, 1897–1923," *Negro History Bulletin* 37 (1974): 254–55.

8. Minutes of the American Negro Historical Society, 25 October 1897, MSS Box 10G, Leon Gardiner Collection, HSP.

9. Ibid., 28 December 1897; 3 January 1898.

10. The public lectures offered by the American Negro Historical Society were often publicized in the *Philadelphia Tribune*; see 12 February 1912, n.p.; 15 February 1913, p. 2; 8 March 1913, p. 1; 21 January 1914,

p. 5; 8 August 1914, p. 4; 24 July 1920, p. 1; 31 July 1920, p. 1; 7 August 1920, p. 1.

11. *The Philadelphia Colored Directory—A Handbook of the Religious, Social, Political, Professional, Business and Other Activities of Negroes in Philadelphia, 1908*, comp. R. R. Wright and Ernest Smith (Philadelphia, 1908), pp. 28–50; *The Philadelphia Colored Directory, 1910*, pp. 20–35; *The Philadelphia Colored Directory, 1913*, pp. 18–23 (HSP).

12. See, for example, *The Philadelphia Colored Directory, 1908*, p. 43.

13. See, *The Philadelphia Colored Directory, 1910*, p. 34.

14. For discussions of these churches and literary societies, see the *Philadelphia Tribune*, 27 January 1912, p. 1; 17 July 1915, p. 1; 10 June 1916, p. 1; 31 January 1920, p. 9; 25 September 1920, p. 1.

15. For information on the lectures of the Pinn Memorial Literary Society, see the *Philadelphia Tribune*, 16 October 1920, n. p.; 7 March 1925, n.p.; 16 February 1928, p. 2. This society was sponsored by Pinn Memorial Baptist Church.

16. Ibid., 10 January 1920, p. 1; 1 and 8 January 1921, p. 1; 5 January 1924, p. 1; 10 January 1925, p. 1; 9 January 1926, p. 1.

17. Ibid., 3 March 1917, p. 1; 1 March 1919, p. 1; 12 February 1921, p. 1; 19 February 1921, p. 2; 27 February 1926, p. 15; 19 February 1927, p. 7.

18. Ibid., 20 February 1926, p. 1. The formation of the Philadelphia branch of the Association for the Study of Negro Life and History, is noted in the *Tribune*, 17 November 1927, p. 2. A description of Negro History Week activities may be found in the *Tribune* on the following dates: 12 January 1928, p. 5; 2 February 1928, p. 16; 23 January 1930, p. 13.

19. For coverage of the activities of the exposition, see the *Tribune* 12 July 1913, p. 1; 6 September 1913, p. 1; 20 September 1913, p. 1; 4 October 1913, p. 1; 18 October 1913, p. 1.

20. Black participation in the Sesquicentennial Celebration (1926), is reviewed in the *Tribune*, 13 February 1926, p. 9; 5 June 1926, p. 5; 12 June 1926, p. 15; 18 September 1926, p. 5. See also, W. E. B. Du Bois, "The Sesquicentennial Exposition," *The Crisis* 33 (December 1926): 65.

21. The first issue of *Black Opals* (Spring 1927) was entitled "Hail Negro Youth," and presented the poetry and prose of a number of young black writers in Philadelphia. One of the leading writers of the Harlem Renaissance was a Philadelphian, Jessie Fauset. Ms. Fauset served as a literary editor of *The Crisis* throughout the 1920s. *The Crisis* and *Opportunity* published many of the important black literary works of the decade.

22. *Philadelphia Tribune*, 12 February 1921, p. 1; 19 April 1924, p. 1; 24 May 1928, p. 3. See also Gerda Lerner, ed., *Black Women in White America—A Documentary History* (New York, 1972), pp. 440–58.

23. For a five-year review of the activities of the Colored Women's Clubs in Philadelphia, see the *Tribune*, 10 April 1915, p. 2; 8 May 1915, p. 2. For the activities of the City Federation of Colored Women's Clubs,

see ibid., 24 February 1917, p. 1; 5 July 1919, p. 1; 12 July 1919, p. 1; 6 March 1920, p. 5; 6 November 1920, p. 1.

24. Specific information on the educational activities of the various community centers was provide by the *Tribune*, 16 November 1912, p. 1; 8 March 1913, p. 1; 10 January 1925, p. 3; 16 May 1925, p. 9.

25. A good example of this situation was the Wissahickon Boys Club, which worked with young men and boys in the black community and had a black staff led by William T. Coleman, but was financed primarily by members of the white community. See the *Philadelphia Tribune*, 19 April 1919, p. 1; 2 April 1927, p. 7. See also Eugene Beaupre, "Negro Boy's Activities at Wissahickon (Boys Club)," *Southern Workman* 58 (1929): 405–14.

26. For the column on church news, see the *Tribune*, 6 January 1912, n.p. ("Churches and Their Pastors"), and 10 February 1912, p. 3; for the "Church Directory," see 15 February 1913, p. 2. They were edited by Rev. Robert H. Peerce.

27. Ibid., 7 June 1924, p. 9.

28. Ibid., see, for example, 27 January 1912, n.p.; 17 February 1912, p. 4; 16 March 1912, p. 4; 13 July 1912, p. 6; 10 August 1912, p. 1.

29. Jesse E. Moorland, "The Young Men's Christian Association among Negroes," *JNH* 9 (1924): 127–38; George Arthur, "The Young Men's Christian Association Movement among Negroes," *Opportunity* 1 (March 1923): 16–18; John Hope, "The Colored YMCA," *The Crisis* 31 (November 1925): 14–17.

30. Ibid.; Campbell C. Johnson, "Negro Youth and Educational Program of the Y.M.C.A.," *JNE* 9 (1940): 354–62.

31. Du Bois, *The Philadelphia Negro*, p. 232.

32. *Philadelphia Tribune*, 20 April 1912, p. 2.

33. Ibid., 24 January 1914, p. 1; see also 7 May 1921, p. 6.

34. The activities of the Christian Street YMCA were reported in the *Tribune* almost weekly throughout this period; however, detailed information may be found on the following dates: 29 November 1924, p. 1; 31 October 1925, p. 1; 7 November 1925, p. 1.

35. Lerner, *Black Women in White America*, pp. 458–97; Channing Tobias, "The Work of the Young Men's and Young Women's Christian Associations with Negro Youth," *The Annals* 140 (November 1928): 283–86; Marion Cuthbert, "Negro Youth and the Educational Program of the Y.W.C.A.," *JNE* 9 (1940): 363–71.

Most of the above sources note that the YWCA was more "interracial" than the YMCA, but give no reason for this. It was probably related to the fact that there was less competition, and thus less possibility of conflict between whites and blacks in the YWCA. There were advantages to this situation for black women in that they had access to greater funds through the YWCA's connection with the white officials. However, the disadvantage was the increased control of the white administration over their activities. In Philadelphia this situation caused several problems; see the *Philadelphia Tribune*, 18 October 1913, p. 4.

36. *The Philadelphia Colored Directory*, 1908, p. 47.

37. *Philadelphia Tribune*, 20 November 1920, p. 7.

38. Ibid., 6 November 1920, p. 3; 27 November 1920, p. 1.

39. The conflict with the Metropolitan branch of the YWCA in Philadelphia was covered in the *Tribune* on the following dates: 15 January 1921, p. 1; 22 January 1921, p. 1; 29 January 1921, p. 1; 1 October 1921, p. 1.

40. As was the case with the YMCA, the activities of the Southwest YWCA were reported on almost a weekly basis in the *Philadelphia Tribune*, but more detailed information may be found on: 21 May 1921, p. 8; 4 June 1921, p. 9; 17 May 1924, p. 1; and 25 July 1925, p. 4.

41. The *Tribune* devoted several columns of almost every issue to the activities of the fraternal organizations in the city; see, for example, 6 January 1912, n.p.; 27 January 1912, n.p. See also Du Bois, *The Philadelphia Negro*, pp. 221–26.

42. Quoted in William C. Hueston, "A Forward Step in Fraternalism," *The Crisis* 34 (July 1927): 149.

43. Scholarships for black students in Philadelphia, for example, were given out by the Fez Club of the Elks, formed in 1949 by Florence C. Franklin, and are still being offered; see "Twenty-fifth Anniversary of the Philadelphia Fez Club, October 20, 1974" (pamphlet in possession of the writer).

44. *Philadelphia Tribune*, 9 June 1927, p. 1; 16 June 1927, p. 1; 7 July 1927, p. 1.

45. Ibid., 25 April 1929, p. 7; 30 May 1929, p. 1; 5 September 1929, p. 1.

46. Ibid., 7 May 1921, p. 1; 28 May 1921, n.p.; 23 May 1925, p. 9.

47. Ibid., 12 April 1924, p. 9; 26 April 1924, p. 9; 19 July 1924, p. 5; 23 May 1925, p. 5; 30 May 1925, p. 1; 9 May 1929, p. 1; 16 May 1929, p. 16.

48. The Philadelphia Association for the Protection of Colored Women, *Report of the Fourth Year's Work, 1908* (Philadelphia, 1909), p. 1. The Historical Society of Pennsylvania has the annual reports for 1908, 1909, 1910, 1911, 1912, 1913, and 1915. It also possesses many of the fliers and bulletins of the organization.

49. *Philadelphia Tribune*, 6 January 1912, n.p.; 10 February 1912, p. 1; 8 May 1915, p. 2.

50. Among the persons who spoke for the Philadelphia Association for the Protection of Colored Women were Chris Perry, editor of the *Tribune* (*Philadelphia Tribune*, 12 April 1919); Ernest Tustin, Philadelphia director of public welfare (10 April 1920); John C. Asbury, representative in the Pennsylvania General Assembly (14 May 1921).

51. One can obtain some information on the activities of the Armstrong Association of Philadelphia from the annual reports, 1910–20, which may be found at the Historical Society of Pennsylvania.

52. Armstrong Association, *Fourth Annual Report, 1912* (Philadelphia, n.d.), passim; *Philadelphia Tribune*, 7 December 1912, p. 1.

53. *Philadelphia Tribune*, 16 January 1926, p. 1; 13 March 1926, p. 7; 18 September 1926, p. 9; 2 October 1926, p. 8; 1 January 1927, p. 1.

54. Ibid. Black and white social work trainees often served their apprenticeships with the Armstrong Association.

55. Ibid., 12 April 1928, p. 1. See also Weiss, *The National Urban League, 1910–1940*, pp. 176–202 passim.

56. For information on the rallies and membership drives of the Philadelphia NAACP, see NAACP Branch Correspondence, Philadelphia Branch, 1913–1930, Boxes G-186 and G-187, NAACP Collection, Library of Congress; and the *Philadelphia Tribune*, 1 February 1913, n.p.; 30 December 1916, n.p.; 3 May 1919, p. 1; 5 February 1921, p. 1.

57. *Philadelphia Tribune*, 15 March 1924, p. 7; 28 June 1924, p. 1; 23 August 1924, p. 13; 16 May 1925, p. 1; 20 February 1926, p. 16; 19 March 1927, p. 7; 31 May 1928, p. 2. See also chapter 3.

58. For examples of joint lectures and activities of the NAACP and other organizations in Philadelphia, see the *Tribune*, 1 November 1924, p. 9; 24 January 1925, p. 4; 7 February 1925, p. 5; 23 May 1925, p. 9; 13 March 1930, p. 2.

59. Ibid., 30 January 1915, p. 4; 13 May 1916, p. 1; 18 September 1920, n.p.; 13 November 1920, p. 10; for specific information on the activities of the "Colored Catholic Schools" in Philadelphia, see 16 March 1912, n.p.; 15 June 1912, p. 1; 28 September 1912, p. 1; 8 February 1913, n.p.; 24 January 1925, p. 2.

60. Ibid., 28 February 1920, p. 2; 19 March 1921, p. 9; 2 July 1921, p. 1; 2 February 1924; p. 7; 27 February 1926, p. 15; 2 February 1928, p. 12. See also Hardin, *Negroes of Philadelphia*, pp. 89–90.

61. *Philadelphia Tribune*, 10 January 1925, p. 6; 14 February 1925, p. 1; 15 January 1927, p. 9; 23 April 1927, p. 9; 2 February 1928, p. 12; 30 January 1930, p. 5.

62. On 24 April 1920, p. 5, the *Tribune* began a regular column entitled "School and Community News." A series on "Christianity and Modern Life" began on 23 August 1924, p. 12. A regular column on health problems began on 18 October 1924, p. 9; and black history series were initiated on that date and on 16 May 1925, p. 9. Extensive series on black education started on 22 August 1925, p. 4, and 2 October 1926, p. 16; for a comprehensive history of the *Tribune* to that date, see the fortieth anniversary issue, 29 November 1924.

63. For information on the hundreds of migrants who came to Philadelphia during the period from 1914 to 1924, see Migration Survey, box 21, PHA Papers, TUUA.

64. U.S. Works Progress Administration, Illinois, "Churches and Voluntary Associations in the Chicago Negro Community" (Chicago, 1940), p. 219 (mimeographed). For other discussions of race versus class conscious organizations, see William O. Brown, "The Nature of Race Consciousness," *Social Forces* 10 (October 1936): 90–97; Elizabeth Ferguson, "Race Consciousness Among American Negroes," *JNE* 7 (1938): 32–40; H.

Viscount Nelson, "Race and Class Consciousness of Philadelphia Negroes with Special Emphasis on the Years between 1927 and 1940" (Ph.D. diss., University of Pennsylvania, 1969); James P. Pitts, "The Study of Race Consciousness: Comments on New Directions," *American Journal of Sociology* 80 (1974): 665–87.

65. *Peoples Advocate*, 13 December 1879, quoted in Linda Marie Perkins, "Quaker Beneficence and Black Control: The Institute for Colored Youth, 1852–1903," in Franklin and Anderson, *New Perspectives on Black Educational History*, pp. 19–43, quotation at p. 31.

Chapter 5. Depression, New Deal, and the Black Community

1. U.S. Department of Labor, Bureau of Labor Statistics, *Bulletin No. 520*, "Social and Economic Character of Unemployment in Philadelphia, April, 1929," by J. Frederick Dewhurst and Ernest A. Tupper (Washington, D.C., 1930), pp. 1–2; Barbara R. Fox, "Unemployment Relief in Philadelphia, 1930–1932: A Study of the Depression's Impact on Voluntarism," *PMHB* 93 (1969): 86–89.

2. Dewhurst and Tupper, "Unemployment in Philadelphia, 1929," p. 1.

3. U.S. Department of Labor, Bureau of Labor Statistics, *Bulletin No. 555*, "Social and Economic Character of Unemployment in Philadelphia, April, 1930," by J. Frederick Dewhurst and Robert R. Nathan (Washington, D.C., 1932), pp. 1–2.

4. "Unemployment in Philadelphia, 1938," *Monthly Labor Review* 49 (1939): 838–40; G. Gordon Brown, *Law Administration and Negro-White Relations in Philadelphia* (Philadelphia, 1947), Table 7, p. 42. See also Gladys L. Palmer, *The Philadelphia Labor Market in 1944*, Research Report No. 8 (Philadelphia, 1945), pp. 28–29.

5. Pennsylvania State Emergency Relief Board, Department of Research and Statistics, "Unemployment in Philadelphia County, February 15, 1934," *Preliminary Results* (Harrisburg, Pa., 1934), Table 4, p. 6. The City and County of Philadelphia are coterminous.

6. Gladys L. Palmer, *Thirty Thousand in Search of Work, 1933* (Harrisburg, Pa., 1933), p. 26.

7. "Long Term Unemployment in Philadelphia," *Monthly Labor Review* 49 (1939): 1079–80. This article was based on the findings of Gladys L. Palmer and Janet H. Lewis, *The Long Term Unemployed in Philadelphia in 1936*, Report P-8, Works Progress Administration, National Research Project, Industrial Research Department, University of Pennsylvania (Philadelphia, 1939).

8. Fox, "Unemployment Relief in Philadelphia," pp. 92–95. See also "Forehanded Philadelphia," *The Survey* 66 (1931): 458–59.

9. Fox, "Unemployment Relief in Philadelphia," pp. 95–96; "How the Cities Stand," *The Survey* 68 (1932): 75.

10. Fox, "Unemployment Relief in Philadelphia," pp. 101–3.

11. Ibid., pp. 104–8; Ewan Clague, "When Relief Stops What Do They Eat?" *The Survey* (1932): 583–85. The statement of the Lloyd Committee upon dissolution was reprinted from the *Philadelphia Record* (20 June 1932) in Report of the Executive Director of the State Emergency Relief Board of Pennsylvania, *Unemployment Relief in Pennsylvania, September 1, 1932–October 31, 1933* (Harrisburg, Pa., 1933), pp. 13–14.

12. Report of the Executive Director of the State Emergency Relief Board, p. 14.

13. Ibid. For a discussion of the history of the enactment of state emergency relief programs in Pennsylvania, see pp. 1–16.

14. Report of the Administrator of the Federal Civil Works Administration of Pennsylvania, *Civil Works Administration Program in Pennsylvania, November 15, 1933–March 31, 1934* (Harrisburg, Pa., 1934), pp. 7–26.

15. Joseph H. Willits, "Some Impacts of the Depression upon the Negro in Philadelphia," *Opportunity* 11 (1933): 201–2.

16. Armstrong Association of Philadelphia, "Report of Negro Population and Industries of Philadelphia," August, 1927, MS, Box 12, f.209 Philadelphia Urban League Papers (Urb I) TUUA; see also chapter 3.

17. "Unemployment in Philadelphia, 1938," *Monthly Labor Review* 49 (1939): 840.

18. Joseph H. Willits, "Some Impacts of the Depression upon the Negro in Philadelphia," pp. 200–204. This article was based on a speech given at the White House Conference on the Economic Conditions of the Negro in 1933.

19. In the 1930 census, blacks listed under the occupations considered "transportation and communications" were usually "chauffeurs and truck and tractor drivers, garage laborers, road, street and steam railroad workers, longshoremen and stevedores." Ibid., p. 200.

20. Ibid.; see also Table 10.

21. Ibid., p. 201; see also Ewan Clague, "A Study of 8,722 Individuals Placed at Made Work," in *Ten Thousand Out of Work*, ed. Ewan Clague and Webster Powell (Philadelphia, 1933), pp. 3–91, passim.

22. Willits, "Some Impacts of the Depression upon the Negro in Philadelphia," pp. 203–4; Webster Powell, "A Study of Financial Resources in the Families of 1,439 Applicants for Made-Work," in Clague and Powell, *Ten Thousand Out of Work*, pp. 95–131 passim.

23. See, for example, George E. Simpson, "Social Changes in the Negro Population in Philadelphia Since 1908," *Opportunity* 14 (1936): 375–77; Hardin, *The Negroes of Philadelphia*, pp. 24–50.

24. See Blanche J. Paget, "The Plight of the Pennsylvania Negro," *Opportunity* 14 (1936): 309–11; Commonwealth of Pennsylvania, Department of Welfare, *Negro Survey of Pennsylvania*.

25. The literature on the New Deal is voluminous. This discussion is based primarily on William E. Leuchtenburg, *Franklin D. Roosevelt and the New Deal, 1932–1940* (New York, 1963), pp. 41–94; and Frank Freidel, *Franklin D. Roosevelt: Launching the New Deal* (Boston, 1973).

26. For discussions of blacks and the New Deal, see Raymond Wolters, *Negroes and the Great Depression: The Problem of Economic Recovery* (Westport, Conn., 1970); Leslie H. Fishel, "The Negro in the New Deal Era," reprinted in *The Negro in Depression and War: Prelude to Revolution, 1930–1945,* ed. Bernard Sternsher (Chicago, 1969), pp. 4–12.

27. Quoted from Priscilla F. Clement, "The Works Progress Administration in Pennsylvania, 1935 to 1940," *PMHB* 95 (1971): 244.

28. Ibid., pp. 244–47; Federal Writers' Project in Pennsylvania, *Philadelphia: A Guide to the Nation's Birthplace* (Philadelphia, 1937), p. 2.

29. U.S. Works Progress Administration, Pennsylvania, *Analytical Report of Older Boy Delinquency, 1934–37* (Harrisburg, Pa., 1938), pp. 5–11.

30. Correspondence on and early typescript drafts of sections of the study on the history of the Negro in Philadelphia may be found in the Philadelphia Housing Association Papers, Box 63, folders 436–37, Box 8, f.140, TUUA. *Philadelphia Tribune,* 28 March 1934, p. 1; 4 January 1938; p. 20.

31. The *Philadelphia Tribune,* a Republican newspaper, was highly critical of the New Deal. See, for example, 31 August 1933, p. 4; 28 September 1933, p. 5; 11 January 1934, p. 1; *The Philadelphia Independent,* began publishing in 1932 and supported the Democratic Party, but was at times critical of the New Deal. See, for example, 2 June 1935, p. 10; 22 December 1935, p. 3.

32. Federal Works Project Administration for Pennsylvania, *Philadelphia Real Property Survey, 1934–37* (Philadelphia, 1934–37); Federal Works Projects Administration, *Philadelphia Real Property Inventory, 1939–40* (Philadelphia, 1940).

33. For a lengthy discussion of New Deal housing programs in the city, see John F. Baumann, "Black Slums/Black Projects: The New Deal and Negro Housing in Philadelphia," *Pennsylvania History* 14 (1974): 311–38.

34. Ibid.; for *Tribune* series on housing conditions, see 28 February 1935, p. 1 for part 1, and 7 March 1935, p. 1 for part 2. For a full-page discussion of the conditions in slum areas, see 14 March 1935, p. 2. For National Negro Congress activities, see 23 April 1936, p. 2; 28 May 1936, p. 1; and especially, 22 October 1936, p. 1.

35. For reports on collapsed houses, see *Philadelphia Tribune,* 21 March 1935, p. 3; 24 December 1936, pp. 1, 4, and 7; and 31 December 1936, p. 1. The federally supported housing projects are discussed in Baumann, "Black Slums/Black Projects," pp. 333–38.

36. *Philadelphia Tribune,* 31 August 1933, p. 3, "Codes Working Hardships on Negro Labor"; 21 September 1933, p. 2, "Negroes Suffer under NRA as Employers Favor Whites."

37. Ibid., 1 February 1934, p. 1; 8 February 1934, p. 1.

38. Ibid., 1 March 1934, p. 1, Editorial: "Colored Citizens Barred by Board of Education on CWA Projects." See also 2 March 1933, p. 14; 6 July 1933, p. 4. Some educational programs of the New Deal were run

by the Board of Public Education, see Melvin R. Maskin, "Black Education and the New Deal: The Urban Experience" (Ph.D. diss., New York University, 1973), pp. 287–311; see also chapter 8.

39. *Philadelphia Tribune*, 18 February 1932, pp. 1, 16; 14 December 1939, p. 4, Editorial: "White Only: Business Must Change and Demand Merit Only"; 21 December 1939, p. 2; 4 January 1940, p. 1.

40. See chapter 8.

41. Quoted in Council for Democracy, *The Negro and Defense, A Test of Democracy* (New York, 1941), p. 1.

42. *Philadelphia Tribune*, 14 March 1940, p. 2, "Jim Crow in Factories Charged . . ."; 21 March 1940, p. 4; Editorial: "Truth—Prejudice Real Reason for Negro Unemployment"; 25 July 1940, p. 10, "WPA Ruling Bans Defense Program Bias."

43. Job discrimination in national defense industries, was discussed at the Hampton Institute Conference on the Participation of the Negro in National Defense (25–26 November 1940), *Findings and Principal Addresses* (Hampton, Va., 1940); see also *Philadelphia Tribune*, 21 November 1940, p. 1.

44. *Philadelphia Tribune*, 14 December 1939, p. 4; 14 March 1940, p. 2; 29 August 1940, p. 4.

45. Ibid., 30 May 1940, p. 4, Editorial: "Government Employs Aliens While Loyal Americans Starve"; 21 November 1940, p. 4.

46. Ibid., 1 November 1941, p. 1, Editorial: "Colored Employees Kept in Worst Paid Positions." This story examined job discrimination at the post offices and navy yards in Philadelphia.

47. See the Hampton Institute Conference on the Participation of the Negro in National Defense, *Findings*, pp. 12–18. *Philadelphia Tribune*, 21 November 1940, p. 1; 5 December 1940, p. 5.

48. *Philadelphia Tribune*, 12 December 1940, p. 1; 2 January 1941, p. 1.

49. Ibid., 28 December 1939, p. 10; 4 January 1940, p. 4; Editorial: "Skilled Workers Needed at Navy Yard"; 19 December 1940, p. 4, Editorial: "Dearth of Skilled Workers 'Other Side' of Unemployment"; p. 20, "Urge Qualified Negroes to Apply for Defense Jobs in Philly Area."

50. Ibid., 14 August 1941, p. 3, "Local Boy Gets Job Following Defense Training"; 29 November 1941, p. 4.

51. Ibid.; see also 13 March 1941, p. 20; chapter 8.

52. Herbert Garfinkel, *When Negroes March: The March on Washington Movement in the Organizational Politics of the FEPC* (Glencoe, Ill., 1959), p. 7; *Philadelphia Tribune*, 26 December 1940, p. 1; 19 June 1941, p. 1; 3 July 1941, p. 1.

53. *Philadelphia Tribune*, 15 May 1941, p. 1; 17 July 1941, p. 8; see also, G. James Fleming, "The Administration of Fair Employment Practice Programs" (Ph.D. diss., University of Pennsylvania, 1948), pp. 6–29. Fleming was the director of the FEPC Office in Philadelphia in the 1940s. Black Philadelphia in the 1940s is discussed in chapter 7.

54. The PTC strike of 1944 is discussed in detail in chapter 7.

55. *Philadelphia Tribune,* 27 March 1930, p. 1 (Allen A.M.E. Church); 23 February 1933, p. 1 (Mother Bethel A.M.E. Church). See also 18 December 1930, p. 1.

56. Ibid., 23 February 1933, p. 3; 30 March 1933, p. 2; 25 May 1933, p. 16.

57. Ibid., 4 May 1933, p. 3; 17 May 1934, p. 12.

58. Ibid., 25 December 1930, p. 2; 1 January 1931, p. 1; 30 December 1937, p. 3.

59. Ibid., 11 June 1931, p. 9; 5 November 1931, p. 1; 12 November 1931, p. 1.

60. *Philadelphia Tribune,* 17 November 1932, p. 1; 12 January 1933, p. 3. Accounts of the merger of the two Negro branches of the YWCA, see 18 May 1933, p. 3. See also Nelson, "Race and Class Consciousness," pp. 285–301.

61. *Philadelphia Tribune,* 2 June 1932, p. 3; 9 March 1933, p. 2; 23 June 1933, p. 3; 25 April 1935, p. 3; 9 May 1935, p. 2.

62. Ibid., 2 July 1931, p. 1.

63. Ibid., 23 June 1933, p. 1.

64. Summaries of the events surrounding the Douglass Hospital's attempts to raise funds are in the *Tribune,* 8 February 1934, p. 1; and 24 March 1938, p. 20. The Department of Public Welfare visited Douglass Hospital to make an inspection and issued a report saying that the hospital facilities were in "terrible shape." Governor Pinchot agreed and held up the hospital's appropriation.

65. In the correspondence between the Philadelphia branch of the NAACP and the national office for the period from 1929 to 1939, there was a preoccupation with the problem of reaching the membership quotas set by the national office; see NAACP Branch Correspondence, Philadelphia Branch, 1929–1939, Box G-187. The financial plight of black welfare organizations was also discussed in the *Philadelphia Tribune;* see 9 October 1931, p. 9; 6 December 1934, p. 14; 7 December 1939, p. 2.

66. For accounts of the "Crusade for Jobs" and "Don't Buy Where You Can't Work" campaigns, see the *Tribune,* 13 February 1930, p. 1; 13 February 1930, p. 1; 20 February 1930, p. 16; 20 March 1930, p. 1; 14 August 1930, p. 1; 9 October 1930, p. 1. See also Ralph J. Bunche, "A Direct-Action Approach to Jobs," reprinted in *Black Protest Thought in the Twentieth Century,* ed. A. Meier, E. Rudwick, and F. Broderick, 2d ed. (New York, 1971), pp. 122–31.

67. *Philadelphia Tribune,* 17 April 1930, p. 1; 1 May 1930, pp. 10, 16; 30 October 1930, p. 9; 11 June 1931, p. 1; 31 January 1935, p. 2; 27 February 1936, p. 1; 19 March 1936, p. 20; 11 June 1936, p. 2. For a discussion of the support of the *Philadelphia Independent* for black self-help campaigns, see Nelson, "Race and Class Consciousness," pp. 87–91, 93–96.

68. For a discussion of the activities of the Armstrong Association, see Nelson, "Race and Class Consciousness," pp. 84–86; *Philadelphia Tribune*, 11 June 1930, p. 9; 13 July 1933, p. 4; 31 January 1935, p. 2; 28 May 1936, p. 1.

69. *Philadelphia Tribune*, 27 February 1936, p. 3; 19 March 1936, p. 4; 6 April 1936, p. 4.

70. Ibid. The first black librarian, Mrs. Ruby Boyd, was hired by the Free Library of Philadelphia in 1944. Ibid., 14 October 1944, p. 1.

71. Ibid., 24 October 1935, p. 12; 14 November 1935, p. 1; 21 November 1935, p. 2.

72. Ibid., 5 December 1935, p. 1; 12 December 1935, p. 1.

73. Ibid., 24 December 1936, p. 18; 25 February 1937, p. 20.

74. The activities of the Philadelphia branch of the National Negro Congress are noted in the *Tribune*, 1 October 1936, p. 4; 22 October 1936, p. 1; 29 October 1936, p. 1; 23 June 1938, p. 1; 18 October 1941, p. 2. See also Nelson, "Race and Class Consciousness," pp. 301–9.

75. For accounts of the boycotts of the civic leagues in Philadelphia, see the *Tribune*, 27 February 1936, p. 1; 1 July 1937, p. 1; 5 August 1937, p. 2; see also 12 August 1937, p. 3.

76. Ibid., 19 August 1937, p. 1. For statement of Magistrate Vincent Girard, see the *Tribune*, 26 August 1937, p. 1. For an account of the conviction of the members of the league, see 23 September 1937, p. 11.

77. Ibid., 25 August 1938, p. 3; 1 September 1938, p. 1; 13 October 1938, p. 17; 20 October 1938, p. 2; See also chapter 8.

78. The campaigns that were launched to improve the well-being of black children in the Philadelphia public schools are discussed in chapter 6.

79. See, for example, Ershkowitz and Zikmund, *Black Politics in Philadelphia* pp. 55–59; James E. Miller, "The Negro in Pennsylvania Politics, with Special Emphasis on Philadelphia Since 1932" (Ph.D. diss., University of Pennsylvania, 1945), pp. 209–20; see also John L. Shover, "Ethnicity and Religion in Philadelphia Politics, 1924–1940," *American Quarterly* 25 (1973): 508–11.

80. For a discussion of the Republican city government in Philadelphia during the period from 1930 to 1951, see James Reichley, *The Art of Government: Reform and Organization Politics in Philadelphia* (New York, 1959), especially pp. 5–21.

81. *Philadelphia Tribune*, 2 October 1930, p. 1; 9 October 1930, p. 1; 30 October 1930, p. 1.

82. Ibid., 6 November 1930, p. 1; see also Shover, "Ethnicity and Religion in Philadelphia Politics," Table 1, p. 505.

83. *The Pennsylvania Manual, 1931* (Harrisburg, Pa., 1931), pp. 528–29. This manual is compiled every two years and provides a great deal of information on elections throughout the state and on the various elected officials.

84. *Philadelphia Tribune*, 19 February 1931, p. 1; 25 June 1931, p. 1.

85. Ibid., 12 March 1931, p. 1; 12 May 1931, p. 1; 28 May 1931, p. 1.

86. Ibid., 2 July 1931, p. 1.

87. Ibid., 8 February 1934, p. 4, Editorial: "Pinchot Must Not Go to the Senate"; 10 May 1934, p. 1, "Gov. Pinchot Hit as Foe of Negroes" by Addie Dickerson and E. W. Rhodes. Pinchot was also rapped by Rhodes at this time for his opposition to the allotting of state funds to Frederick Douglass Hospital.

88. Shover, "Ethnicity and Religion in Philadelphia Politics," Table 1, p. 505.

89. Ibid.; *Philadelphia Tribune*, 8 November 1934, p. 1.

90. *Pennsylvania Manual, 1935–1936*, pp. 447–48. The black representatives elected in 1934 were: Marshall Shepard (D), 18th District, Philadelphia; Samuel Hart (R), 6th District, Philadelphia; Walker K. Jackson (R), 7th District, Philadelphia; Hobson Reynolds (R), 21st District, Philadelphia; and Homer S. Brown (R), 1st District, Allegheny County. For an excellent brief discussion of the competition for black votes in 1934 and the willingness of the two parties to acquiesce to black demands, see E. Washington Rhodes, "Pennsylvania Politics As of the Year 1934," *The Crisis* 41 (July 1934): 212.

91. These appointments and elections were covered in the *Tribune* on the following dates: 13 December 1934, p. 1; 14 February 1935, p. 1; 7 February 1935, p. 1; 7 November 1935, p. 1. John Cooper was the last black to serve on the City Council, ending his term in 1919.

92. For the passage of the equal rights bill, see ibid., 6 June 1935, p. 1; and 13 June 1935, p. 1. For the passage of the Hart National Guard bill, see 28 March 1935, p. 1; 6 June 1935, p. 1. The equal rights law is reprinted in Hardin, *The Negroes of Philadelphia*, pp. 152–53.

93. These events are discussed in detail in chapter 6.

94. *Pennsylvania Manual, 1937*, pp. 195–203. The black representatives elected in 1936 were: Marshall Shepard (D), 18th District, Philadelphia; John Brigerman (D), 21st District, Philadelphia; Edwin Thompson (D), 13th District, Philadelphia; Samuel D. Holmes (D), 6th District, Philadelphia; and Homer S. Brown (D), 1st District, Allegheny County.

95. Shover, "Ethnicity and Religion in Philadelphia Politics," Table 1, p. 505; Miller, "The Negro in Pennsylvania Politics," pp. 209–20.

96. *Philadelphia Tribune*, 4 February 1937, p. 1; 18 March 1937, p. 1; 1 April 1937, p. 1; 27 May 1937, p. ; 8 July 1937, p. 2.

97. Ibid., 30 December 1937, p. 1.

98. The *Philadelphia Tribune* gave its complete support to the candidacy of Edward Henry, and detailed accounts of his campaign may be found on the following dates: 7 April 1938, p. 1; 19 May 1938, p. 1; 11 August 1938, p. 1; 6 October 1938, p. 1; 3 November 1938, p. 1; 10 November 1938, p. 1. See also G. W. McKinney, "The Negro in Pennsylvania Politics," *Opportunity* 17 (1939): 50–51.

99. *Pennsylvania Manual, 1939*, pp. 167–72. The black representatives elected in 1938 were: William A. Allmond (D), 7th District, Philadelphia; Crystal Bird Fauset (D), 18th District, Philadelphia; Hobson Reynolds (D), 21st District, Philadelphia; E. Washington Rhodes (R), 6th District,

Philadelphia; Edwin Thompson (D), 13th District, Philadelphia; and Homer S. Brown (D), 1st District, Allegheny County.

100. For a brief biographical sketch of Representative Crystal Bird Fauset, see *The Pennsylvania Manual, 1939*, p. 761.

101. *The Pennsylvania Manual, 1941*, pp. 167–73. The black Representatives elected in 1940 were: William A. Allmond (D), 7th District, Philadelphia; Ralph T. Jefferson (D), 21st District, Philadelphia; Marshall Shepard (D), 18th District, Philadelphia; Edwin Thompson (D), 13th District, Philadelphia; Edward C. Young (D), 6th District, Philadelphia; and Homer S. Brown (D), 1st District, Allegheny County.

102. The political powerlessness of the black community following the defection to the Democratic Party is briefly examined in the Epilogue.

Chapter 6. The Campaign to End Public School Segregation

1. W. E. B. Du Bois, ed., *The Negro Common School* (Atlanta, Ga. 1901).

2. The U.S. Bureau of Education published several investigations of black education in the period before 1903; see, for example, J. L. M. Curry, "The Negro Since 1860 and the Education of the Negro," in the *Report of the Commissioner of Education, 1895–1896* (Washington, D.C., 1897), 3:2081–2118; Kelly Miller, "The Education of the Negro," in the *Report of the Commissioner of Education, 1901* (Washington, D.C., 1902), pp. 731–859.

3. Horace Mann Bond, *The Education of the Negro in the American Social Order* (1933; reprint ed., New York, 1956), p. 257.

4. For an excellent recent examination of the status of the private black colleges, see Daniel C. Thompson, *Private Black Colleges at the Crossroads* (Westport, Conn., 1973).

5. U.S. Department of the Interior, Bureau of Education, Bulletin Nos. 38–39 (1916), *Negro Education: A Study of the Private and Higher Schools for Colored People in the United States*, prepared by Thomas J. Jones (Washington, D.C., 1916); idem, Bulletin No. 7 (1928), *Survey of Negro Colleges and Universities*, prepared by Arthur J. Klein (Washington, D.C., 1929).

6. The conclusions of the National Advisory Committee on Education were discussed in detail by W. E. B. Du Bois; see "Education," *The Crisis* 39 (January 1932): 468, 474.

7. For an example of the reaction of blacks to the filing of the minority report by the black college presidents, see *Philadelphia Tribune*, 26 November 1931, p. 1; 3 December 1931, p. 16.

8. Quotations from the minority report come from Du Bois, "Education," pp. 468, 474. See also Thomas E. Posey, "The Negro Land Grant Colleges," *Opportunity* 10 (1932): 14–17.

9. For examinations of the strategy of the NAACP in litigating cases of school segregation, see R. L. Stokes, "Decision of the Missouri Court on

the Admission of Negroes to State Universities," *School and Society* 48 (3 December 1938): 26–27; Genna Rae McNeil, "Charles Hamilton Houston," *Black Law Journal* 4 (1974): 123–31. A detailed analysis of the NAACP cases leading up to the *Brown* decision is found in Richard Kluger, *Simple Justice: The History of Brown v. Board of Education and Black America's Struggle For Equality* (New York, 1976).

10. For detailed discussions of the racial beliefs of white Americans and the pseudoscientific experiments to demonstrate the inferiority of blacks, see Frederickson, *The Black Image in the White Mind*; Newby, *Jim Crow's Defense*; Stanton, *The Leopard's Spots*; Haller, *Outcasts of Evolution*.

11. For a discussion of racist ideologies, see W. Vander Zander, "The Ideology of White Supremacy," *Journal of the History of Ideas* 20 (1959): 385–402.

12. The work and ideas of Franz Boas are examined in Thomas Gossett, *Race: The History of an Idea in America* (Dallas, 1963), pp. 409–27.

13. William B. Provine, "Geneticists and the Biology of Race Crossing," *Science* 182 (23 November 1973): 790–96. See also David M. Reimers, ed., *Racism in the United States: An American Dilemma?* (New York, 1972).

14. Quoted in Howard H. Long, "Race and Mental Tests," *Opportunity* 1 (1923): 22. See also Lewis Terman, "Were We Born That Way?" *World's Work* 44 (1922): 660, for the entire statement.

15. Long, "Race and Mental Tests," p. 25.

16. Ibid., pp. 25–28.

17. Carl Bingham, *A Study of American Intelligence* (Princeton, 1923).

18. Quoted in Horace Mann Bond, "What the Army 'Intelligence' Tests Really Measured," *Opportunity* 2 (1924): 197.

19. Ibid., pp. 198–202. See also Howard Long, "On Mental Tests and Racial Psychology: A Critique," *Opportunity* 3 (1925): 134–38.

20. A partial list of some of the more important articles of these writers during this period are: H. Long, "Test Results of Third-Grade Negro Children Selected on the Basis of Socioeconomic Status," *JNE* 4 (1935): 192–212; H. Long, "Intelligence of Colored Elementary Pupils in Washington, D.C.," *JNE* 3 (1934): 205–22; Martin D. Jenkins, "Intelligence of Negro Children," *Educational Method* 19 (1939): 106–12; Martin D. Jenkins, "Educational Achievement of a Group of Gifted Negro Children," *Journal of Educational Psychology* 25 (1934): 585–97; M. D. Jenkins, "A Socio-Psychological Study of Negro Children of Superior Intelligence," *JNE* 5 (1936): 175–90; Charles Thompson, "The Conclusions of Scientists Relative to Racial Differences," *JNE* 3 (1934): 494–512; Doxey Wilkerson, "Racial Differences in Scholastic Achievement," *JNE* 3 (1934): 453–77.

21. Martin D. Jenkins, "The Mental Ability of the American Negro,"

JNE 8 (1939): 511–80. The July issue of the *Journal of Negro Education* for 1939 was devoted to "The Mental and Physical Abilities of the American Negro." For a detailed analysis of the efforts of black psychologists and educators to expose the fallacies of mental testing, see Vincent P. Franklin, "Black Social Scientists and the Mental Testing Movement, 1920–1940" in *Black Psychology*, ed. Reginald Jones, 2d ed. (New York, 1980).

22. The ongoing debate among blacks over the issue of segregation is examined by Charles Johnson, *The Patterns of Negro Segregation* (New York, 1943), pp. 22–25.

23. For a discussion of Marcus Garvey and the UNIA, see Meier, Rudwick, and Broderick, "Marcus Garvey: The Challenge of Black Nationalism," in *Black Protest Thought in the Twentieth Century*, pp. 100–109; and Tony Martin, *Race First* (Westport, Conn., 1977).

24. W. E. B. Du Bois, "Segregation," *The Crisis* 41 (January 1934): 20.

25. Walter White, from "Segregation, A Symposium," *The Crisis* 41 (February 1934): 80–81.

26. Quoted from J. St. Clair Price, "General Summary and Conclusions," *JNE* 1 (1932): 334.

27. Editorial, "An Educational Conference," *Opportunity* 12 (June 1934): 167. See also Harold Ickes, "Why a National Conference on the Education of Negroes," *JNE* 3 (1934): 576–78.

28. See especially Charles Thompson, "Court Action the Only Reasonable Alternative to Remedy Immediate Abuses of the Negro Separate School," *JNE* 4 (1935): 419–34.

29. The issue of segregation continued to be debated among black leaders and educators. For a discussion of the nature of the debate after 1939, see Franklin, "The Persistence of School Segregation in the Urban North," pp. 61–68.

30. Du Bois, "Segregation," p. 20; White, "Segregation," p. 81.

31. See PBPE, *Annual Report, 1931*, "Report of the President," pp. 10–16.

32. PBPE, *Annual Report, 1933*, "Report of the President," pp. 9–15.

33. Ibid., p. 15.

34. Ibid., p. 16.

35. For progress in the development of the junior high school, see PBPE, *Annual Report, 1921*, "Report of the Superintendent of Schools," pp. 27–29.

36. *Philadelphia Tribune*, 17 September 1931, pp. 1, 16; 24 September 1931, pp. 1, 16.

37. *Philadelphia Tribune*, 8 October 1931, pp. 1–2; 15 October 1931, pp. 1–2.

38. Ibid., 24 September 1931, p. 1.

39. Ibid., 3 December 1931, p. 16; 10 December 1931, p. 16; 24 December 1931, p. 6.

40. Floyd Logan to William Rowen, president of the Board of Public Education, 6 January 1932, in PBPE Minutes of Meeting of 9 February 1932, KC.

41. Quoted from the *Philadelphia Tribune*, 14 January 1932, p. 1.

42. Ibid., 28 January 1932, p. 1.

43. For information on the Berwyn School Case, see NAACP Branch Correspondence, Bryn Mawr, Pennsylvania branch, 1932–1935, Box G-179, NAACP Papers, Library of Congress; Williamson, "The History of the Separate Schools for Negroes in Pennsylvania," pp. 72–82; *Philadelphia Tribune*, 24 March 1932, p. 1; 21 April 1932, p. 1; 19 May 1932, p. 2; 4 August 1932, p. 1.

44. Ibid., *Philadelphia Tribune*, 13 October 1932, p. 1.

45. *Philadelphia Tribune*, 15 December 1932, p. 3.

46. Ibid., 29 December 1932, pp. 1.

47. Ibid., 26 January 1933, p. 1; 2 February 1933, p. 1; 9 March 1933, p. 1.

48. Rallies held in support of the Berwyn parents are described ibid., 11 May 1933, p. 1; 25 May 1933, pp. 1, 16.

49. Quoted from letter of Walter White to Arthur Spingarn, 1 April 1932, Box G-188; see also, I. Maximillian Martin to Walter White, 14 April 1933, Box G-188, NAACP Branch Correspondence, Philadelphia Branch, 1930–39. See also *Philadelphia Tribune*, 16 March 1933, p. 1.

50. *Philadelphia Tribune*, 13 April 1933, p. 9; 20 April 1933, p. 1; 27 April 1933, p. 1.

51. Ibid., 11 May 1933, p. 1; 1 June 1933, p. 1. Floyd Logan suggested that the *Tribune* Defense Fund be used to support the Berwyn School Case, but the Defense Committee did not concur; see ibid., 24 August 1933, p. 1; 19 October 1933, p. 1.

52. Ibid., 14 September 1933, p. 1; 21 September 1933, p. 1; 28 September 1933, p. 1.

53. Ibid., 5 October 1933, p. 1; 12 October 1933, p. 1.

54. Ibid., 19 October 1933, p. 1. The NAACP was not pleased that the ILD also was involved in the Berwyn case. See ibid., 9 November 1933, p. 16.

55. Ibid., 9 November 1933, p. 3; 7 December 1933, p. 1.

56. Ibid., 15 February 1934, p. 3; 15 March 1934, p. 1; 29 March 1934, p. 1; 19 April 1934, p. 1; 3 May 1934, p. 1. At the beginning of the 1934–35 school year, Italian and black parents protested that they were not allowed to enroll their children at any school in the Berwyn school districts. The issue was quickly resolved when the pupils were allowed to enroll at the school of the parents' choice. See ibid., 6 September 1934, p. 1; 13 September 1934, p. 1; 27 September 1934, p. 3.

57. Ibid., 8 November 1934, p. 1.

58. The Educational Equality League also tried to get the school board to rescind its order to move Central High School out of a predominantly black area to the northern section of the city. The school had the

highest enrollment of black males in the city high schools. The school board did not rescind the order, and the school was moved. See ibid., 25 February 1937, p. 4; 4 March 1937, p. 10; 1 April 1937, p. 4. See also Nelson, "Race and Class Consciousness," pp. 167–68.

59. Bureau of Municipal Research, *Philadelphia's Government, 1932* (Philadelphia, 1932), pp. 4, 53, 64.

60. The political affiliations of the judges of the Common Pleas Court are indicated in *The Pennsylvania Manual, 1935–1936*, p. 336.

61. The Republican party's use of appointments to gain the support of various groups in the city is described in detail in David H. Kurtzman, *Methods of Controlling Votes in Philadelphia* (Philadelphia, 1935), pp. 102–14.

62. *Philadelphia Tribune*, 8 March 1928, p. 1. Appointments to the school board were staggered, and members were elected for six-year terms. Every two years five members were appointed or reappointed, Bureau of Municipal Research, *Philadelphia's Government, 1932*, pp. 68–69.

63. *Philadelphia Tribune*, 24 November 1932, p. 1; 7 September 1933, p. 1.

64. Ibid., 29 September 1927, p. 16; 8 January 1931, p. 9; 15 January 1931, p. 8.

65. Ibid., 31 August 1933, p. 1; 7 September 1933, p. 4. The president of the school board, William Rowen, had passed away.

66. Ibid., 1 February 1934, p. 1.

67. *The Pennsylvania Manual, 1935–1936*, p. 447.

68. *Philadelphia Tribune*, 1 May 1926, p. 1. In February 1935 Walter Gay was appointed assistant district attorney in Philadelphia. This was considered a minor appointment.

69. The appointment of Dr. Turner is discussed in the *Tribune* on 13 June 1935 and in the *Independent* on 16 June 1935, p. 2. The members of the PBPE in December 1934 were: Joseph Catherine (president), Edward Martin (vice-president), Solomon Solis-Cohen, Nichola D'Ascenzo, W. Finley Downs, Aloysius L. Fitzpatrick, Morris Leeds, Mrs. J. Frederick Lewis, Anna Lane Lingelbach, William H. Loesche, Howard McClenahan, Robert B. Pollock, Walter Biddle Saul, William H. Ziegler. Dr. Turner replaced Chester A. Farr.

70. *Philadelphia Tribune*, 20 September 1934, p. 4. The letter sent by John Christopher to black teachers who applied for the junior high school examinations was excerpted by the editor of the *Tribune*.

71. Cf. ibid., 14 June 1934, p. 3; and 6 June 1925, p. 1.

72. Speech of John Francis Williams at PBPE meeting, 12 June 1934, in Minutes of the meeting, KC.

73. See, for example, *Philadelphia Tribune*, 11 July 1935, p. 4, Editorial: "105 to 1." In this editorial, it was pointed out that in the 1934–35 school year, 105 appointments were made to the junior high schools and one to the elementary schools by the PBPE. See also 28 February 1935, p. 4; 11 April 1935, p. 1.

74. Ibid., 10 October 1935, p. 1. See also Nelson, "Race and Class Consciousness," pp. 177–78.

75. For information on the continued activities of the Educational Equality League and others in opposition to the dual lists, see the *Tribune*, 14 November 1935, p. 3; 26 December 1935, p. 1; 27 February 1936, p. 1; 28 May 1936, p. 3; 9 July 1936, p. 3; 22 October 1936, p. 1. See also *Philadelphia Independent*, 10 May 1936, p. 11; 12 July 1936, p. 9.

76. For a report on the evening schools in the city, see the *Philadelphia Tribune*, 26 September 1935, p. 3. See also 28 October 1937, p. 11.

77. Ibid., 9 December 1937, p. 3; 20 January 1938, p. 4; 24 February 1938, p. 1. See also Nelson, "Race and Class Consciousness," pp. 171–72.

78. Ibid., 13 January 1938, p. 17. See also Maskin, "Black Education and the New Deal," pp. 287–311; and chapter 7.

79. *Philadelphia Tribune*, 14 November 1935, p. 3; 15 October 1936, p. 4.

80. Ibid., 18 March 1937, p. 1; *Philadelphia Independent*, 21 March 1937, p. 3. The typescript Minutes of the meetings of the PBPE Department of Superintendence for 1937 indicate that the shift in policies was carried out smoothly, with no great bureaucratic problems. These Minutes are located in the superintendent's office at the PBPE building in Philadelphia.

81. In December 1937, it was announced that starting in 1943, four years of college would be required for teaching positions in the elementary public schools; see *Philadelphia Tribune*, 30 December 1937, p. 3.

82. Ibid., 1 April 1937, p. 4; *Philadelphia Independent*, 4 April 1937, p. 4.

83. *Philadelphia Independent*, 23 May 1937, p. 11; *Philadelphia Tribune*, 8 April 1937, p. 13; 22 April 1937, p. 20; 13 May 1937, p. 20.

84. *Philadelphia Tribune*, 20 May 1937, p. 4; 24 June 1937, pp. 2, 3; 8 July 1937, p. 2; *Philadelphia Independent*, 6 June 1937, p. 3; 11 July 1937, p. 3. Mannie Bradshaw, Joe Rainey, Magistrate Edward Henry, and Wayne Hopkins headed the citizens' committee.

85. *Philadelphia Tribune*, 10 June 1937, p. 20.

86. Ibid., 15 July 1937, p. 20.

87. Ibid., 22 July 1937, p. 20; 16 September 1937, p. 1.

88. *Philadelphia Tribune*, 2 December 1937, p. 1; 21 July 1938, p. 1; *Philadelphia Independent*, 24 July 1937, p. 2.

89. *Philadelphia Tribune*, 8 September 1938, p. 1; 15 September 1938, p. 1; 6 October 1938, p. 1.

90. Ibid., 15 July 1937, p. 1.

91. See chapter 9.

92. According to Floyd Logan of the Educational Equality League, several leading Democratic politicians, including Judge Francis Biddle and Rev. Marshall Shepard, had offered the league their support, if it became necessary to take the issue of the separate schools and the problems for black teachers to the state legislature.

93. For an excellent examination of Marcus Garvey and the UNIA, see Martin, *Race First*; for the Socialists and Communists in the 1920s, see Theodore Kornweibel, *No Crystal Stair: Black Life and the Messenger, 1917–1928* (Westport, Conn., 1977); and Philip Foner, *American Socialism and Black Americans* (Westport, Conn., 1977), esp. pp. 265–311.

94. Racial violence in the U.S. during the depression years is examiend in Allen P. Grimshaw, *Racial Violence in the United States* (Chicago, 1969), pp. 116–35.

Chapter 7. Race Relations and Intercultural Education

1. Palmer, *Philadelphia Workers in a Changing Economy*, Appendix Table 15, p. 163; Appendix Table 16, p. 164.

2. Ibid., Appendix Table 16, p. 164.

3. Ibid., pp. 96–118. See also Gladys L. Palmer and Samuel Cohn, *War Labor Supply Problems of Philadelphia and Its Environs* (Philadelphia, 1942); Palmer, *The Philadelphia Labor Market in 1944*.

4. Palmer, *Philadelphia Workers in a Changing Economy*, Appendix Table 16, p. 164.

5. See table 2. See also PHA, *Philadelphia's Negro Population: Facts on Housing* (Philadelphia, 1953), p. 5.

6. PHA, *Philadelphia's Negro Population*, pp. 6–8.

7. Idem, "Housing for Negroes in Philadelphia—Data Based on 1940 Census," 10 November 1947 (copy), Box 47, f.256, PHA Papers, TUUA.

8. Ibid.

9. Armstrong Association of Philadelphia, "Some Basic Facts Concerning the Negro Population of Philadelphia" (1955), p. 1 (copy), Box 12, f. 209, Philadelphia Urban League Papers, TUUA.

10. Ibid.; see also PHA, *A Report on the Housing of Negro Philadelphia* (Philadelphia, 1953), n.p. (pamphlet).

11. Brown, *Law Administration and Negro-White Relations in Philadelphia*, Table 7, p. 42; Table 8, p. 45.

12. For a discussion of black employment in defense and wartime industries in Philadelphia, see chapter 8.

13. Hardin, *The Negroes of Philadelphia*, p. 52.

14. Armstrong Association, Industrial Research Department, "Industrial Employment Gains of Negro Workers in Philadelphia During the War Years, 1941–1944" (1944). A summary of this report may be found in James Gross, "Negro Labor and the Industrial Department of the Armstrong Association" (M.B.A. thesis, Temple University, 1957), pp. 8–12.

15. Carolyn D. Moore, "The NAACP in Philadelphia," May 1944, MS Box 7, f. 149, Philadelphia NAACP Papers, TUUA. For information on the founding and early years of the Armstrong Association of Philadelphia, see Emlen, "The Movement for the Betterment of the Negro in Philadelphia," pp. 81–92.

16. Thomas Dabnay of the Interracial Commission of Philadelphia, to the PBPE, 9 November 1927; and "Resolution on Segregation and the Negro Passed by the Interracial Conference held at the Southwest Y.W.C.A., Friday, 28 October 1927, Philadelphia" (MSS) in Minutes of PBPE Meeting on 14 November 1927, KC. See also *Philadelphia Tribune,* 5 December 1929, p. 1.

17. *Philadelphia Tribune,* 13 February 1930, p. 1; 1 February 1934, p. 5.

18. Ibid., 3 May 1934, p. 2; 30 December 1937, p. 2.

19. The Race Relations Institute at Swarthmore College, and other activities of the Society of Friends are discussed ibid., 30 April 1931, p. 1; 31 August 1933, p. 5; 3 May 1934, p. 2; 12 June 1941, p. 4. It should also be noted that although the Quakers were active in trying to improve race relations, they did not allow blacks to attend their elementary and secondary schools in Philadelphia until 1945; see ibid., 1 April 1944, p. 3; 7 April 1945, p. 1.

20. Ibid., 28 May 1936, p. 15; 26 September 1935, p. 3; 30 May 1940, p. 1.

21. Ibid., 20 February 1941, p. 1; 3 April 1941, p. 1; 8 May 1941, p. 20; see also 22 November 1941, p. 5; 6 December 1941, p. 3; 20 December 1941, p. 3.

22. Ibid., 22 May 1941, p. 3; 24 January 1942, p. 3; 11 December 1943, p. 2; 1 February 1947, p. 9.

23. For information on the background and activities of the Interracial Church, see ibid., 24 October 1935, p. 1; 7 November 1935, p. 3; 22 October 1936, p. 1.

24. Ibid., 26 November 1936, p. 3; 29 April 1944, p. 2; 30 September 1944, p. 7; 14 October 1944, p. 1; 24 March 1945, p. 2; 6 October 1945, p. 2; 16 March 1946, p. 4; 23 March 1946, p. 1; 21 October 1947, p. 9; 14 June 1949, p. 1 See also Leo Marsh, *Steps Taken to Improve Racial Practices in the YMCA, 1946–1959* (New York, n.d.), p. 4 (pamphlet).

25. *Philadelphia Tribune,* 17 April 1941, p. 3; 20 March 1943, p. 1; 9 September 1944, p. 3; 2 December 1944, p. 5. See also Maurice B. Fagan, "Intercultural Education Is a Process," *Education* 68 (1947): 184–85.

26. The founding and activities of the Fellowship Commission are detailed in Fagan, "Intercultural Education," pp. 182–87. Fagan was acting director of the commission. The eight original constituent organizations were: Philadelphia Federation of Churches, the Society of Friends, Fellowship House, Philadelphia Jewish Community Relations Council, Philadelphia NAACP, International Institute of Philadelphia, National Conference of Christians and Jews (Philadelphia Office), and the Council for Equal Job Opportunity.

27. Ibid., pp. 184–85. For other information on the activities of the Fellowship Commission, see the *Philadelphia Tribune,* 8 January 1944, p.

2; 24 June 1944, p. 20; 31 March 1945, p. 3; 28 May 1946, p. 16; 4 June 1946, p. 5.

28. *Philadelphia Tribune,* 17 July 1943, p. 1. Dr. Duckrey was formerly the principal of the Paul Lawrence Dunbar Public School in North Philadelphia.

29. Edward T. Myers, "Schoolmen Study Intercultural Problems in Philadelphia," *Nation's Schools* 36 (September 1945): 47; *Philadelphia Tribune,* 8 April 1944, p. 2.

30. The members of the Committee were: Dr. Edwin Adams, associate superintendent of public schools; Dr. Tanner Duckrey; Maurice Fagan; William M. Gerber, chairman of the Intercultural Education Committee; Capt. Thomas Gibbons, Crime Prevention Association; J. Francis Finnegan, director, Crime Prevention Association; Wayne Hopkins, Armstrong Association; Carolyn D. Moore, Philadelphia NAACP; Marjorie Penney, director of Fellowship House; Robert C. Taber, director of Pupil Personnel and Counseling, PBPE. See Minutes of the Committee on School and Community Tensions, Meeting Held September 14, 1944, Box 8, f.138, Philadelphia Urban League Papers, TUUA.

31. Minutes of Committee on School and Community Tensions, 14 September 1944, n.p.

32. Minutes for meetings from September 1944, to 11 June 1948 may be found in Box 8, f. 138, Philadelphia Urban League Papers, TUUA.

33. E. Washington Rhodes, Chairman of Pennsylvania State Temporary Commission, to Edmund Bacon, Philadelphia Housing Association, August 11, 1943, Box 43, f. 214, PHA Papers, TUUA.

34. Pennsylvania State Temporary Commission on the Conditions of the Urban Colored Population, "Suggestions for Interracial Committees," (1943) Box 43, f. 214, PHA Papers, TUUA. See also *Philadelphia Tribune,* 28 August 1943, p. 1; 16 December 1944, p. 1.

35. *Philadelphia Tribune,* 24 July 1943, p. 1; 21 August 1943, p. 1; 25 December 1943, p. 1. For minutes of various meetings of the City-Wide Interracial Committee, see Boxes 43 and 44, f. 214 and f. 215, PHA Papers, TUUA. In the Detroit Race Riot of 1943, over thirty-five persons were killed; see Grimshaw, *Racial Violence in the United States,* pp. 116–35.

36. *Philadelphia Tribune,* 8 August 1934, p. 1; 16 August 1934, p. 1.

37. Ibid., 2 January 1941, p. 3.

38. Ibid., 21 March 1942, p. 1; 20 March 1943, p. 1. The City-Wide Interracial Committee reported at the meeting of the executive committee on 15 October 1943, that sixty-five racial incidents occurred in the city between May 1943 and 15 October 1943. See Minutes of Executive Committee of City-Wide Interracial Committee, October 15, 1943 (MS), Box 72, f. 103, PHA Papers, TUUA.

39. *Philadelphia Tribune,* 1 May 1941, p. 9; 24 January 1942, p. 3; 12 December 1942, p. 20.

40. Ibid., 12 December 1942, p. 20. See also Allen M. Winkler, "The

Philadelphia Transit Strike of 1944," *Journal of American History* 59 (June 1972): 75.

41. Winkler, "The Philadelphia Transit Strike," p. 76; see also Louis Ruchames, *Race, Jobs and Politics: The Story of the FEPC* (New York, 1953), pp. 100–20.

42. *Philadelphia Tribune*, 18 March 1944, p. 1; 25 March 1944, p. 4; 6 May 1944, p. 1; 15 July 1944, p. 1; 22 July 1944, p. 1.

43. *Philadelphia Tribune*, 5 August 1944, p. 1; 12 August 1944, p. 1; 19 August 1944, p. 1; see also Winkler, "The Philadelphia Transit Strike," pp. 81–86. There were several contemporary accounts of the transit strike; see, for example, "Race Trouble in Philadelphia Brings Test of Wartime Powers," *Newsweek* 24 (14 August 1944): 36; "Trouble in Philadelphia Transportation Strike," *Time* 44 (14 August 1944): 22–23.

44. For statements on the need for a FEPC in Philadelphia in 1944, see the *Tribune*, 8 April 1944, p. 1; 29 April 1944, p. 1; 20 May 1944, p. 9.

45. See chapter 5. See also Garfinkel, *When Negroes March*.

46. *Philadelphia Tribune*, 3 July 1941; 17 October 1942, p. 1. The national politics and the creation of the FEPC are examined in Ruchames, *Race, Jobs, and Politics*, and Louis C. Kesselman, *The Social Politics of FEPC: A Study in Reform Pressure Movements* (Chapel Hill, N. C., 1948).

47. Kent M. Lloyd, *State FEPC Public Education Programs: A Comparative Civil Rights Study* (Seattle, 1957), p. 29.

48. For accounts of the FEPC measure in the Pennsylvania legislature, see the *Philadelphia Tribune*, 6 January 1945, p. 1; 27 January 1945, p. 1; 28 April 1945, p. 1; 1 December 1945, p. 2; 19 April 1947, p. 1; 6 May 1947, p. 1; 22 May 1948, p. 1; 12 June 1948, p. 2; 1 January 1949, p. 3; 29 March 1949, p. 1; 9 April 1949, p. 1; 28 January 1950, p. 4; 25 July 1950, p. 2; 19 December 1950, p. 2; 26 December 1950, p. 3. For a discussion of the bill that was eventually passed in 1955, see Lloyd, *State FEPC*, pp. 28–46, 184–85.

49. *Philadelphia Tribune*, 3 November 1945, p. 1.

50. Ibid., 1 December 1945, p. 2; 8 December 1945, p. 10; 19 January 1946, p. 20; 16 March 1946, p. 1; 20 April 1946, p. 1; 11 May 1946, p. 2; 28 January 1947, p. 2; 18 February 1947, p. 1; 4 November 1947, p. 9.

51. Ibid., 8 November 1947, p. 1; 17 January 1948, p. 1; 21 February 1948, p. 1; 9 March 1948, p. 1; 13 March 1948, p. 1. See also Philadelphia Fair Employment Practices Commission, *First Annual Report, June 1, 1948–May 31, 1949* (Philadelphia, 1949), pp. 2–3.

52. Philadelphia FEPC, *First Annual Report*, pp. 4–6.

53. Ibid., pp. 5–10; Philadelphia Commission on Human Relations, *First Annual Report, 1952* (Philadelphia, 1953), n.p.

54. See Gossett, *Race*, pp. 19–51.

55. See chapters 2 and 6.

56. Quoted in Stanford M. Lyman, *The Black American in Sociological Thought* (New York, 1972), pp. 43–44.

57. For a detailed discussion of Park's "Race Relations Cycle," see ibid., pp. 27–70.

58. Gunnar Myrdal, *An American Dilemma: The Negro Problem and Modern Democracy*, 2 vols. (New York, 1944), 1: xliii–xliv; 2: 1023–24.

59. Ibid.; Lyman, *The Black American in Sociological Thought*, pp. 99–120. There were hundreds of books and articles published on intercultural education during the 1930s and 1940s. A few that the writer found helpful were: William W. Brickman, "Educational Literature Review; Intercultural Education," *School and Society* 66 (27 July 1946): 67–71; Hymen Alpern, "Role of High Schools in Improving Intercultural Education," *Journal of Educational Sociology* 16 (1943): 363–67; William Kirkpatrick, "Conflict Areas in America's Intercultural Life," *Journal of Educational Sociology* 16 (1943): 340–44; Herbert L. Seamans, "Education and Intergroup Relations," *Educational Record* 27 (1946): 87–95; Theodore B. Brameld, *Minority Problems in the Public Schools: A Study of Administrative Policies and Practices in Seven School Systems* (New York, 1946); William E. Vickery and Stewart G. Cole, *Intercultural Education in American Schools: Proposed Objectives and Methods* (New York, 1943).

60. Fagan, "Intercultural Education Is a Process," p. 186. For educational materials issued by the Philadelphia Fellowship Commission, 1941–51, see Box 53, f. 318; Box 85, f. 379–81, PHA Papers, TUUA.

61. Philadelphia Fellowship Commission, "Evaluation of the Services of the Fellowship Commission to the Public Schools of Philadelphia, 1947–1948" (copy), Box 85, f. 379; see also, Philadelphia Fellowship Commission, "The Intercultural Climate in Philadelphia" (14 October 1947) (copy), Box 53, f. 318, PHA Papers, TUUA.

62. Fagan, "Intercultural Education Is a Process," pp. 184–85; see also PBPE, *For Every Child: The Story of Integration in the Philadelphia Public Schools* (Philadelphia, 1961), p. 10 (pamphlet). For a discussion of the Bureau of Intercultural Education, see Ronald K. Goodenow, "The Progressive Educator and Racial Tolerance: Intercultural Education, 1930–1941" (paper delivered at the American Educational Research Association meeting, March 1975), pp. 2–15. See also *Philadelphia Tribune*, 24 June 1944, p. 20; 4 June 1946, p. 5; 4 March 1950, p. 1.

63. *Philadelphia Tribune*, 21 August 1943, p. 1; 28 August 1943, p. 1.

64. Ibid., 29 April 1944, p. 2; 30 September 1944, p. 7; 14 October 1944, p. 1; 6 October 1945, p. 2; 14 June 1949, p. 1.

65. Myers, "Schoolmen Study Intercultural Problems," pp. 47–48. See also *Philadelphia Tribune*, 16 December 1944, p. 4; 12 January 1946, p. 4; 26 January 1946, p. 2; 23 February 1946, p. 10.

66. Fagan, "Intercultural Education Is a Process," p. 185; *Philadelphia Tribune*, 2 December 1944, p. 5; 20 December 1949, p. 2; 31 January 1950, p. 9.

67. For examples of statements by various black leaders and educators in support of interracial activities in Philadelphia, see the *Tribune*, 10 November 1932, p. 7; 19 May 1938, p. 4; 18 January 1940, p. 4; 12 December 1940, p. 4; 7 August 1941, p. 8; 13 March 1943, p. 1; 3 June 1944, p. 1;

9 September 1944, p. 5; 28 April 1945, p. 4 11 August 1945, p. 4; 12 January 1946, p. 4.

68. The resurgence of the Ku Klux Klan in post-World War II Philadelphia is described in the *Tribune*, 3 September 1946, p. 1; 7 September 1946, p. 4; 21 September 1946, p. 4; 30 March 1948, p. 9.

69. Brown, *Law Administration and Negro-White Relations in Philadelphia*, pp. 47–52; see also chapter 9.

70. See chapter 9. See also Franklin, "The Persistence of School Segregation in the Urban North," pp. 51–67.

Chapter 8. Secondary Education, Vocational Training, and the Problems of Black Youth

1. Hardin, *The Negroes of Philadelphia*, p. 103; *The Final Report on the Urban Colored Population*, pp. 413-15.

2. *The Final Report on the Urban Colored Population*, pp. 411–15, and Appendix II, Table 16.

3. See table 2; PBPE, *Annual Report, 1950*, p. 134. Although the breakdown of black enrollment in the Philadelphia public secondary schools in 1950 is not available, in 1956 it was reported that blacks were 38 percent of the enrollment in the junior high schools, 30 percent in the senior high schools, and 35 percent in the vocational-technical schools. See PBPE, Department of Research and Development, *Distribution of Negro Pupils in the Philadelphia Public Schools, 1956–1965* (Philadelphia, 3 January 1966), p. 11 (pamphlet).

4. See, for example, William R. Odell, director, *Educational Survey Report for the Philadelphia Board of Public Education* (Philadelphia, 1965), pp. 28–31.

5. *The Final Report on the Urban Colored Population*, pp. 413–14. The commission was formed in 1939 by the General Assembly of Pennsylvania in order to get some indication of the overall social conditions of blacks in the state. However, a great part of the report deals with the situation of blacks in Philadelphia.

6. U.S. Commission on Civil Rights, *Racial Isolation in the Public Schools*, vol. 1 (Washington, D.C., 1967), p. 9, Table 3.

7. *The Final Report on the Urban Colored Population*, p. 414.

8. The *Philadelphia Tribune* published a special report on black students in the public schools by Dr. Daniel Brooks, principal of Reynolds School. Brooks reported that in 1945 William Penn and Benjamin Franklin High Schools were three-fourths black, and Vaux Junior High School was 98 percent black; Barratt, 82; Sulzberger, 77; Stoddart, 73; Fitzsimmons and Shoemaker junior high schools, 55 percent, See 13 April 1946, p. 10.

9. For information on the occupational aspirations of black pupils in Philadelphia in the 1930s, see John Brodhead, "Educational Achievement and Its Relationship to the Socio-Economic Status of the Negro" (Ed.D. diss., Temple University, 1937), pp. 128–31.

10. Junior Employment Service, School District of Philadelphia, *When Philadelphia Youth Leave School at 15 and 16* (Philadelphia, 1941), pp. 29–31; see also Hardin, *The Negroes of Philadelphia*, p. 69; "Employment Status of Philadelphia Public School Graduates of 1935," *Monthly Labor Review* 46 (1938): 389–91.

11. *PBPE*, Department of Superintendence, Division of Industrial Arts, *Industrial Opportunities for Negro Youth in the Manufacturing Industries of Philadelphia* (Philadelphia, 1939), p. 18. A copy of this pamphlet may be found in the Philadelphia Urban League Papers, Box 9, f. 151, TUUA.

12. PBPE, *Negro Employment: A Study of the Negro Employment Situation in Philadelphia and Its Relation to the School Program* (Philadelphia, 1942), p. 9.

13. Ibid., p. 37.

14. *Philadelphia Tribune*, 9 February 1924, p. 1; 16 February 1924, p. 1.

15. For examples of these and other discriminatory practices in the secondary schools, see the *Tribune*, 13 November 1915, p. 1; 31 January 1925, p. 1; 16 January 1926, p. 2; 2 November 1933, p. 1; 15 November 1934, p. 1; 3 December 1936, p. 1.

16. *The Final Report on the Urban Colored Population*, pp. 428–29.

17. Ibid., pp. 443–44.

18. Ibid., p. 444.

19. Armstrong Association of Philadelphia, "Enrollment of Negro Pupils in Vocational Schools of Philadelphia, April, 1940," copy, Philadelphia Urban League Papers, Box 12, f. 210, TUUA.

20. The activities and programs offered at the Berean School are discussed in the *Philadelphia Tribune*, 23 February 1924, p. 1; 20 June 1925, p. 5; 27 March 1926, p. 4; 12 January 1928, p. 1; 19 January 1928, p. 16.

21. I. Maximillian Martin, "Student Placement at Berean School," *Journal of Business Education* 14 (June 1939): 23–24; Hardin, *The Negroes of Philadelphia*, pp. 113–14.

22. *The Final Report on the Urban Colored Population*, pp. 380–81; *Philadelphia Tribune*, 11 June 1921, p. 1.

23. For an excellent discussion of the school, see S. Shalett and J. S. McIlvaine, "They Salvage Forgotten Children: Downingtown Industrial School," *Saturday Evening Post* 223 (38 October 1950): 38–39, 117, 121.

24. Parris and Brooks, *Blacks in the City*, pp. 210–14.

25. For accounts of the activities during Vocational Opportunity Week in Philadelphia, see the *Philadelphia Tribune*, 28 March 1940, p. 20; 4 April 1940, p. 4; 23 January 1941, p. 20; 13 March 1941, p. 20; 27 March 1941, p. 10; 28 March 1942, p. 2; 13 March 1943, p. 19.

26. Armstrong Association, "Enrollment of Negro Pupils in Vocational Schools in Philadelphia, April, 1940." See also *The Final Report on the Urban Colored Population*, pp. 414–15.

27. U.S. Works Project Administration for Pennsylvania, *One Year of*

the Works Projects Administration in Pennsylvania, July 1, 1935–June 30, 1936 (Harrisburg, Pa., 1936), pp. 85–87.

28. Maskin, "Black Education and the New Deal," pp. 303–11; Philadelphia Tribune, 23 April 1936, p. 2; 13 August 1936, p. 3; 25 March, 1937, p. 2.

29. Charles F. Bauder, "Philadelphia Program of Vocational Education for Defense," Industrial Arts and Vocational Education 31 (March 1942): 83.

30. Ibid., pp. 83–87; see also James K. Satchell, "Defense Training in Philadelphia during 1940 and 1941," Industrial Arts and Vocational Education 31 (February 1942): 42–44.

31. Minutes of the Meeting of the State Advisory Council on Negro Affairs, 28 October 1939, p. 4 (copy), Box 6, f. 97, Philadelphia Urban League Papers, TUUA.

32. Philadelphia Tribune, 4 January 1940, p. 1; 2 May 1940, p. 17; 9 May 1940, p. 2; 22 May 1940, p. 3; 15 August 1940, p. 1; 22 August 1940, p. 2; 29 August 1940, p. 3.

33. Armstrong Association, Industrial Research Department, "Placenemt of Negro Workers in Skilled and Semi-skilled Jobs," prepared by Charles Shorter, 16 April 1941, p. 1 (copy), Box 11, f. 192, Philadelphia Urban League Papers, TUUA.

34. Ibid., p. 2.

35. Franklin O. Nichols, "Report Dealing with Activities in the City of Philadelphia," 22–29 April 1941, p. 2 (copy), Box 11, f. 186, Philadelphia Urban League Papers, TUUA. This report was made to a meeting on the "Participation of the Negro in the Defense Industries of the Eastern United States," held in the city during that week by the Urban League.

36. The Final Report on the Urban Colored Population, pp. 509–10.

37. Ibid., p. 510.

38. Ibid., pp. 519–20.

39. Hardin, The Negroes of Philadelphia, p. 51.

40. Ibid., pp. 51–53.

41. Brown, Law Administration and Negro-White Relations, pp. 48–49; Seymour Wolfbein, "Postwar Trends in Negro Employment," Monthly Labor Review 65 (1947): 663–65.

42. U.S. War Manpower Commission, Final Report of the National Youth Administration, Fiscal Years, 1936–1943 (Washington, D.C., 1944), pp. 10–11.

43. For information on the background to the youth programs of the New Deal, see Betty and Ernest Lindley, A New Deal for Youth (New York, 1938).

44. John A. Salmond, "The Civilian Conservation Corps and the Negro," Journal of American History 52 (1965): 75.

45. President Roosevelt, quoted in Lindley, A New Deal for Youth, p. 3.

46. *Final Report of the NYA*, p. 13.

47. Salmond, "Civilian Conservation Corps and the Negro," pp. 75–88 passim; see also Marian T. Wright, "Negro Youth and the Federal Emergency Programs: CCC and NYA," *JNE* 9 (1940): 397–407.

48. *Final Report of the NYA*, pp. 16–20.

49. Ibid., Table 15, p. 56. For general information on blacks and the NYA, see Walter G. Daniel and Carroll L. Miller, "The Participation of the Negro in the National Youth Administration Program," *JNE* 7 (1938): 357–65.

50. PBPE, *Report of the Bureau of Compulsory Education, 1930*, p. 134.

51. Ibid., 1931, pp. 134–35.

52. Ibid., 1933, p. 30.

53. We cannot use the issuance of employment certificates as a measure of the employment of youth in Philadelphia after 1935 because the Pennsylvania Child Labor Law was amended in that year. After that date children under sixteen years of age were not allowed to be employed during school hours. Certificates were then given only to students between sixteen and eighteen years of age who had found jobs. See PBPE, *Report of the Bureau of Compulsory Education, 1936*, p. 15.

54. The *Philadelphia Tribune* published a number of articles and editorials on juvenile delinquency in the early 1930s; see, for example, 6 March 1930, p. 1; 23 March 1933, p. 7; 10 August 1933, p. 3; 18 October 1934, p. 2; 29 November 1934, p. 2; 14 February 1935, p. 3.

55. "Exhibit No. 11, prepared by Phillip Wallis, Frank S. Brown, and Robert Taber of the Municipal Court, Philadelphia, Pennsylvania, 'The Care of Negro Children,'" in *The Final Report on the Urban Colored Population, pp.* 604–5.

56. Ibid., p. 269.

57. Ibid., p. 305.

58. Ibid., p 322.

59. One of the earliest gangs discussed in the *Tribune* was the "40 Thieves," which engaged in several burglaries. See the *Philadelphia Tribune*, 2 February 1933, p. 1; 9 February 1933, p. 1.

60. Ibid., 14 January 1937, p. 4; 21 December 1939, p. 4; 25 April 1940, p. 1; 24 April 1943, p. 2; 22 January 1944, p. 1; 3 October 1950, p. 2. See also Brown, *Law Administration and Negro-White Releations*, pp. 75–77.

61. *Philadelphia Tribune*, 27 April 1946, p. 10. This is a discussion of juvenile delinquency by Dr. Daniel Brooks.

62. Quoted in Maskin, "Black Education and the New Deal," p. 306.

63. National Youth Administration, Philadelphia Area, "Annual Report, 1935–1936" (copy), Box 32, f. 245, Wharton Centre Papers, TUUA.

64. Quoted from "The Constitution of the Pennsylvania State Negro Council" (copy), Box 4, f. 76, Philadelphia Urban League Papers, TUUA.

The leaders of the council were Leslie Pinckney Hill of Cheyney and Wayne Hopkins of the Armstrong Association.

65. *Philadelphia Tribune*, 11 June 1936, p. 2.

66. Ibid., 14 January 1937, p. 2; 21 January 1937, p. 3; 24 June 1937, p. 2.

67. Ibid., 28 March 1935, p. 3; 3 October 1940, p. 2; 6 February 1943, p. 2; 16 October 1943, p. 7; 27 November 1943, p. 3; 13 January 1945, p. 3; 20 April 1946, p. 3; 2 April 1949, p. 9; 1 November 1949, p. 9.

68. Ibid., 21 June 1949, p. 3; 27 June 1950, p. 16.

69. Information on the activities of the YMCA, YWCA, and Wharton Centre in helping black youth may be found in the papers of these organizations, which are located at TUUA. The *Philadelphia Tribune* began a column entitled "In the Community Centers" on 14 October 1947, p. 5, which twice a week reported on the activities in the various community centers in the black community. For other detailed accounts of the work of these centers with black youth, see 29 October 1936, p. 2; 16 September 1937, p. 20; 20 June 1940, p. 3; 24 October 1940, p. 2; 11 October 1941, p. 19; 10 October 1942, p. 2; 23 October 1943, p. 20; 20 October 1945, p. 17.

70. Ibid., 23 April 1936, p. 2; 28 May 1936, p. 20, National Negro Congress Youth Section; 8 May 1943, p. 2; 8 September 1945, p. 2, the Elks; 1 July 1937, p. 2; 27 January 1938, p. 8, Youth Council of the NAACP. See also 20 March 1943, p. 3; 1 May 1943, p. 1, church groups; 10 October 1950, p. 2, women's clubs.

71. Ibid., 30 November 1939, p. 3; 23 January 1941, p. 2; 24 April 1941, p. 2; 15 May 1941, p. 3; 5 December 1942, p. 20.

72. Ibid., 1 April 1944, p. 3; 17 November 1945, p. 10; 15 December 1945, p. 1; 5 January 1946, p. 3.

73. See also ibid., 27 February 1936, p. 1; 1 July 1937, p. 1; 5 August 1937, p. 2.

74. Ibid., 4 February 1937, p. 20; 4 March 1937, p. 2; 5 August 1937, p. 2. See also Nelson, "Race and Class Consciousness," pp. 265–71.

75. *Philadelphia Tribune*, 4 April 1940, p. 20; 2 May 1940, p. 3; 6 June 1940, p. 3; 4 July 1940, p. 20; 19 December 1940, p. 2.

76. Ibid., 20 March 1941, p. 2; 10 April 1941, p. 2; 14 August 1941, p. 8; 28 August 1941, p. 8.

77. Ibid., 20 September 1941, p. 2; 27 September 1941, p. 10; 26 September 1942, p. 1; 25 September 1942, p. 1; 2 October 1943, p. 1.

78. Ibid., 7 March 1942, p. 2; 27 March 1943, p. 2; 3 April 1943, p. 2; 30 October 1943, p. 2.

79. For some general information on community organizations and the problems of black youth, see E. R. Moses, "Community Factors in Negro Delinquency," *JNE* 5 (1936): 220–27; John Lovell, "Youth Program of Negro Improvement Groups," *JNE* 9 (1940): 379–87.

80. See, for example, the *Philadelphia Tribune*, 5 December 1940, p.

1; 23 January 1941, p. 2; 20 February 1941, p. 4; 17 April 1941, p. 10; 18 October 1941, p. 20; 25 April 1942, p. 16; 28 August 1943, p. 2; 25 September 1943, p. 16; 9 December 1944, p. 10; 20 January 1945, p. 1; 21 September 1948, p. 3; 21 October 1950, p. 16.

81. Municipal Court of Philadelphia, *Thirty-seventh Annual Report . . . for the Year 1950*, ed. Frank S. Brown (Philadelphia, n.d.), pp. 28–29.

82. Ibid., p. 30.

83. Ibid., Table 5, p. 77; *The Final Report on the Urban Colored Population*, pp. 604–5. See also Mary Huff Diggs, "Some Problems and Needs of Negro Children as Revealed by Comparative Delinquency and Crime Statistics," *JNE* 14 (1950): 290–97. This article discusses the 1948 report of the municipal court of Philadelphia on juvenile delinquency.

Chapter 9. Change and Continuity in Black Philadelphia

1. W. E. B. Du Bois, "Of Our Spiritual Strivings," in *The Souls of Black Folk* (1903; reprint ed., Millwood, N.Y., 1973), pp. 3–4.

2. The need for Negro improvement is explicit in names of the two largest black social advancement organizations: the National Association for the Advancement of Colored People and the Universal Negro Improvement Association. Booker T. Washington's most famous autobiographical work, *Up from Slavery*, is the story of a black individual who had advanced. William Crogman's 1898 history of blacks in America, *Progress of a Race*, was another example of the obvious concern for improvement. For related discussions, see Houston Baker, "Men and Institutions: Booker T. Washington's *Up from Slavery*," in *Long Black Song: Essays on Afro-American Literature and Culture* (Charlottesville, Va., 1974), pp. 84–95; and Robert A. Hill, "The First England Years and After, 1912–1916" in *Marcus Garvey and the Vision of Africa*, ed. John H. Clarke and Amy J. Garvey (New York, 1974), pp. 38–70.

3. Du Bois, *The Philadelphia Negro*, pp. 389–90.

4. Philadelphia Commission on Human Relations, *Philadelphia's Negro Population: Facts on Housing* (Philadelphia, 1953), pp. 6–8.

5. Philadelphia Commission on Human Relations, *A Report on the Housing of Negro Philadelphia* (pamphlet), (Philadelphia, 1959), p.p.

6. Armstrong Association of Philadelphia, "Report on the Negro Population and the Industries of Philadelphia," pp. 5–6 (copy), Box 12, f. 209 Philadelphia Urban League Papers, TUUA.

7. William J. McKenna, "The Negro Vote in Philadelphia Elections," in Ershkowitz and Zikmund, *Black Politics in Philadelphia*, pp. 73–83; Reichley, *The Art of Government*, pp. 68–72.

8. *Philadelphia Tribune*, 11 January 1947, p. 1; 11 November 1950, p. 1.

9. Charles A. Ekstrom, "The Electoral Politics of Reform and Machine: The Political Behavior of Philadelphia's 'Black' Wards, 1943–1969," in Ershkowitz and Zikmund, *Black Politics in Philadelphia*, pp. 91–96.

10. Reichley, *The Art of Government*, pp. 11–12.

11. Ibid.; see also Ekstrom, "The Electoral Politics of Reform and Machine"; and Oscar Glantz, "Recent Negro Ballots in Philadelphia," pp. 60–72, 84–108.

12. The most significant victory for the Educational Equality League during the 1940s took place in Chester, Pa., in 1946. Following numerous complaints to the local school board about the hazardous fire conditions at the Watts School for black children, black parents began a boycott of the school in March 1946 and demanded that their children be allowed to attend the predominantly white schools. The league provided lawyers for the parents, who finally were able to desegregate the public school system in the face of opposition from the local Ku Klux Klan chapter. See the *Philadelphia Tribune*, 6 April 1946, pp. 1, 3–4; 1, 8, 11, and 29 June 1946; 27 July; 3, 7, 10, 14, 17, 21, 24, 28 September; 1 and 5 October 1946.

13. For extended reports on the lack of black teachers in the public secondary schools, see the *Tribune* 25 December 1944, p. 1; 15 January 1944, p. 14; and 21 October 1944, p. 4.

14. This discussion is based on interviews with Dr. Ruth Wright Hayre and Mr. Floyd L. Logan. Correspondence surrounding this case and other complaints about the testing procedures for appointments to the public secondary schools are in the papers of the Educational Equality League. See also the *Tribune*, 25 December 1943, p. 1; 5 February 1944, p. 2; and 2 September 1944, p. 1.

15. For full-page coverage of the appointment of Ruth Wright Hayre to William Penn High School, see the *Tribune*, 2 February 1946, p. 1; for other appointments, 7 July 1945, p. 1; 23 July 1946, p. 1; and 8 July 1950, p. 1.

16. For reports by Dr. Daniel Brooks on the growing number of predominantly black secondary schools, see ibid., 11 December 1943, p. 20; 15 January 1944; and 30 March 1946, p. 1.

17. Educational Equality League, "Some Pertinent Facts about Philadelphia Schools (1950)," p. 1, Box 15, f. 375, Philadelphia NAACP Papers, TUUA.

18. *Philadelphia Tribune*, 31 January 1948, p. 1; 11 May 1948, p. 3; 5 June 1948, p. 3; 19 July 1949, p. 14; 15 November 1949, p. 1. For statement of W. B. Saul, see 9 May 1950, p. 1. Saul presented his views on public education in Philadelphia in 1950 in an essay entitled, "I'll Stick Up for the Schools," *Saturday Evening Post* 223 (15 April 1950), pp. 22–23.

19. In many interviews with black teachers who desegregated the staffs of predominantly black secondary schools, they pointed out that there were occasions when overtly racist statements had been made by white teachers and administrators and they felt obliged to speak out in protest. These black educators did not regret the subsequent transfer of many of the white teachers to predominantly white schools.

20. Chapter 8 discussed the educational efforts of black social organizations to help prevent juvenile delinquency among black youth. For other

important educational activities of black social organizations during the period from 1930 to 1950, see the *Philadelphia Tribune,* 1 February 1934, p. 5; 7 February 1935, p. 9; 18 February 1937, p. 17; 17 February 1938, p. 1 (Negro History Week activities); 6 February 1943, p. 1; 9 February 1946, p. 2; 31 January 1948, p. 2; 19 June 1948, p. 2; 5 February 1949, p. 1; 14 February 1950, p. 4 (National Freedom Day activities); 8 April 1944, p. 2; 9 September 1944, p. 3; 18 November 1944, p. 3; 5 May 1945, p. 2 (United Peoples Action Committee activities); 7 October 1944, p. 1; 29 March 1947, p. 1; 1 April 1947, p. 1 (Pennsylvania State Negro Council activities); 28 March 1940, p. 1; 2 October 1943, p. 20; 22 January 1944, p. 20; 6 December 1949, p. 2; 14 January 1950, p. 2; 15 August 1950, p. 1; 12 September 1950, p. 1 (activities of several other black social organizations of the period).

21. In October 1949 the Pennsylvania Association of Teachers of Colored Children changed its name to the Association of Pennsylvania Teachers, but according to some black teachers this change only hastened its demise. *Philadelphia Tribune,* 1 November 1949, p. 3.

22. See, for example, Kenneth Kusmer, *A Ghetto Takes Shape: Black Cleveland, 1870–1930* (Urbana, Ill., 1976), pp. 157–89; August Meier and Elliot Rudwick, *From Plantation to Ghetto,* rev. ed. (New York, 1970) pp. 211–50; Allan Spear, *Black Chicago: The Making of A Ghetto, 1890–1920* (Chicago, 1967), pp. 167–230. For a discussion of several flaws in this research on blacks in American cities, see Vincent P. Franklin, "Ghetto on Their Minds: Afro-American Historiography and the City," *Afro-Americans in New York Life and History* 1 (1977): 111–20.

23. Franklin, "The Philadelphia Race Riot of 1918," pp. 115–23. As was mentioned in chapter 7, there was a minor race riot on Ridge Avenue in North Philadelphia in 1932.

24. See, for example, R. Freeman Butts, "Public Education and Political Community," *History of Education Quarterly* 14 (1974): 165–84; Merle L. Borrowman, "Studies in the History of American Education," *Review of Education* 1 (1975): 56–66; Wayne J. Urban, "Some Historiographical Problems in Revisionist Education History," *American Educational Research Journal* 12 (1975): 337–50; Sol Cohen, "The History of the History of American Education 1900–1976: The Uses of the Past," *Harvard Educational Review* 46 (1976): 322–30.

25. Christopher Jencks et al., *Inequality: A Reassessment of the Effect of Family and Schooling in America* (New York, 1972), especially pp. 135–75; Milton Gordon, *Assimilation in American Life* (New York, 1964), pp. 10–83; Colin Greer, *The Great School Legend: A Revisionist Interpretation of American Public Education* (New York, 1972); Michael Katz, *Class, Bureaucracy, and Schools: The Illusion of Educational Change in America* (New York, 1971); and Edgar B. Gumbert and Joel H. Spring, *The Superschool and the Superstate: American Education in the Twentieth Century, 1918–1970* (New York, 1974).

26. August Meier in his *Negro Thought in America 1880–1915* (Ann

Arbor, Mich., 1963) discusses the so-called accommodationist black leaders. But in most instances these leaders were spokespersons for white interests, even in the face of opposition from other black leaders.

27. In my informal interviews with various members of the Philadelphia black community, they often distinguished the "race men" from those other so-called race leaders who did not always work for the interests of the entire community.

Epilogue

1. For a history of the Brown decision, see Richard Kluger, *Simple Justice: The History of Brown v. Board of Education;* See also H. Rodgers and C. Bullock, "School Desegregation: Nine Parts Deliberation and One Part Speed," in *Law and Social Change: Civil Rights Laws and Their Consequences* (New York, 1972), pp. 69–111; U.S. Commission on Civil Rights, *Civil Rights, U.S.A.: Public Schools, Southern States* (Washington, D.C., 1964); Gary Orfield, *The Reconstruction of Southern Education: The Schools and the 1964 Civil Rights Act* (New York, 1969); and Betty Showell, "The Courts, The Legislature, The Presidency, and School Desegregation Policy," *School Review* 84 (1976): 401–16.

2. U.S. Commission on Civil Rights, *Civil Rights, U.S.A.: Public Schools—North and West* (Washington, D.C., 1962); and *Racial Isolation in the Public Schools*, pp. 20–25, 199, 202–4; David Kirby, et al., *Political Strategies in Northern School Desegregation* (Lexington, Mass., 1973); and Franklin, "The Persistence of School Segregation in the Urban North," pp. 51–64.

3. Among the surveys of the conditions in the Philadelphia public school system were the Greater Philadelphia Movement, *A Citizens' Study of Public Education in Philadelphia* (Philadelphia, 1962); Special Committee on Nondiscrimination, *Report to the Board of Public Education* (Philadelphia, 1964); and William R. Odell, *Educational Survey Report for the PBPE;* for statistics on the changing black enrollment in the Philadelphia public schools, see esp. pp. 4–7, 23–31. For a discussion of the "minority status" in American society, see S. J. Makielski, Jr., *Beleaguered Minorities: Cultural Politics in America* (San Francisco, 1973), pp. 13–23.

4. For a discussion of the case, *Chisholm v. Philadelphia Board of Education*, see Albert P. Blaustein, "Philadelphia," in U.S. Commission on Civil Rights, *Civil Rights, U.S.A.: Public Schools: North and West*, pp. 129–41.

5. The attempt to decentralize the Philadelphia public school system is analyzed in detail by Fred Foley, Jr., in "The Failure of Reform: Community Control and the Philadelphia Public Schools," *Urban Education* 10 (1976): 389–402.

6. There have been several accounts of this incident; see, for example, Peter Binzen, *Whitetown, U.S.A.* (New York, 1970), pp. 272–81; and

Conrad Weiler, *Philadelphia: Neighborhood, Authority, and the Urban Crisis* (Philadelphia, 1974), pp. 88–89.

7. Weiler, *Philadelphia*, pp. 89–102.

8. Quote from John H. Strange, "Blacks and Philadelphia Politics, 1963–1966," in Ershkowitz and Zikmund, *Black Politics in Philadelphia*, p. 131. The essays in this volume by William McKenna, "The Negro Vote in Philadelphia Elections," and Harry A. Bailey, Jr., "Poverty, Politics, and Administration: The Philadelphia Experience," also support Strange's conclusions. See also Reichley, *The Art of Government*, pp. 68–72.

9. Strange, "Blacks and Philadelphia Politics," p. 139.

10. An entire file of correspondence, legal briefs, and newspaper clippings on the Girard College case may be found in the papers of the Educational Equality League. See also *Philadelphia Inquirer*, 12 September 1968, p. 3, for an article on the first black students at Girard College.

11. This summary of the findings of the Special Committee on Nondiscrimination is quoted from Weiler, *Philadelphia*, p. 85. Copies of the report are available at the Pedagogical Library at the Board of Education Building.

12. Odell, *Educational Survey Report*, pp. 16–17.

13. For a discussion of the movement for quality integrated education in the late 1960s, see Joseph Cronin, *The Control of Urban Schools: Perspective on the Power of Educational Reformers* (New York, 1973), pp. 181–97.

14. William Penn High School Home and School Association, *Wings to Excellence* (Philadelphia, 1959). This pamphlet and other materials on Project WINGS were made available to the author by Dr. Ruth Wright Hayre.

15. Quote from Henry S. Resnick, *Turning on the System: War in the Philadelphia Public Schools* (New York, 1970), p. 121. This book contains an entire chapter on the work of Marcus Foster at Gratz High School. Resnick, a journalist, visited many Philadelphia schools during the late 1960s, and the book is an account of what he found. This discussion is based on the chapter, and on conversations with teachers and students who worked with the late Marcus Foster.

16. For discussion, see Weiler, *Philadelphia*, pp. 92–101.

17. Housing policies in Philadelphia and the impact on blacks and other groups are examined in Kirk Petshek, *The Challenge of Urban Reform: Policies and Programs in Philadelphia* (Philadelphia, 1973); and Weiler, *Philadelphia*, pp. 103–27.

18. For information on the roles of Dawson, Powell, and Nix in the U.S. Congress, see Maurine Christopher, *America's Black Congressmen* (New York, 1971), pp. 185–193, 194–208, and 215–20 respectively.

19. W. E. B. Du Bois, "The Tragedy of 'Jim Crow,'" *The Crisis* 26 (August 1923): 170.

A Note
on Sources

Historians and other scholars used to complain about the dearth of primary and secondary materials on the black experience in the United States. This is generally no longer the case. The recent upsurge in interest in one's "roots" has heightened people's awareness of the importance of keeping and preserving personal, family, and organizational records. In gathering historical materials for this examination of the education of the Philadelphia black community, I found that I had to be selective in utilizing the vast amount of information that is available. In the selected bibliography, that follows, I have listed the more important primary and secondary sources that are cited in the notes. This listing will, I hope, provide some indication of the types of resources that yield information on community educational activities.

As was noted in the Introduction, one of the more important sources of information on black public and community education was the *Philadelphia Tribune*. Although newspapers are not the best sources for detailed and accurate information on some subjects, such as political maneuverings and social change, they are quite useful in documenting community-wide educational activities. Usually an event, conference, or meeting was announced in the newspaper a few weeks ahead of time, and one or more accounts of activities were published following the event. In the absence of organizational reports and records, newspaper accounts become important sources of information. The high standards of the editorial staff of the *Tribune* enhance the value of this newspaper to historians of black Philadelphia.

As is the case with most histories of contemporary American society, new archival and organization records and materials became available following the completion of research for this study. Fortunately I was able to utilize some of the papers of Floyd L. Logan and the Educational Equality League that are now housed at Temple University Urban Archives (TUUA), but a detailed account of the activities of the League should be written in the near future. The papers of the Philadelphia branch of the Universal Negro Improvement Association

(UNIA), recently unearthed in Germantown by Leon Brown, should provide some much-needed information on the education of Garveyites in the city during the 1920s and 1930s. Although the UNIA was not active in the various campaigns to desegregate the businesses, industries, and public school system in Philadelphia, the organization had a large membership in the city and was engaged in many activities for the social advancement of African peoples throughout the world. TUUA has recently been involved in the collection of organizational records, such as those of the Belmont and Southwest Young Women's Christian Association and the Philadelphia Urban League, and should continue to be an important repository of historical materials on the social and educational development of black Philadelphia.

Unpublished Materials

Manuscript Collections

American Negro Historical Society Papers, Leon Gardner Collection, HSP.

National Association for the Advancement of Colored People Papers, Branch Correspondence, Bryn Mawr, Pennsylvania Branch, 1930–1939, Library of Congress (Washington, D.C.).

National Association for the Advancement of Colored People Papers, Branch Correspondence, Philadelphia Branch, 1913–1939, Library of Congress (Washington, D.C.).

National Association for the Advancement of Colored People, Philadelphia Branch Papers, 1940–1950, TUUA.

Philadelphia Board of Public Education, Minutes of Meetings, 1920–1945. Kennedy Center, Philadelphia, Pa. (PBPE).

Philadelphia Housing Association (Delaware County Housing Association) Papers, TUUA.

Philadelphia Urban League Papers, TUUA.

Wharton Centre (Wharton Settlement House) Papers, TUUA.

Dissertations and Theses

Alexander, John K. "Philadelphia's Other Half: Attitudes toward Poverty and the Meaning of Poverty in Philadelphia, 1760–1800." Ph.D. dissertation, University of Chicago, 1973.

Brodhead, John. "Educational Achievement and Its Relationship to the Socio-Economic Status of the Negro." Ed.D. dissertation, Temple University, 1937.

Conyers, Charlene H. "A History of the Cheyney State Teachers College, 1837–1951." Ed.D. dissertation, New York University, 1960.

Fleming, G. James. "The Administration of Fair Employment Practice Programs." Ph.D. dissertation, University of Pennsylvania, 1948.

Gross, James. "Negro Labor and the Industrial Department of the Armstrong Association." M.B.A. thesis, Temple University, 1957.

Maskin, Melvin R. "Black Education and the New Deal: The Urban Experience." Ph.D. dissertation, New York University, 1973.

Miller, James E. "The Negro in Pennsylvania Politics, with Special Emphasis on Philadelphia Since 1932." Ph.D. dissertation, University of Pennsylvania, 1945.

Nelson, H. Viscount. "Race and Class Consciousness of Philadelphia Negroes with Special Emphasis on the Years between 1927 and 1940." Ph.D. dissertation, University of Pennsylvania, 1969.

Silcox, Harry C. "A Comparative Study of School Desegregation, 1800–1881: The Boston and Philadelphia Experience." Ed.D. dissertation, Temple University, 1972.

Williamson, Etta. "The History of the Separate Public Schools for Negroes in Pennsylvania." M.A. thesis, Howard University, 1935.

Published Materials

Organizational and Institutional Reports and Publications

Armstrong Association of Philadelphia. A Comparative Study of the Occupation and Wages of Children of Working Age in Potter and Durham Schools in Philadelphia. Philadelphia, 1913.

————. Annual Reports, 1910–1920, Philadelphia, 1910–1920 (HSP).

Bacon, Benjamin C. Statistics of the Colored People of Philadelphia. Philadelphia, 1856 (pamphlet).

Cheyney Training School for Teachers (Cheyney State Teachers College). Annual Reports, 1900–1920. (Cheyney, Pa., 1901–1921) (HSP).

Fuller, William. "The Negro Migration to Philadelphia, 1924." Philadelphia Housing Association Pamphlet Collection (TUUA).

Junior Employment Service, School District of Philadelphia. When Philadelphia Youth Leave School at 15 and 16. Philadelphia, 1941.

Municipal Court of Philadelphia. Annual Reports, 1930–1950. Philadelphia, 1931–51.

Odell, William R. Educational Survey Report for the Philadelphia Board of Public Education. Philadelphia, 1965.

Philadelphia Association for the Protection of Colored Women. Annual Reports, 1908–1915. Philadelphia, 1908–15 (HSP).

Philadelphia Board of Public Education (PBPE). Annual Reports, 1900–1950. Philadelphia, 1900–1950 (Pedagogical Library, Board of Public Education, Philadelphia).

————, Department of Research and Development. Distribution of Negro Pupils in the Philadelphia Public Schools, 1956–1965. Philadelphia, 1966.

————, Department of Superintendence, Division of Industrial Arts. Industrial Opportunities for Negro Youth in the Manufacturing Industries of Philadelphia, Philadelphia, 1939.

————. For Every Child: The Story of Integration in the Philadelphia Public Schools. Philadelphia, 1961.

Philadelphia Commission on Human Relations. *First Annual Report, 1952.* Philadelphia, 1953.

Philadelphia Fair Employment Practices Commission. *Annual Reports,* 1949, 1950, and 1951. Philadelphia, 1949–52.

Philadelphia Housing Association (Delaware County Housing Association). *Annual Reports,* 1915–1945, Philadelphia, 1915–45 (TUUA).

Public Education Association of New York. *A Description of the Bureau of Compulsory Education of the City of Philadelphia, Showing How Its Organization and Administration Bear Upon the Problems of Compulsory Education in the City of New York.* Prepared by Howard W. Nudd. New York, 1913.

Public Education Association of Philadelphia and the Department of Education of the Civic Club of Philadelphia. *Compulsory Education.* Philadelphia, 1898.

Government Publications

Commonwealth of Pennsylvania. *The Common School Laws of Pennsylvania and Decisions of the Superintendent with Explanatory Instructions and Forms.* Prepared by Henry C. Hickok. Harrisburg, Pa. 1857.

————, Department of Welfare. *Negro Survey of Pennsylvania.* Harrisburg, Pa. 1927.

————. *Final Report of the Pennsylvania State Temporary Commission on the Conditions of the Urban Colored Population.* Harrisburg, Pa. 1943.

Philadelphia Commission on Human Relations. *Philadelphia's Negro Population: Facts on Housing,* Philadelphia, Pa., 1953.

————. *A Report on the Housing of Negro Philadelphia,* Philadelphia, Pa., 1953.

Report of the Administrator of the Federal Civil Works Administration of Pennsylvania. *Civil Works Administration Program in Pennsylvania, November 15, 1933–March 31, 1934.* Harrisburg, Pa. 1934.

Report of the Executive Director of the State Emergency Relief Board of Pennsylvania. *Unemployment Relief in Pennsylvania, September 1, 1932–October 31, 1933.* Harrisburg, Pa., 1933.

U.S. Commission on Civil Rights. *Racial Isolation in the Public Schools.* 2 vols. Washington, D.C., 1967.

U.S. Department of Commerce, Bureau of the Census. *Immigrants and Their Children, 1920.* By Niles Carpenter. Census Monograph Series. Washington, D.C., 1927.

————. *Negro Population, 1790–1915.* Washington, D.C., 1918.

————. *Thirteenth Census of the United States.* Vol. 4. *Population: Occupation Statistics.* Washington, D.C., 1914.

U.S. Department of the Interior, Bureau of Education. *Bulletins No. 38–39, 1916. Negro Education: A Study of the Private and Higher Schools for Colored People in the United States.* Prepared by Thomas J. Jones. Washington, D.C., 1916.

————. Bulletin No. 7, 1928. *Survey of Negro Colleges and Universities.* Prepared by Arthur Klein. Washington, D.C., 1929.

U.S. Department of Labor, Bureau of Labor Statistics Bulletin No. 520. *Social and Economic Character of Unemployment in Philadelphia, April, 1929.* Prepared by J. Frederick Dewhurst and Ernest A. Tupper, Washington, D.C., 1930.

————. Bulletin No. 555. *Social and Economic Character of Unemployment in Philadelphia, April, 1930.* Prepared by J. Frederick Dewhurst and Robert R. Nathan. Washington, D.C., 1932.

U.S. Works Progress Administration, Pennsylvania. *Analytical Report of Older Boy Delinquency, 1934–1937.* Harrisburg, Pa., 1938.

————. *One Year of the Works Projects Administration in Pennsylvania, July 1, 1935–June 30, 1936.* Harrisburg, Pa., 1936.

U.S. Works Projects Administration, Pennsylvania. *Philadelphia Real Property Inventory, 1939–1940.* Philadelphia, 1940.

————. *Philadelphia Real Property Survey, 1934–1937.* Philadelphia, 1934–1937.

————, Writers' Project in Pennsylvania. *Philadelphia: A Guide to the Nation's Birthplace.* Philadelphia, 1937.

Newspapers

North American (Philadelphia), 1918–22.
Philadelphia Evening Bulletin, 1918–22.
Philadelphia Independent, 1932–42.
Philadelphia Inquirer, 1918–19.
Philadelphia Press, 1918–19.
Philadelphia Public Ledger, 1918–19.
Philadelphia Record, 1918–19.
Philadelphia Tribune, 1912–51.

Books and Pamphlets

Aptheker, Herbert, ed. *A Documentary History of the Negro People in the United States from the Colonial Period to the Establishment of the NAACP.* Secaucus, N.J., 1951.

Bacon, Margaret. *History of the Pennsylvania Society for Promoting the Abolition of Slavery; the Relief of Negroes Unlawfully Held in Bondage; and for Improving the Condition of the African Race.* Philadelphia, 1959.

Bailyn, Bernard. *Education in the Forming of American Society.* New York, 1960.

Baker, Houston, Jr. *Long Black Song: Essays in Black American Literature and Culture.* Charlottesville, Va., 1972.

Bixler, Edward G. *An Investigation to Determine the Efficiency with Which the Compulsory Attendance Law Is Enforced in Philadelphia.* Philadelphia, 1913.

Blassingame, John W. *The Slave Community: Plantation Life in the Antebellum South.* New York, 1972.

Bond, Horace Mann. *The Education of the Negro in the American Social Order.* 1934. Reprint ed., New York, 1970.

Brameld, Theodore B. *Minority Problems in the Public Schools: A Study of Administrative Policies and Practices in Seven School Systems.* New York, 1946.

Brigham, Carl. *A Study of American Intelligence.* Princeton, N. J., 1923.

Brookes, George. *Friend Anthony Benezet.* Philadelphia, 1937.

Brooks, Charles. *The Official History of the First African Baptist Church of Philadelphia.* 1922.

Brown, G. Gordon. *Law Administration and Negro-White Relations in Philadelphia.* Philadelphia, 1947.

Brown, Ira. *The Negro in Pennsylvania History.* Gettysburg, Pa., 1970.

Bureau of Municipal Research, *Philadelphia's Government, 1932.* Philadelphia, 1932.

Callahan, Raymond. *Education and the Cult of Efficiency: A Study of the Social Forces That Have Shaped the Administration of the Public Schools.* Chicago, 1962.

Chicago Commission on Race Relations. *The Negro in Chicago.* Chicago, 1922.

Council for Democracy. *The Negro and Defense, A Test of Democracy.* New York, 1941 (pamphlet).

Cremin, Lawrence. *American Education: The Colonial Experience, 1607–1783.* New York, 1970.

———. *Public Education.* New York, 1976.

———. *Traditions of American Education.* New York, 1977.

———. *The Transformation of the School: Progressivism in American Education, 1876–1957.* New York, 1961.

Cronin, Joseph M. *The Control of Urban Schools: Perspective on the Power of Educational Reformers.* New York, 1973.

Davis, Allen F., and Haller, Mark H., eds. *The Peoples of Philadelphia: A History of Ethnic Groups and Lower Class Life, 1790–1940.* Philadelphia, 1973.

Davis, Arthur P. *From the Dark Tower: Afro-American Writers, 1900–1940.* Washington, D.C., 1974.

Dorsell, Lyle W., ed. *The Challenge of the City, 1860–1910.* Lexington, Conn., 1968.

Drake, St. Clair, and Cayton, Horace. *Black Metropolis: A Study of Negro Life in a Northern City.* New York, 1945.

Drake, Thomas. *Quakers and Slavery in America.* New Haven, 1950.

Du Bois, W. E. B. *The Philadelphia Negro—A Social Study.* 1899. Reprint ed., New York, 1967.

Dusinberre, William. *Civil War Issues in Philadelphia, 1856–1865.* Philadelphia, 1965.

Dutcher, Dean. *The Negro in Modern Industrial Society: An Analysis of Changes in the Occupations of Negro Workers, 1910–1920.* Lancaster, Pa., 1930.

Ensign, Forrest C. *Compulsory School Attendance and Child Labor.* Iowa City, Iowa, 1921.

Ershkowitz, Miriam, and Zikmund, Joseph, eds. *Black Politics in Philadelphia.* New York, 1973.

Franklin, Vincent P., and Anderson, James D., eds. *New Perspectives on Black Educational History.* Boston, 1978.

Frederickson, George. *The Black Image in the White Mind: The Debate on Afro-American Character and Destiny, 1817–1914.* New York, 1971.

Freidel, Frank. *Franklin D. Roosevelt: Launching the New Deal.* Boston, 1973.

Garfinkel, Herbert. *When Negroes March: The March on Washington Movement in the Organizational Politics of the FEPC.* Glencoe, Ill., 1959.

George, Carol V. R. *Segregated Sabbaths: Richard Allen and the Rise of Independent Black Churches, 1760–1840.* New York, 1973.

Gossett, Thomas. *Race: The History of an Idea in America.* Dallas, 1963.

Graham, Patricia. *Community and Class in American Education, 1865–1918.* New York, 1974.

Grant, Robert B., ed. *The Black Man Comes to the City: A Documentary Account from the Great Migration to the Great Depression.* Chicago, 1972.

Green, Constance M. *The Secret City: A History of Race Relations in the Nation's Capitol.* Princeton, N. J., 1967.

Greer, Colin. *The Great School Legend—A Revisionist Interpretation of American Public Education.* New York, 1972.

Gumbert, Edgar B., and Spring, Joel H. *The Superschool and the Superstate: American Education in the Twentieth Century, 1918–1970.* New York, 1974.

Haller, John. *Outcasts of Evolution: Scientific Attitudes of Racial Inferiority, 1859–1900.* Urbana, Ill., 1971.

Hardin, Clara A. *The Negroes of Philadelphia: The Cultural Adjustment of a Minority Group.* Bryn Mawr, Pa., 1945.

Harrison, Bennett. *Education, Training and the Urban Ghetto.* Baltimore, 1972.

Huggins, Nathan. *Harlem Renaissance.* New York, 1971.

James, Sidney V. *A People among Peoples: Quaker Benevolence in Eighteenth Century America.* Cambridge, Mass., 1963.

Johnson, Charles. *The Patterns of Negro Segregation.* New York, 1943.

Katz, Michael. *Class, Bureaucracy, and Schools: The Illusion of Educational Change in America.* New York, 1971.

Katznelson, Ira. *Black Men, White Cities: Race, Politics and Migration in the United States, 1900–1930; in Britain, 1948–1968.* New York, 1973.

Kennedy, Louise V. *The Negro Peasant Turns Cityward.* 1930. Reprint ed., New York, 1971.

Kesselman, Louis C. *The Social Politics of FEPC: A Study in Reform Pressure Movements.* Chapel Hill, N.C., 1948.

Lerner, Gerda, ed. *Black Women in White America—A Documentary History.* New York, 1972.

Leuchtenburg, William E. *Franklin D. Roosevelt and the New Deal, 1932–1940.* New York, 1963.

Lubove, Roy. *The Progressives and the Slums: Tenement House Reform in New York City, 1890–1917.* Pittsburgh, Pa., 1962.

Lyman, Stanford M. *The Black American in Sociological Thought.* New York, 1972.

McCadden, Joseph J. *Education in Pennsylvania, 1801–1835, and Its Debt to Roberts Vaux.* Philadelphia, 1937.

Myrdal, Gunnar. *An American Dilemma: The Negro Problem and Modern Democracy.* 2 vols. New York, 1944.

Nash, Charles. *The History of Legislative and Administrative Changes Affecting The Philadelphia Public Schools, 1869–1921.* Philadelphia, 1943.

Newby, I. A. *Jim Crow's Defense: Anti-Negro Thought in America, 1900–1930.* Baton Rouge, La., 1965.

Newman, Bernard J. *Housing of the City Negro.* Philadelphia, 1915 (pamphlet).

Osofsky, Gilbert. *Harlem: The Making of a Ghetto, Negro New York, 1890–1930.* New York, 1963.

Parris, Guichard, and Brooks, Lester. *Blacks in the City: A History of the National Urban League.* Boston, 1971.

Penn, I. Garland. *The Afro-American Press and Its Editors.* 1891. Reprint ed., New York, 1969.

Petshek, Kirk. *The Challenge of Urban Reform: Policies and Programs in Philadelphia.* Philadelphia, 1973.

Reichley, James. *The Art of Government: Reform and Organization Politics in Philadelphia,* New York, 1959.

Reimers, David M., ed. *Racism in the United States: An American Dilemma?* New York, 1972.

Richardson, Clement, ed. *The National Cyclopedia of the Colored Race.* Vol. 1. Montgomery, Ala., 1919.

Ross, Frank V., and Kennedy, Louise V. *A Bibliography of Negro Migration.* New York, 1934.

Ruchames, Louis. *Race, Jobs, and Politics: The Story of the FEPC.* New York, 1953.

Ryan, William. *Blaming the Victim.* New York, 1971.

Scott, Emmett J. *The Negro Migration during the War.* New York, 1920.

Simpson, George. *The Negro in the Philadelphia Press.* Philadelphia, 1936.

Spear, Allan H. *Black Chicago: The Making of A Ghetto, 1890–1920.* Chicago, 1967.

Spring, Joel. *Education and the Rise of the Corporate State.* Boston, 1972.

Stanton, William. *The Leopard's Spots: Scientific Attitudes toward Race in America, 1815–1859.* Chicago, 1960.

Stone, Chuck. *Black Political Power in America.* New York, 1968.

Turner, Edward. *The Negro in Pennsylvania, Slavery-Servitude-Freedom, 1639–1861.* 1911. Reprint ed., New York, 1969.

Tyack, David B. *The One Best System: A History of American Urban Education.* Cambridge, Mass., 1974.

Warner, Sam Bass. *The Private City: Philadelphia in Three Periods of Growth.* Philadelphia, 1968.

Weber, Adna F. *The Growth of Cities in the Nineteenth Century: A Study in Statistics.* 2d ed. Ithaca, N.Y., 1965.

Weiler, Conrad. *Philadelphia: Neighborhood, Authority, and the Urban Crisis.* Philadelphia, 1974.

Weiss, Nancy. *The National Urban League, 1910–1940.* New York, 1974.

West, Earl. *The Black American and Education.* Columbus, Ohio, 1972.

Wickersham, James. *A History of Education in Pennsylvania.* Lancaster, Pa., 1886.

Wolters, Raymond. *Negroes and the Great Depression: The Problem of Economic Recovery.* Westport, Conn., 1970.

Woodson, Carter G. *The Education of the Negro Prior to 1861.* 1914. Reprint ed., New York, 1968.

———. *The Mis-Education of the Negro.* 1933. Reprint ed., New York, 1972.

Woody, Thomas. *Early Quaker Education in Pennsylvania.* New York, 1920.

Woofter, T. J., and Priest, Madge H. *Negro Housing in Philadelphia.* Philadelphia, 1927 (pamphlet).

Wright, Richard R., Jr. *The Negro in Pennsylvania: A Study in Economic History.* New York, 1969.

Zilversmit, Arthur I. *The First Emancipation: The Abolition of Slavery in the North.* Chicago, 1967.

Articles

Baumann, John F. "Black Slums/Black Projects: The New Deal and Negro Housing in Philadelphia." *Pennsylvania History* 41 (1974): 311–38.

Binder, Frederick. "Pennsylvania Negro Regiments in the Civil War." *JNH* 27 (1952): 383–417.

Blaustein, Albert P. "Philadelphia, Pennsylvania." In *Civil Rights U.S.A.; Public Schools, Cities in the North and West,* U.S. Commission on Civil Rights, pp. 107–73. Washington, D.C., 1963.

Brown, Ira. "Pennsylvania and the Rights of the Negro, 1865–1887." *Pennsylvania History* 28 (1961): 45–57.

Brown, William O. "The Nature of Race Consciousness." *Social Forces* 10 (1936): 90–97.

Clement, Priscilla F. "The Works Progress Administration in Pennsylvania, 1935–1940." *PMHB* 95 (1971): 244–60.

Cohen, Sol. "The Industrial Education Movement, 1906–1917." *American Quarterly* 20 (1968): 95–110.

Ekstrom, Charles A. "The Electoral Politics of Reform and Machine: The Political Behavior of Philadelphia's Black Wards, 1943–1969." In *Black Politics in Philadelphia*, ed. M. Ershkowitz and J. Zikmund, pp. 84–108. New York, 1973.

Farley, Reynolds. "The Urbanization of Negroes in the United States." *Journal of Social History* 1 (1968): 241–58.

Fishel, Leslie. "The Negro in the New Deal Era." In *The Negro in Depression and War: Prelude to Revolution, 1930–1945*, ed. Bernard Sternsher, pp. 4-12. Chicago, 1969.

———. "The Negro in Northern Politics, 1870–1900." *Mississippi Valley Historical Review* 42 (1955): 466–89.

———. "Northern Prejudice and Negro Suffrage, 1865–1870." *JNH 34* (1954): 8–26.

Foner, Philip. "The Battle to End Discrimination Against Negroes on Philadelphia Street Cars: (Part I) Background and Beginning of Battle." *Pennsylvania History* 40 (1973): 261–90.

———. "The Battle to End Discrimination Against Negroes on Philadelphia Street Cars: (Part II) The Victory." *Pennsylvania History* 40 (1973): 355–79.

Fox, Barbara R. "Unemployment Relief in Philadelphia, 1930–1932: A Study of the Depression's Impact on Voluntarism." *PMHB* 93 (1969): 86–108.

Franklin, Vincent P. "American Values, Social Goals, and the Desegregated School: A Historical Perspective." In *New Perspectives on Black Educational History*, ed. Vincent P. Franklin and James D. Anderson, pp. 193–201. Boston, 1978.

———. "The Persistence of School Segregation in the Urban North—A Historical Perspective." *Journal of Ethnic Studies* 1 (1974): 53–68.

———. "The Philadelphia Race Riot of 1918." *PMHB* 99 (1975): 336–50.

Glantz, Oscar. "Recent Negro Ballots in Philadelphia." In *Black Politics in Philadelphia*, ed. M. Ershkowitz and J. Zikmund, pp. 60–72. New York, 1973.

Golab, Caroline. "The Immigrant and the City: Poles, Italians, and Jews in Philadelphia, 1870–1920." In *The Peoples of Philadelphia: A History of Ethnic Groups and Lower Class Life, 1790–1940*, ed. Allen Davis and Mark Haller, pp. 203–30. Philadelphia, 1973.

Hershberg, Theodore. "Free Blacks in Antebellum Philadelphia." In *The Peoples of Philadelphia*, ed. Davis and Haller, pp. 111–33. Philadelphia, 1973.

Issel, William. "Modernization in Philadelphia School Reform, 1882–1905." *PMHB* 94 (1970): 358–83.

Kutler, Stanley. "Pennsylvania Courts, The Abolition Act, and Negro Rights." *Pennsylvania History* 30 (1963): 14–27.

McKenna, William J. "The Negro Vote in Philadelphia Elections." In

Black Politics in Philadelphia, ed. M. Ershkowitz and J. Zikmund, pp. 73–83. New York, 1973.

Perkins, Linda M. "Quaker Beneficence and Black Control: The Institute for Colored Youth, 1852–1903." In *New Perspectives on Black Educational History*, ed. Vincent P. Franklin and James D. Anderson, pp. 19–43. Boston, 1978.

Pitts, James P. "The Study of Race Consciousness: Comments on New Directions." *American Journal of Sociology* 80 (1974): 665–87.

Provine, William. "Geneticists and the Biology of Race Crossing," *Science* 182 (23 November 1973): 790–96.

Runcie, John. "Hunting the Nigs in Philadelphia: The Race Riot of August 1934." *Pennsylvania History* 39 (1972): 187–218.

Salmond, John A. "The Civilian Conservation Corps and the Negro." *Journal of American History* 52 (1965): 75–88.

Shover, John L. "Ethnicity and Religion in Philadelphia Politics, 1924–1940." *American Quarterly* 25 (1973): 499–515.

Silcox, Harry C. "Delay and Neglect: Negro Public Education in Antebellum Philadelphia, 1800–1860." *PMHB* 97 (1973): 444–64.

———. "Philadelphia Negro Educator: Jacob C. White, Jr." *PMHB* 97 (1973): 75–98.

Smith, Timothy L. "Immigrant Social Aspirations and American Education, 1880–1930." *American Quarterly* 21 (1969): 523–43.

———. "Native Blacks and Foreign Whites: Varying Responses to Educational Opportunity in America, 1880–1950." *Perspectives in American History* 6 (1972): 309–35.

Spady, James. "The Afro-American Historical Society: The Nucleus of Black Bibliophiles, 1897–1923." *Negro History Bulletin* 37 (1974): 254–57.

Stolarik, M. Mark. "Immigration, Education, and Social Mobility of Slovaks, 1870–1930." In *Immigrants and Religion in Urban America*, ed. R. Miller and T. Marzik, pp. 103–16. Philadelphia, 1977.

Strange, John H. "Blacks and Philadelphia Politics: 1963–1966." In *Black Politics in Philadelphia*, ed. M. Ershkowitz and J. Zikmund, pp. 109–44. New York, 1973.

Sutherland, John F. "The Origins of Philadelphia's Octavia Hill Association: Social Reform in the 'Contented' City." *PMHB* 99 (1975): 20–44.

Vander Zander, W. "The Ideology of White Supremacy." *Journal of the History of Ideas* 20 (1959): 385–402.

Varbero, Richard A. "Philadelphia's South Italians in the 1920s." In *The Peoples of Philadelphia*, ed. Allen F. Davis and Mark H. Haller, pp. 255–76. Philadelphia, 1973.

Winkler, Allen M. "The Philadelphia Transit Strike of 1944." *Journal of American History* 59 (1972): 73–89.

Index